# TWO WHEELS IN THE DUST

## From Kathmandu to Kandy

*Anne Mustoe*

First published in Great Britain in 2001 by
Virgin Publishing Ltd
Thames Wharf Studios
Rainville Road
London W6 9HA

A catalogue record for this book is available
from the British Library.

ISBN 1 85227 926 5

Typeset by TW Typesetting, Plymouth, Devon
Printed and bound in Great Britain by
Mackays of Chatham PLC

# Contents

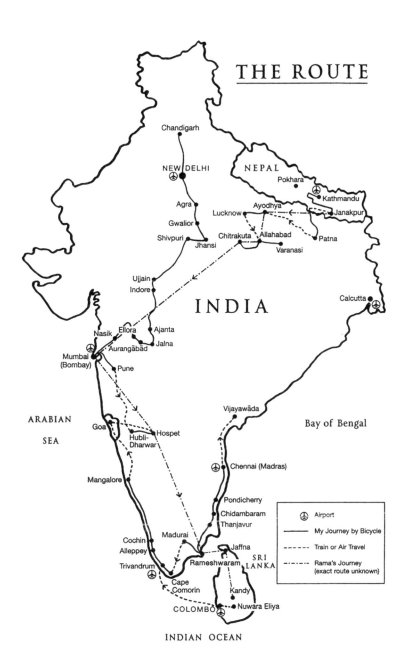

# THE ROUTE

Chandigarh

NEW DELHI

NEPAL

Pokhara

Kathmandu

Agra

Lucknow    Ayodhya
Janakpur

Gwalior

Shivpuri    Chitrakuta    Allahabad    Patna

Jhansi    Varanasi

INDIA

Ujjain

Indore    Calcutta

Nasik    Ellora    Ajanta

Aurangābād    Jalna

Mumbai
(Bombay)

Pune

ARABIAN    Vijayawāda    Bay of Bengal

SEA    Goa

Hubli-    Hospet
Dharwar

Mangalore    Chennai (Madras)

Pondicherry

Chidambaram
Thanjavur

Cochin    Madurai
Alleppey    Jaffna

Trivandrum    Rameshwaram    SRI
LANKA

Cape    Kandy
Comorin

COLOMBO    Nuwara Eliya

INDIAN OCEAN

| | | |
|---|---|---|
| ✈ | | Airport |
| ——— | | My Journey by Bicycle |
| - - - | | Train or Air Travel |
| -·-·- | | Rama's Journey (exact route unknown) |

# Prologue: The Pilgrimage Begins

MY PILGRIMAGE BEGAN one morning in the dust of the Deccan. It was January 1992, and I was on my bicycle, trying to make my way out of the centre of Ujjain into open country. In the morning rush hour, I was fighting for my few inches of space in the turmoil of the narrow street. There was every conceivable sort of motorised vehicle, plus bicycles, cycle-rickshaws, bullock-carts, horses, camels and handcarts. Horns were honking, cycle-bells jangling, whips cracking and impatient drivers shouting. What little pavement there was, was so jam-packed with shoe repairers, barbers, fortune-tellers with their parrots, beggars, underwear salesmen, sleepers and homeless families cooking their breakfasts, that pedestrians had nowhere to walk but the road. They surged through the traffic in anxious clumps, compounding the confusion. Then there were the animals. Bristly black pigs rooted in the heaps of stinking garbage, grunting at the crows who cawed and pecked at them. Stray dogs yelped and dodged between the cartwheels. And through the middle of everything sauntered the peaceable holy cows of India, sacrosanct and unperturbed, pausing to chew a paper bag here and a cabbage leaf there. It was the usual Indian assault on the senses.

I had been in India for some months and had learned that it was no place for the faint-hearted cyclist. I just had to grit my teeth and barge along the road like everyone else. But that morning, the dust was so thick and acrid with wood-smoke that I had to pull up to wipe my eyes. It was then that I noticed him.

He stood barefoot in his torn grey shirt and trousers, with a check scarf wound round his head and tied under his chin. The crowds were pouring past, parting round him, then rejoining and pressing on with little clicks of annoyance. The man stood his ground, eyes closed, hands together, lips moving, praying with the unselfconsciousness of a child. At the end of his prayer, he raised his joined hands to his forehead, lips and heart, then strode into the morning rush.

I pushed my bicycle across to the roadside shrine, to find out which of the multitude of Hindu gods could produce such rapt devotion in the middle of a crowded street. I peered through the iron grille and saw a hectic vermilion face with staring black eyes. It was Hanuman, the monkey god, garlanded with marigolds and dressed in a golden frock.

My knowledge of the Hindu religion was fairly vague at the time. I knew that Hanuman was worshipped as the faithful friend. He was the divine helper, the solver of problems. The worried man in the check scarf had laid his troubles before Hanuman, then gone on his way with a lighter step.

I was suddenly curious to know more about this god; and my curiosity was to lead me through the entire Indian subcontinent, from Nepal to Sri Lanka, and back three millennia in time, to the origins of *The Ramayana*, India's favourite story.

# Introduction

*T*HE RAMAYANA (Rama's Journey) is a gripping adventure story, a wonderful yarn in which the heroes are incredibly heroic and the villains monumentally villainous. Rama is the perfect man, Sita the perfect woman, Lakshmana the perfect brother and Hanuman the perfect friend. At the other end of the spectrum, Ravana, the Demon King, has ten heads, twenty arms, teeth like young moons and copper-coloured eyes. He and his man-eating army are so fierce that even the gods are terrified of them.

On my long cycle-rides, I always try to follow historical routes, to give an extra dimension to my travels. But in India, a country which fascinated me in a vague sort of way, there were no roads of real significance, apart from the Grand Trunk Road, and I had already cycled that. But if I turned to mythology for a change, I had the perfect journey.

Sita, the heroine of *The Ramayana*, was born in present-day Nepal, while Rama came from Uttar Pradesh in the north of India. Hanuman, his divine monkey helper, lived in Karnataka, in the centre, and Ravana, the villain of the plot, reigned in Sri Lanka. So the incidents in the epic span the whole of the Indian subcontinent, from north to south. I did my background research in London, mostly in the library of the School of Oriental and African Studies, but to follow the entire route of Rama's journey, from Sita's birthplace to the lair of the Demon King, I had to spend five winters in India.

I could have covered the distance in far less time, had I rushed about in cars and trains. But I chose my favourite means of transport, my well-travelled bicycle, because I value the insights that a bicycle brings – and I also find it less stressful than fighting my way on to India's heaving buses and trains. Everyone talks to a cyclist, especially in India, where the bicycle is the most common form of transport. Sharing the road, we somehow share a fellow-feeling, that transcends barriers of race and wealth. My bicycle takes me through the countryside and brings me into contact with village people and their customs in a way which would not be possible if I swept through on four wheels; I find out much more and have more time to think about it as I wheel my peaceful way along country roads. For poking around, meeting people and learning the inside story, there is no introduction quite so effective as the modest bicycle. Yet this is not a cycling book, written primarily for fellow cyclists. Anyone who is thinking of cycling in India will, I hope, find the book encouraging and will certainly be able to glean some practical information from its pages. But my bicycle is no more the book's *raison d'être* than the flights and bus journeys of other writers are the *raisons d'être* of theirs. It is simply the vehicle from whose saddle I have taken a free-wheeling, personal view of contemporary India.

Rama and Sita travelled from north to south, beginning in Sita's hometown of Janakpur in Nepal and ending their journey in the central highlands of Sri Lanka. My own travels took a slightly erratic course, because I was unaware of the Nepalese connection until I got chatting with a Nepalese businessman during my third Indian winter. This meant that I cycled the central part of the route first, then the southern sections, and ended with the northern run down from Nepal to the Ganges. But as *The Ramayana* has been the spur to my travels in India, I shall exercise a certain literary licence and bring my own journey into line with the wanderings of my epic characters.

On the surface, *The Ramayana* is a magical, much-loved fairy tale, where Good triumphs over Evil and Hanuman's monkey tricks add the comic element. But because Rama is the incarnation of a Hindu god, his story arouses darker passions. In recent years it has been the cause of rioting and bloodshed between Hindus and Muslims in Ayodhya, Rama's birthplace, and in other cities across north India. Sri Lanka is engaged in a civil war between the Buddhist Sinhalese and the Hindu Tamils. So my route begins and ends in religious conflict, which spills over into politics.

As *The Ramayana* is the inspiration for my journey, it obviously dictates the route, leading me to some of the holiest Hindu pilgrim sites. But it must also govern perspective and the choice of material for inclusion. India is a heady, fomenting brew of peoples, languages, religions, cultures and landscapes, and no single book could possibly encompass the whole. *Two Wheels in the Dust* leans towards those areas of life where the ancient epic is still influential, even today. It is an exploration of the world's most ancient living religion, as well as a passing view of everyday life in modern India. To the Hindu, there is no difference between the two. God is all-pervading and is both.

I first crossed the Indian subcontinent from Karachi to Calcutta in 1988, as part of my West-to-East cycle-ride around the world. Pakistan, with its Muslim monotheism, seemed an easier country to come to terms with. When I crossed the border into India, I was perplexed by the Hindus with their complicated religion (33 million gods in some estimates) and shocked by the rules of caste. I cycled through the country in a fog, uncomprehending and unsympathetic. Although I was courteously received, I felt out of touch, an outsider. *The Ramayana* has changed all that. My search for Hanuman, which began in a crowded street in Ujjain, has given me a topic of conversation which is deeply fascinating to Indians of all religions. It has taken me to parts of India I should never otherwise have visited and it has provided the key to at least some aspects of this ancient and complex civilisation. *The Ramayana* has been my passport to India.

*Two Wheels in the Dust* is really two books in one, because there is a book within a book. Each stage of Rama's journey is followed by an account of my own travels through that particular region. The two strands have been printed in two different types, so that the short epic sections can be picked out very easily. They can be read in sequence as a separate story or they can be skipped altogether by any readers whose interests are limited to the present day. But I hope that the two accounts will be taken together in the order in which they appear. Indian civilisation is deeply rooted in its ancient traditions and it is difficult to understand the contemporary scene without reference to the mythical past. By intertwining the two, and working in a few sections on Hindu religion, I have tried to shed a glimmer of light on at least a few of India's current problems.

*The Ramayana* is such an important classic, and so much scholarly work has been produced on its content and background, that the present book can only hope to scratch the surface. For those whose interest has been stimulated, I have added a bibliography for further reading.

For the cyclist, I have given the specifications of my bicycle and a luggage list in an appendix. When I read through the first draft of the book, I was struck by the loving detail in which I had described my meals and Kingfisher beers in the restaurants where I dined, but cyclists will know that food and drink are extremely important! As for accommodation, I cycled through parts of the country where tourists had never been seen and hotels were non-existent. I was not carrying a tent, so the problem of where I was going to spend the night dominated many of my afternoons. But this very remoteness and vulnerability led to some of my most interesting encounters, when I was taken in and treated with the greatest kindness by people who had never come into contact with a foreigner before. Their hospitality was heart-warming. Even so, it was always a great relief to a townie like myself to arrive in a city, where I knew I could count on a hotel bed and water for a shower.

India is not a comfortable country. It is overwhelming in its size, beauty and diversity. There are palaces and temples, but their backdrop is poverty and the cardboard shacks of the slums. The noise, dirt and beggars, the staring crowds and the bureaucracy of petty officials can fray even the strongest nerves. Yet the atmosphere is never threatening. The eyes spark with interest and humour, never with hatred or resentment of the richer foreigner. At times, I longed to escape – but once I was back home in the sanitised West, the vibrant colours, the smiles, the scent of spices and jasmine, and the swish of silken saris in the dust haunted me until I returned. Love it or hate it, India is the ancient, fascinating, complex, irritating country which everyone should visit at least once in a lifetime.

# 1 *The Ramayana*

*'He who reads the story of Rama, which imparts merit and purity, is freed from all sin.'*

THE RAMAYANA IS ONE OF THE OLDEST stories in the world. Like the *Iliad* and the *Odyssey*, the epic began as a series of folk tales which were passed down from generation to generation by wandering storytellers. Some scholars have traced its origins back as far as the fifteenth century BC, but more recent work on the language and style of the poem, together with its political, sociological and geographical content, has narrowed down the period of its evolution to around 750–500 BC.

According to tradition, the epic was composed in Sanskrit verse by the poet Valmiki. No one knows whether Valmiki actually existed as a historical person, but internal stylistic evidence does suggest that the central core of the story, Books Two to Six of *The Ramayana*, is indeed the work of a single poet, who wrote it down between the second century BC and the second century AD. Books One and Seven are generally agreed to be later additions.

Valmiki's tale is secular and heroic. Rama is the perfect man – valiant, steadfast, truthful, just, faithful, gentle, handsome, learned in the holy scriptures, loved by everyone (Valmiki devotes hundreds of lines to descriptions of Rama and his virtues) – while his wife, the beautiful Sita, is the model of fidelity and loving compliance. Each was the other's only love, so that they have come to stand for constancy in marriage. At Hindu weddings, even today, the bride and groom are seen as embodiments of Sita and Rama and are worshipped on that day by the wedding guests. The form of words used by Sita's father, King Janaka, when he gave his daughter to Rama, are still part of the Hindu marriage ceremony.

Over the centuries, there was a shift in interpretation. Rama became an avatar, or incarnation, of the great god Vishnu and Sita an incarnation of Vishnu's consort, the goddess Lakshmi. Rama's battle with Ravana came to be seen as an allegory of the struggle between Good and Evil, in which the Good triumphs under God's leadership on earth.

Valmiki's epic has come down to us in three differing versions and there have been many later interpretations of the poem in the vernacular. The most important are Kamban's twelfth-century version in Tamil (which the south Indian writer RK Narayan has shortened and rendered most delightfully in English) and the *Ram Carit Manas* (*The Lake of Rama's Deeds*), written in Hindi in the sixteenth century by Tulsi Das. In Tulsi Das, Rama is consistently divine and the aim of the *Ram Carit Manas* is to encourage devotion to Rama as an incarnation of Vishnu. All the conflicts, discrepancies and character flaws in the original epic are eliminated to produce a harmonious, lyrical poem in praise of God.

In addition to the poetic versions, there are innumerable folk versions, which are recited at festivals all over India, each one with a different message or emphasis. For instance, folk versions sung by women often strengthen the role of Sita and portray her as a more independent and more spirited woman than she appears in the brahminic literary versions.

Zeus and Hera, with their retinue of Olympian gods, ceased to be worshipped at the fall of Greece, and even their shadows have faded now from our literary and poetic traditions. Homer's heroes, Achilles and Odysseus, are no longer in any vital sense a part of our Western consciousness. But the Hindu gods and heroes are still as alive in modern India as they were in the days of Valmiki. The story of Rama and Sita is told to children at bedtime and performed at village fairs. *The Ramayana* is studied as a devotional text and used to illustrate moral precepts. 'Ram Ram' is a common form of greeting in north India and 'He Ram' were the last words uttered by Mahatma Gandhi, when he fell to an assassin's bullet in 1948. When *The Ramayana* was serialised in the 1980s on Doordarshan, the Indian government television service, it was the most popular series ever shown and the streets of India were deserted once a week, as people crowded round the nearest television set. Now, video tapes of the series are played in homes and teastalls on days sacred to Rama and Hanuman, when to watch them is considered as much an act of devotion as a visit to the temple. The epic is currently being put on to the Internet.

*The Ramayana* is a long and complicated story, an epic of some 50,000 lines, almost twice the length of the *Iliad* and the *Odyssey* combined. It was my companion on my travels across India and I shall return to it again and again in the course of my narrative. But, as a preliminary, I shall try to condense into one paragraph the tale of Rama and Sita, the perfect couple, and Rama's faithful friend, Hanuman, that magical monkey in the golden frock who set his match to my fuse.

### The Plot

*Rama, a prince of the Kingdom of Kosala, was about to be installed as prince regent by his aged father, King Dasaratha, when he fell victim to a palace plot and was forced into exile for fourteen years. He left the capital city, Ayodhya, accompanied by his wife, Sita, and his devoted younger brother, Lakshmana. While the three were living as hermits in the forest, Sita was tricked by Ravana, the ten-headed King of the Demons, who abducted her in his aerial car to his palace in Sri Lanka, where he tried to persuade her to forget Rama and marry him instead. Rama and Lakshmana assembled an army of forest creatures to search for Sita. Their general was Hanuman, chief adviser to the monkey king, Sugriva. By his supernatural powers as a son of the Wind God, Hanuman was able to clear the straits to Sri Lanka in one prodigious leap and discover where Sita was held captive. His army of monkeys and bears built a bridge over the sea, so that Rama could reach Sri Lanka and defeat Ravana in single-handed combat. When Sita submitted to an ordeal by fire, to prove that she had remained faithful to Rama, the Fire God, Agni, rose in person from the flames, with Sita safe in his arms. The happy couple returned to Ayodhya, where Rama began his glorious reign of eleven thousand years.*

This is considered to be Valmiki's original story. It belongs, geographically, to north-east India, as is clear from Valmiki's detailed knowledge of the countryside in the early books and his vagueness about places further south. Historically, it may be an allegory of the southward thrust of the invading Aryans. These fair-skinned Indo-European peoples filtered through Bactria and Afghanistan into north India from about 1,500 BC and gradually spread southwards, supplanting the shorter, darker, indigenous Dravidians of south India and the Veddahs of Sri Lanka. In this context, Rama is obviously the victorious Aryan, while Ravana and his Rakshasas are the Dravidians and Veddahs. Hanuman's forest creatures may be the aboriginal tribal peoples, who formed an alliance with the Aryans against their Dravidian overlords.

Sadly, I have no Sanskrit, but the charm of the original language does creep through in translation. Sanskrit and Greek are members of the same linguistic family and their epics are clearly born of the same, or similar, poetic traditions. Like Homer, Valmiki makes great use of conventional epithets, similes and metaphors, to brighten the text and help with the scansion. But whereas the Greek words and phrases are all firmly embedded in nature, those in Valmiki often have a metaphysical flavour, which is distinctively Indian. Homer's heroes rush into the attack like straightforward lions or rivers in flood. Valmiki's heroes fight 'like Time at the dissolution of the worlds'. Even everyday objects become things of poetic fancy: 'golden lamps which resembled gamblers absorbed in their dice'. Valmiki's similes are so picturesque that I sometimes find them irresistible and quote them in full in my own brief summaries of the text.

Flights of fancy appear in the contents too. Valmiki treats factual consistency and probability with scorn, and his numbers are too huge for contemplation. But the vivid imagination and staggering embellishment are all part of what the Sanskrit scholar Winternitz describes as 'a true popular epic, the property of the whole Indian people, high and low, of all religions'.

I have relied chiefly on the unabridged three-volume translation of *The Ramayana of Valmiki* by Professor Hari Prasad Shastri (published by Shanti Sadan, 1953).

# 2 Downhill through Nepal

(Winter 1998)

*Kathmandu – Mugling – Narayangadh – Royal Chitwan National Park – Hetauda – Janakpur*

'WHAT IS THIS ANGIOPLASTY, please? I am not understanding the term.'

We flew into Kathmandu in mid-November, when King Birendra of Nepal was in London for medical treatment. The newspapers were printing daily bulletins on his progress after successful angioplasty, but none of them thought to explain what angioplasty was. So as soon as the locals heard we were from London, we became immediate experts. Their eyes opened wide in wonder, as we did our best to describe the procedure – the little balloon which is threaded up from the thigh to one of the coronary arteries, then inflated to clear the obstruction.

'What a wonderful thing! We are not doing that in Nepal.'

The Nepalese are inscrutable. They were awestruck at the medical technology, but none of them expressed any views at all to foreigners like us about the King himself, neither relief at his good progress, nor antagonism towards his rule. He was simply there, and it was difficult to tell whether he was above comment, below it, or just irrelevant to their lives.

Arriving in Kathmandu for the first time, I found it a disturbing city. I was not surprised at the lack of angioplasty, because I knew that medical facilities in general were thin on the ground, with few hospitals and only something like one doctor to every 15,000 Nepalese. Illiteracy was up around the 75 per cent mark and education, welfare and public services were all depressingly lacking. The only thing that flourished, and it flourished startlingly in a city which was still mediaeval at heart, was information technology. Technology produced the most extraordinary contrasts. Tourists picked their way through filthy, garbage-strewn streets to send off e-mails or surf the net in cyber-cafés, while others climbed out of cycle-rickshaws, pedalled by ragged skeletons of men, to watch satellite television in smart hotels. Bills for Carlsberg, steak and chips and pancakes with chocolate sauce were cleared by Visa in the restaurants where the tourists gathered, while the pavement vendors scrabbled in ancient cigarette tins for their few rupees of change. Even the outsiders fell into two sharply contrasting groups – the well-fed, mountain-booted West-erners, mostly young and male, so different from the slight Tibetan refugees, who were trying to scrape a living by selling cheap quilted jackets and Buddhist prayer wheels. It all felt somehow out of joint, and I was glad that I didn't have to spend much time in the place.

My Ramayana pilgrimage was to begin in Janakpur, the birthplace of Sita. It lies in Nepal, just north of the border with India, and is a very awkward town to reach. I could either struggle across India with my bicycle on trains and buses, then cross the Nepalese border from the south, or I could fly into Kathmandu and cycle there through Nepal. One look at the map gave me the answer. I saw that the Kathmandu Valley stood at an altitude of 1,370 metres, while Janakpur lay down on the Gangetic Plain. What a wonderful downhill ride!

I usually cycle alone, but this winter I was joined by two friends, Shirley and Suzanna. Suzanna and I travelled to-gether from London to Vienna, where we joined up with Shirley, who had flown there from her home in Ankara. None of us had been to Nepal before, but I knew the Indian subcontinent well and Suzanna had trekked in Ladakh. It was Shirley who suffered the culture shock, when we were mobbed by hotel touts and drivers of every sort of ramshackle conveyance immediately we left the airport building in Kathmandu. Using our bikes as battering rams, we scattered them all and forced our way through to the road. Then we cycled bravely into the city centre and found our own way to the Fuji Guest House, a deservedly popular mid-range hotel with a flowery little breakfast patio.

Since travel became my main occupation in life, twelve years ago, I have learned to focus my sightseeing. I think of the world as a giant, sumptuous fruit-cake, crammed with sights, scents, sounds, peoples and cultures, and the only way to enjoy it is to take it a modest slice at a time. The slice can be vertical, an in-depth exploration of a particular spot; or it can be horizontal, a thin sliver pared off a wide surface. My Ramayana slice was horizontal, covering the entire length of the Indian subcontinent, but limited in every place I visited to one particular topic. In Nepal, my only concerns were Rama, Sita and Hanuman, and they never visited Kathmandu. So, in that warm November week, I was free to enjoy the city, without having to worry too much about its history or styles of architecture. I could even switch off from it altogether and sit in the hotel patio with a novel if I felt like it.

My Kathmandu list was short: the Hanuman Dhoka (the old Royal Palace), named after the statue of Hanuman at the main gate, and the giant statue of the sleeping Vishnu, Rama's great Original, just outside the city at Budhanilkantha.

Poor Hanuman turned out to be no more than a large heap of red cloaks, trimmed with gold tinsel, under a red and gold umbrella. Even his eyes, the most important feature for a Hindu worshipper, were buried under a pile of marigold garlands. Inside the palace, we cast a professional eye over King Tribhuvan's bicycles, which were gathering dust in a jumble of His Master's Voice gramophones, standard lamps and other Western paraphernalia, then took a taxi out to the sleeping Vishnu. A five-metre giant, the four-armed Vishnu was reclining in a water tank, supported by the immense coils of the serpent king, Ananta. As we were obviously not Hindus, we were not allowed to cross the stepping-stones into the tank. We had to peer at him from a distance, through the railings. But at least we could have a look, unlike King Birendra. The Kings of Nepal are revered as incarnations of Vishnu, but none of them has dared look on this holy likeness since a seventeenth-century monarch dreamed that death would follow the view.

Souvenir-hunting is a problem for cyclists. For me, having two small panniers imposes a welcome discipline and I'm glad to have the excuse not to go shopping. But my two friends found temptation in every chowk, and one of my abiding memories of the trip is the rustle of their plastic bags, as they struggled to stuff their panniers, agonising over what to throw away to make room for the latest Nepali waistcoat, embroidered hat or hand-woven shawl – all of them totally unwearable at home. On our last afternoon in Kathmandu, I left them to it and took a rickshaw-ride to Durbar Square, to the small gilt-roofed temple of Maru Ganesh. The elephant-headed Ganesh is the god of auspicious beginnings and I queued up with the other departing travellers to crack a coconut at his shrine and pray for a safe journey. With no doctors out there, no detailed maps and no idea where we should spend our nights, I felt that we needed all the help we could get.

And Ganesh smiled on us. We had fought our way through the morning rush from our hotel in Thamel, along Kath-mandu's main artery, the Kanti Path, on to the main Pokhara highway, and were just starting the great climb out of the Kathmandu Valley, when my chain came off, three times. We all stopped and peered. Central Kathmandu is as flat as a pancake and I had never needed to change gear on the ride in from the airport. So it was only now, on my first steep hill, that the broken lever on my derailleur came to light. It had been snapped in two on the flight. As luck, or Ganesh, would have it, we were just opposite a small cycle-repair shed.

'Broke,' said the cycle-man.

'Broke,' said I.

'Come.'

With that monosyllabic exchange, he wheeled my bicycle a few doors up the road to another little shed, where there was a welder. A piece of tin was found and, between them, they cut out a perfect patch and welded it on. The whole operation took about ten minutes and cost me a few pence. I sailed away, my patched lever working like a dream, reflecting that in England I should probably have had to buy a complete new derailleur, or parts which would have taken a month to arrive! Travel in the developing world certainly has its advantages.

Suzanna turned out to be a strong cyclist, who could breeze up hills that I could never contemplate and speed along the flat like a cheetah. And I knew from past experience that my ballerina friend Shirley was always professionally fit and agile, and could outcycle me any day of the week. So, although I was the most experienced cyclist, I was by far the slowest and had to do the most pushing on mountain roads. Yet we somehow managed to accommodate ourselves to one another: either they went ahead and waited for me under a shady tree, or they let me lead our small caravan and cruised along behind at the pace I set. To my relief, it was never a problem and I never felt under pressure to speed up.

It took us the whole morning to climb out of the Kathmandu Valley. Pollution gets trapped in the hollow and for the first 20 kilometres we choked and gasped as trucks belched even more diesel fumes into the acrid haze. As we climbed, we could look down on the pall of dirty grey which swallowed all the capital's landmarks. Then, suddenly, near the top of the pass, we broke clear. The air sparkled, the sky was a brilliant blue and we saw the majestic mountains, piled range upon snowy range, from Ganesh Himal in the east right round to the twin peaks of Manaslu Himal in the west. At the summit, we sat on a wall, eating chocolate and dried apricots. The highway below us seemed almost vertical, a series of dizzying bends. Trucks and buses crawled cautiously round them, looking as small as Dinky toys from our eagle's eyrie. We overtook them all when we whirled down towards the rushing white waters of the Mahesh river. On mountain switchbacks, two wheels feel safer and are much more manoeuvrable than four.

By mid-afternoon, we had swept down the highway to Naubise, our Nepalese ordeal by fire. We had grown soft in Kathmandu, where every amenity was available to the Western tourist: clean, comfortable beds, en-suite bathrooms, and well-cooked food of every nationality. So it was a bit hard to meet our severest test of character on our very first day out. In Naubise, we had our worst lodgings of the whole trip.

We had decided to spend our first night there, as it stood at the junction of the Prithvi Highway to Pokhara, which we were following, and the Tribhuvan Highway, the oldest, most mountainous of Nepal's main roads, which leads directly south into India. Although no hotels were mentioned in our guide books, we reasoned that such an important junction must have a few modest places to stay. And, in any case, there were no guide-book recommendations before Mugling, which was another 80 kilometres along the highway, much too great a distance to cover in the afternoon when we were already tired after the climb out of Kathmandu.

There were two open-fronted transport cafés, which a local boy assured us were lodges. As group leader, I was deputed to inspect the first. An old one-eyed man, who was stirring a pot at the front of the café, said, 'Go to Kathmandu.' But he reluctantly sent a small boy to lead me to the accommodation. I groped my way through to the back of the unlit building, where I felt rather than saw a slatted-wood staircase, which had no handrail and led up to even inkier blackness. My courage failed me.

We inspected the next place together. It was run by a grimy couple, and the woman was considerably more positive than the man. She led us through the café, over the flowing stream from a hosepipe (used for washing-up), past a stinking latrine which was leaking across the corridor, and up a similar wooden staircase to next-door's. This staircase was more manageable, as it had an electric light. Above was a large loft, most of it a grain store, though there were two small cubicles for guests. Each had two wooden plank beds with pillows and quilts of unspeakable filthiness.

I have travelled in many remote places and slept in some awful accommodation, but I had never seen a lodge quite so depressing as this one. We were in despair, particularly as we were sure that the grain would be a nesting place for rats. But what could we do? We could cycle no further and we were not carrying tents. I think, if I had been alone, I might perhaps have chickened out and caught the next bus to Mugling. I would have been too worried to spend the night on my own in such a hovel, when I was unfamiliar with the Nepalese and had no idea what sort of behaviour to expect. But there was safety in numbers. Catching a bus seemed like cheating, and we would have missed cycling a spectacular mountain road. So we swallowed hard and agreed to take the two rooms. At least we had sleeping mats and bags, so we could zip ourselves into our own clean spaces.

We filled up the rest of the daylight hours by strolling back up the hill to the last village we had swept through, which was slightly more salubrious, but had no accommodation. There we had our first meal of *dhal bhat*, the lentil, rice and curried vegetable dish which is the staple food of Nepal. There was a student there who spoke good English, so the unemployed of the village gathered round for tea and a chat. The student told us that he had really wanted to read medicine, and had good enough grades to do it. But the Kathmandu medical school was the only one in Nepal, and it took in only twenty students a year. To get one of those twenty places required the kind of influence which his family didn't have, so he had settled for microbiology.

'My parents are so disappointed in me,' he said sadly. 'They are poor farmers, illiterate people, who have saved up all their lives, and got themselves into debt, to send me to university to become a doctor. That has been their dream. But they don't understand the system. They don't realise that you haven't a chance unless you're related to the King or one of the ministers. And they don't even know what microbiology is. I do my best. I've found a side-job now in Kathmandu and that brings in a bit of money to help us along.'

We took our evening meal (*dhal bhat* again) in our own café, in the company of a sociable young Nepali, who drove lorries in Qatar. The rest of the locals drank quietly under the gimlet eyes of our hostess. Their tipple was neat, colourless alcohol, which came out of the fridge in triangular plastic packets. We three travellers had just one bottle of beer between us, as the prospect of a night expedition down the rickety stairs to the filthy latrine was too grim to contemplate. Then we screwed up our courage for bed. Blackouts are frequent in Nepal, but our luck was in and we climbed to the loft by the light of the dim bulb. I took one of the two rooms on my own, while Shirley and Suzanna opted to share.

Some time after midnight, there was stumbling on the stairs and my bedroom door was kicked open. An irate truck driver in a navy-blue shell suit burst into the room and towered over my bed shouting. He was much the worse for drink and he had a prostitute in tow. As far as I could gather, he was accusing me of occupying a bed which he had booked for himself and was ordering me out of it. I refused to budge. He then began to plead with me.

'Come out here, just for five minutes, just to talk,' he wheedled.

My two friends came to the rescue. The Nepalis are short, small-boned men and we were three tall, hefty women. Our size and determination soon had the poor little truck driver cowering. He retreated down the loft steps muttering indignantly, while his lady friend stared at us and giggled. The rest of the night was uneventful, except for scuffling in the granary, followed by horrendous shrieks and howls, which we took to be the resident cats performing their rodent duties.

Morning brought the sun and, with it, optimism and a feeling of confidence. If we could manage the Naubise lodge, we could manage anything. The mountain scenery was unbelievably beautiful and we had ten days' spectacular cycling. As far as Narayangadh, there was always a tumbling, white-water river beside us – first the Mahesh Khola, then the Trisuli, then the mighty Narayani. And for three days, our ride was dominated by the magnificent Annapurnas. Down on the flat Terai, we went on an elephant safari to see the rhinos in the Royal Chitwan National Park; and for three hours we prowled the jungle on foot, under the protection of two park rangers. It was a fascinating day, but we were disappointed to see no tigers.

We had one more alarming nocturnal visit, when policemen burst into our room in another basic lodge, searching for teak poachers (the Nepalese accuse the Indians of poaching teak, while the Indians accuse the Nepalese of poaching tigers). We peered at them through our mosquito nets like three startled Miss Havishams through the cobwebs. Then I rose from my bed and towered above them.

'I am not a poacher,' I said. 'I am a headmistress.'

They withdrew submissively. The rest of our nights were undisturbed.

Mountain bikers, for whom the antique Tribhuvan High-way from Naubise to Hetauda seems to be the ultimate Nepalese challenge, will no doubt despise us for taking the long and easy way round. The friendly Motel Avocado at Hetauda had a cyclists' log book, where the macho riders who had climbed to Daman, then on to the 2,840-metre Simbhaniyang Pass, noted their times and the numbers of broken spokes and punctures. We followed the rivers round those fearsome mountains, pedalling along good surfaces financed by the Indian and Chinese Governments. We covered 201 kilometres from Naubise to Hetauda, as against their 123, but for lazy cyclists it was well worth the detour.

The Nepalese lived up to their reputation for friendliness. We met a retired Gurkha corporal, who had set up a roadside teastall on his British Army pension. In Narayangadh, we shared Uncle's Lodge with a team of social workers, who were running a conference for small-town chemists on how to recognise AIDS and encourage safe sex. In Nijgarh, we spent a pleasant evening with the two proprietors of the local independent, English-medium school, whose own daughter was at a boarding school in Darjeeling, where the standards and facilities were better than in Nepal. And in our second-worst roadside lodge in the Terai, we were pounced on by a bossy Rajput from Ajmer, with a splendid Rajasthani moustache, who marched us across the irrigation dykes, on an evening of fireflies, to visit a leper hospital.

'The doctors will be extremely happy to see you. Not just happy. Extremely happy,' he declared.

Back in our lodge, he told us that he was an orthopaedic surgeon, but the doctors up at the hospital wouldn't employ him, because he drank too much. The lodge-keeper winked and made the 'screw-loose' sign.

The only Western traveller we met across the whole of rural Nepal was the Russian Ambassador. He was an enthusiastic Anglophile after a twelve-year tour of duty in London and was delighted to have a chat with us in our smart hotel in Bharatpur. He told us that his son had attended Holland Park Comprehensive.

'It was not too good. It was rather a socialist school,' he said disdainfully.

He was driving across the Terai to attend a conference in Lumbini, the birthplace of the Buddha. He explained, to our surprise, that Russia has a tiny Buddhist minority and he had been asked to represent their interests.

Altogether, it was a varied and eventful ride, but I never somehow connected with Nepal; the empathy was lacking. So it was a happy morning for me when we wheeled into Janakpur and I could make a start on the real business of the trip.

CB EO

### The Miraculous Birth and Marriage of Sita

*Janaka was King of Videha, an ancient state which lay between the Gandak and Kosi Rivers and comprised part of present-day Nepal as well as northern Bihar. His capital was Mithila, now Janakpur, a Hindu pilgrimage city just north of the Nepalese border with India.*

*King Janaka was a wealthy, wise and virtuous monarch. One day, as he was ploughing a field as part of a sacrificial ritual, he found a baby girl lying in a furrow. He took her home, called her Sita (furrow) and brought her up as his own daughter. She grew in grace and beauty, 'her eyes as large as the petals of the water lily, her face like a flower, bright as the full moon, and her feet as lovely as lotus buds'. King Janaka was overwhelmed with suitors seeking her hand in marriage.*

*To solve the problem, he decided to set a test. He had a gigantic bow in his palace, which had once belonged to the great god Shiva and was the terror of all the Immortals. He proclaimed that he would give Sita in marriage to the man who could lift and string this mighty weapon. Every suitor failed in the attempt and, as the years went by, the King became worried that Sita would never find a husband.*

*Then along came Rama, a prince of Kosala. He and his brother Lakshmana had been living in the forest under the tutelage of the virtuous sage Vishvamitra. Vishvamitra took the two boys to Mithila, as he had been invited to assist King Janaka in a sacrifice. He asked the King to show the divine bow to Rama. The bow, garlanded with flowers and scented with sandalwood, was* kept in an iron box and it took five hundred men to draw the eight-wheeled waggon on which it lay. Rama opened the box and, to the amazement of King Janaka and the assembled courtiers, lifted the giant bow with one hand and 'smiling with a slight effort' bent it with such force that it snapped in two. There was a crash like Indra's thunderbolt and the onlookers, stunned by the reverberations, fell unconscious to the ground.

'Oh blessed sage,' cried King Janaka. 'I have witnessed the strength of Rama, the son of Dasaratha, who has performed an unimaginable feat. It will be the glory of my dynasty that Sita receive Rama as her lord! Sita, whom I love more than my life, shall be given to Rama.'

King Dasaratha gave his consent to the marriage and travelled to Mithila to attend the celebration. Rama was married to Sita and, at the same wedding ceremony, Lakshmana was married to Sita's sister, Urmila, and Rama's other two brothers, Bharata and Satrughna, were married to King Janaka's nieces, Mandavi and Shrutikirti.

For each of his sons, King Dasaratha gave a hundred thousand cows to the brahmins, each cow with gilded horns and accompanied by a calf. King Janaka gave magnificent dowries of cows, carpets, fine fabrics and dresses, gold, silver, pearls and coral, male and female slaves, and an entire army with elephants, horses, chariots and infantry of celestial splendour, all laden with precious ornaments. When the happy couples were united, a rain of flowers fell down from heaven, where the nymphs danced and sang for joy. Then King Dasaratha, with Rama and Sita and the other brides and grooms, returned to his city of Ayodhya.

In the earliest narrations of the epic, Sita would have been a human princess, just as Rama was a human prince. But as Rama gradually, over the centuries, became identified with the god Vishnu, so Sita became an incarnation of his consort, Lakshmi. The connection between the two is clear. Sita's name (furrow) associates her with the earth, fertility and abundance. Lakshmi, who was born like Aphrodite from the foam of the sea, seated on a blossoming lotus and carrying lotus flowers in her hands, represents the vitality of vegetation and wealth in the form of water. She is worshipped as the goddess of material well-being and good fortune.

# **3** The Kingdom of Videha

*Janakpur – Motihari – Muzafarpur – Patna*

JANAKPUR HAD CLEARLY GONE DONWHILL since King Janaka's glorious days. As we rattled into the town over the level crossing, the potholes and the skiddy stretches of sand where the road had once been, it was difficult to see the place as the former capital of a great kingdom. King Janaka was so rich that he could afford to give dowries of jewels, elephants and entire armies. Today's inhabitants looked as if they would have to save up to endow so much as a mop and bucket. But it was a nice, tranquil little town for all that, protected from noisy traffic by a ring road. At its heart lay the great temple to Sita and the sacred bathing tanks which, according to legend, King Janaka had excavated for the guests at her wedding. At festival times, the town is thronged with pilgrims from all over Nepal and India. They come in devout droves to celebrate the marriage of Sita to Rama at the Vivaha Panchami in late November or early December, and to watch the magnificent processions on Rama's birthday, Rama-navami, in late March or early April, depending on the state of the moon. Unfortunately, we had just missed the wedding celebrations. The town was back to its usual sleepy self and we were able to take our pick of its mediocre hotels.

We chose the Hotel Rama, which seemed more welcoming than the Welcome, and had just settled down in the garden to recover from the day's ride over a well-earned Pepsi, when along came Dolly. Dolly was an A-level science student. She was a niece of the Rama's owner and seemed to haunt the garden in search of tourists. As she was learning English, she offered to be our guide in Janakpur, in return for the chance to practise her conversation.

We realised how seriously she was taking her duties when she appeared at our bedroom doors early next morning, to take us to her home for breakfast. Morning not being our best time, we would rather have breakfasted quietly on our own in the hotel. But we dressed hastily, anxious to oblige, and jumped on our bicycles to follow her neat little cycling figure in its Punjabi trouser suit. We went out through a maze of narrow alleys to the ring road, where Dolly took a side turning up a dusty, unmade track and led us into a big yard at the back of a factory.

Her home was more like a row of sheds than a house. Each shed was one room with its own door leading out into the yard; there was no interconnection. When we arrived, Dolly's mother was at the outdoor well in her nightdress, drawing water under the evil yellow gaze of a goat. There was a very young calf, which was suspended from two poles in a sort of body sling, to prevent it from putting weight on a broken leg. And there was a younger brother, who was doing wheelies on his little BMX. Otherwise, the great yard was empty of everything but rusting machine parts from the silent factory. It was Saturday morning.

We went into Dolly's room, where there was a bed, a table which she could use only if she sat in the lotus position at the bed's foot, and a row of three hard wooden chairs. All Dolly's books and clothes were kept in suitcases on a high shelf. She climbed up on the bed and fished out some of her paintings to show us, stylised flowers in what we took to be traditional designs. As we were admiring these, her father arrived to help entertain us. He spoke no English and he perched on the bed beside Dolly, dressed only in a vest and a pair of rather revealing underpants. Dolly's elder brother was propelled reluctantly into the room by his mother; he was in a great sulk because he wanted to go on an outing with his friends and was not being allowed to. Finally, Dolly's mother joined us and handed round Nepalese tea which, like Indian tea, is a mixture of water and milk, boiled up with tea leaves and swamped in sugar. It was served with excruciatingly sweet biscuits and handfuls of *chaat,* spicy nibbles which were by far the best part of the meal. With the exception of the grumpy elder brother, they were all very welcoming, but it was a heavy social occasion and we were relieved when we could decently pay our compliments and go. Dolly led us back to our hotel and promised to come after lunch to show us the temples.

She arrived in the afternoon, dressed in another elegant Punjabi suit, this one in palest grey, with the long overshirt cut on the bias. She was so small and trim that we felt positively lumpen by comparison. The contrast between our ungainly selves and the tidy little Nepalese people was heightened by the fact that we were the only Westerners in Janakpur, apart from a retired Belgian schoolmaster called Jos. We clomped down the street like three female Gullivers in Lilliput.

Dolly led us straight to Sita's vast white marble temple, the Janaki Mandir. Although it was completed as recently as 1911 and was a Hindu temple, its style was high Moghul, with rococo flourishes for good measure. The massive towers, more like the watchtowers of a fortress than the corners of a temple, were surrounded by octagonal parapets and crowned with chattris, while galleried arcades of regal splendour overlooked the courtyards; and to pile decoration on decoration, even the multifoil Moghul arches were covered in exuberant red and green arabesques. I found it all a bit overwhelming, which was no doubt the intention of its founder, the Maharani of the one-time princely state of Tikamgarh. It was a temple which looked tawdry and Disneylike in the strong light of early afternoon, but it took on a mellow charm in the evenings, when the marble turned gold in the sunset and the mouldering garbage was less visible. Then, the silver gates of the inner sanctum were opened to reveal the image of Sita, and there was a small trickle of devotees with offerings of sweets and flowers.

Next door stood another startling building, the marriage pavilion, or Vivaha Mandap. With its Nepalese pagoda roof, it looked more at home in its setting than its imposing mosque-like neighbour, but it had glass walls, like an elegant bus shelter. We walked up the avenue of trees draped in fairy lights and peered at the figures of Rama and Sita, sitting together on a couch in their red wedding finery with great gold crowns on their heads. They were dolls with porcelain faces, identical except that the Sita doll was wearing a small gold ring in its nose. The same incongruous white faces peered out at us from all the pavilion's minor shrines. Rama's brothers and their wives were the same model, from the same doll factory. It was a popular model, because it appeared in many shrines across north India. Rama and Sita, as members of the Indo-Aryan race, would have been on the pale side of brown; or as incarnations of Vishnu and Lakshmi, they might have been blue, the colour of heaven and the immortal gods. So what was the point of the ghastly sepulchral white? Was it wishful thinking? The matrimonial advertisements in Indian newspapers make it clear that fair skin is the Indian ideal. Did Rama and Sita have to be fairer than fair? Or were these sickly white-faced dolls the only models available? It was not the kind of question I could put to Dolly. She said a quick prayer before the shrine to Durga in Rama's temple, but was keener to be photographed and visit the market stalls than she was to discuss theology.

The temple buildings were lifeless and we soon left them, to stroll in the shade of the palm trees around the great tanks. These were the real social centres of the town. Worshippers entering the water to perform their ritual cleansing jostled for space on the steps with the dhobi wallahs doing the laundry, women washing the dishes and shampooing their children, sellers of lentils and spinach, and the odd goat or cow. We strayed one morning, without Dolly, to the far side of one of the tanks, when we were looking for the post office, and started to trip over human bones poking through the sand. We had stumbled on the burning ghats and were just in time to see the holy water put to another use. A woman's body on a woven stretcher (a woman, because the shroud was red) was being immersed by her family before they cremated her. Immersion in one of the sacred rivers of India frees the deceased from sin. As there was no river in Janakpur, the tank had to do – but at least it was a very holy tank, being in such an important pilgrim centre. With cries of 'Ram Nam Satya Hai' (Rama's name is truth) they carried her over to the pyre, at which point we beat a tactful retreat. New temples were going up all round the tanks, built of prestressed concrete and painted raspberry pink. Dominating one of them was a giant statue of Hanuman with ten extra heads, five small monkey faces sprouting from each ear, in addition to the normal-sized head on his neck.

Finding our way around Janakpur was not easy. It took us two whole afternoons to find the post office, and when we found it, it was closed because the postal workers were on strike. Then there was the money-changing problem. We took rickshaws out to the one bank which was supposed to deal in foreign exchange, only to find that the facility had been moved to a bank in the winding alleys of the town centre. By the time we tracked it down, it had closed for the day. Like most of Asia, Nepal was a country where even the simplest tasks took a frustrating amount of time. And people ask me how I fill up my days on my long trips!

There was one holy pilgrim site about 20 kilometres outside the town. This was Dhanukha, the very spot where Rama bent Shiva's mighty bow and qualified to be Sita's husband. We thought of cycling out there, but I was given so many conflicting sets of directions that I despaired of finding it. So I booked a jeep and we all set off across the paddy fields. The road began as potholed tarmac, but soon deteriorated into deeply rutted sand. We forded streams and swooped down precipitous banks into dried-up river beds. And if crossing the countryside was unnerving, the villages we passed through were even worse. I have never seen so many small children milling about, dashing out in front of the jeep, along with the goats, cows, pigs and chickens. How we managed to get to Dhanukha and back without mowing down at least a dozen small creatures I shall never know. Jos the Belgian said that he got to Dhanukha on a local bus, without fording any streams, so we must have taken some adventurous short cuts in our jeep.

Dhanukha was a village with one dirt road, standing in the middle of open country. The jeep driver parked outside the teastall and pointed to a distant peepul tree surrounded by a high wall. The wall, like those of Janakpur's new temples, was painted in what is obviously the sacred colour of south Nepal, bright blancmange pink. We walked across the field to the enclosure and found the remains of Shiva's bow, an immense arc of what appeared to be solidified lava. It was strewn with decaying marigold garlands and the remnants of candles and incense sticks. Nearby was a modest temple, with the names 'Rama' and 'Sita' baked on its tiled columns, and a *dharamshala,* or hostel for pilgrims. We were the only visitors that morning and we enjoyed the quiet fields and the shady clumps of woodland. It was peaceful too without Dolly, whose attentions were becoming wearing.

She visited our hotel three times a day. She would pop in to see us at 6 a.m. on her way to school, again at lunchtime, and again in the evening. Shirley and Suzanna were sharing a room in the hotel, and their door was nearer to the entrance than mine, so that was where Dolly made her first appearance. I took to pretending that I hadn't heard her and stayed in my room with the door locked. She pressed us constantly to visit her home again. I managed to avoid it, but the others were kinder. Shirley went there early one morning with gifts of warm jerseys and woollen trousers that she and Suzanna had worn on the journey out and no longer needed in Nepal. On our last afternoon, we took Dolly into the bazaar and bought her a Chicago Bulls windcheater, which she had had her eye on for some days. We thought that would be the end of Dolly, but we were wrong.

We had done most of our packing and had just settled down to a nice pre-dinner glass of whisky when she appeared yet again, this time with her parents in their best clothes.

'My father is a businessman,' she said proudly. 'Import export.'

'What does he export?'

'Men. Workpeople.'

We were stunned into silence. No one noticed and Dolly went on to tell us that her mother also worked. She ran the family planning clinic, fighting a losing battle against Janakpur's enthusiasm for large families.

They brought us presents of glass bangles from Varanasi, which were designed for small-boned Indians and embarrassingly difficult for us to get over our beefy English wrists. We couldn't offer whisky to serious Hindus, nor did we feel that we could carry on drinking in their presence, so we made polite conversation for what seemed an eternity, while the Rama's mice scurried round our feet and even jumped over them, totally unafraid.

The family finally went on their way – but it was still not the end of Dolly. Like clockwork, at 6 a.m., she came racing along the hotel corridor, the proud sporter of Shirley's camel trousers and her own new Chicago Bulls jacket, to bid us one final farewell on her way to school.

For me, Janakpur was a disappointment. I had visited many of India's holy cities and been moved by the masses of pilgrims, the buzz, the stir, the flowers, the incense, the bells and the high drama when the doors of the inner sanctum were thrown open to reveal the god. Even out of festival times, they were places of spiritual intensity. But Janakpur was a desert of the soul: no priests or sadhus, few devotees and none of the mystic aura of sites trodden by the feet of pilgrims over the centuries. It seemed to have no place in the sacred geography of India, perhaps because it was no longer a part of India. It was a very ordinary little town.

After four days in Janakpur, we were glad to be on the road again. We cycled out of town through fifteen kilometres of brilliant-green paddy fields and peaceful grazing to the Indian border at Jaleshwar and our next frustration. The guide books said that the border at Jaleshwar was closed to foreigners, but I had consulted the Nepalese Embassy and the Indian High Commission in London and been assured by both that we would be allowed through on our bicycles. We cruised through Jaleshwar's bazaar and across no-man's-land without being challenged and were just beginning to congratulate ourselves on our good fortune, when we came to a road block and a small clutch of officials who told us that we must go to Birganj to cross. This was a great blow, as it meant we had to go all the way back along the Mahendra Highway to Hetauda, a journey of nearly 200 kilometres, before turning south again to the Indian border. We protested and were referred to the CDO (the Nepalese, like the Indians, love initials).

Back in Jaleshwar town, we tracked down the Chief District Officer, who was holding court on the upper balcony of a rickety wooden building. Being European and, particularly, English, is still very useful in those parts, so Shirley and I were led by a brisk soldier to the front of the queue. Suzanna stayed outside to guard the bicycles, hemmed in by a mob of ragged Nepalese, who were waiting to cross into India for work. She said it reminded her of a bad day at the Paddington benefits office.

The CDO, in his beige jumper and sandals, was full of concern. He offered us tea and rang his superiors for advice. If we understood his halting English correctly, the problem seemed to be that the Nepalese could stamp us out of Nepal, but there was no immigration office on the other side which could stamp us into India. He told us to go back to Janakpur and make an appointment with the chief of police. Our hearts sank. Even if we managed to find the police chief in that maze of a town, it seemed unlikely that he would be able to solve what was in fact a problem on the Indian side. It was just not worth the effort. We ate our lunch of bananas under a tree, then turned back wearily towards Janakpur. The landscape which had seemed so idyllic in the morning had changed with our mood and was now nothing more than a succession of dreary fields to be cycled past.

We couldn't face returning to the Hotel Rama and Dolly, so we decided to check in at the Welcome and hide there until we had made our onward travel arrangements. But kindly Ganesh, the remover of obstacles, remembered my offering in Kathmandu and came to our rescue again. On our way into Janakpur, we passed the bus station, stopped to make enquiries and found that there was an express coach to Birganj leaving in five minutes. The conductor rushed us to the ticket office, our bicycles were heaved up on to the roof and we just had time to take our seats before the bus lurched out of the yard. The road which had taken us three days to cycle flashed by in the sunset and by 11 p.m. we were installed in a triple room in a tolerable Birganj hotel. We had no Nepalese rupees to pay the bill, but that was a problem which could be left until morning.

Needless to say, it took two hours of rickshaw-riding around Birganj to change money, even though we were accompanied by the obliging young hotel manager. Then we cycled to the border. Our passports were stamped on the Nepalese side and we wove in and out of the stream of ox carts and ponies and traps into the filthy tip of a town on the Indian side, Raxaul Bazaar. There we searched for the immigration office until we could stand the noise and the diesel fumes no longer. We escaped into open country without getting an Indian stamp in our passports. For all the administrative good the journey to Birganj had done us, we might just as well have crossed the border at Jaleshwar!

The frontier between Nepal and India is no more than a line on the map. In Bihar, we found ourselves in the same terrain, among the same people speaking the same languages. The main difference, from our perspective, was the shocking state of the highways.

Bihar is the most poverty-stricken and the most corrupt of all the Indian states, where major criminals hold parliamentary seats, and state subsidies for the provision of services such as education and road building go straight into the pockets of the political leaders. Mr Laloo Prasad Yadav, Bihar's former chief minister, was the most notorious crook of them all. He continued for years to enjoy all the luxuries of high office in India, despite being on bail on embezzlement charges, to the tune of £180 million on one fodder scam alone. When he was finally forced out of office for gross corruption in 1997, he simply arranged for his wife, Rabri Devi, to take over as chief minister, and nothing changed. The proportion of illiterates in the state continued to soar and potholes the size of bomb-craters continued to sink in the roads. Even where roads were repaired, the work was done on the cheap, without a smooth top surface. So we rattled along in Bihar on beds of irregular, hand-broken stones, held together with a dribble of tar. The panniers jumped off our bikes, screws worked loose and we feared for our tyres. When we stopped cycling at night, our teeth were rattling in our heads and even as we lay in bed our limbs were still vibrating. Rural Nepal might be just as poor as Bihar, but at least there were decent highways there.

When King Dasaratha hurried from Ayodhya to Janakpur for Rama's wedding, Valmiki says that he completed the journey in four days, but he gives no indication of the route. So we were free to travel to Ayodhya in any way we pleased. There was nothing of historical interest along the most direct cross-country roads and we knew that their condition would be appalling. In addition, banditry in the state was so rampant that even motorists were afraid to be out in country places alone. The only safe and sensible course was to cycle down the main road to the state capital, Patna, and take the train from there. It looked like a three-day ride, with large enough towns on the way to provide a choice of hotels.

Our first night was almost a disaster. We thought, when we wheeled into Motihari in the dark (and a power-cut for good measure), that the town's only claim to fame was that George Orwell was born there. Not so. A glittering Bollywood film star also came from Motihari and she had chosen that day to come home for her wedding. We pushed our bicycles from one hotel to another, picking up all the teenaged boys in the town as we went, only to find that every bed had been booked months before by the wedding guests. One hotel manager seemed kinder and more concerned than the others, so we asked if we could doss down in reception. But reception was booked up too, as overflow dormitory space.

'Go to the railway station,' he said. 'Report to the railway police. They'll look after you. You'll be safe there.'

Our safety was his prime concern, which shows how bad the law-and-order situation was in Bihar. Fortunately, we had our youthful escort. They exhausted us with questions, when we were already so tired that we could scarcely put one foot in front of the other, but they were eager and well meaning, and we were grateful for their protection along the pitch-black roads. They marched us to the station and turned us over to the duty police sergeant.

Motihari railway station had a retiring room, but permission to use it could be given only by the station-master, who had gone home. I made a written application: we were three English ladies, travelling alone by bicycle, and we had nowhere safe to spend the night. I elaborated on our plight, and wrote a letter which would have wrung the heart of even the sternest station-master. It was taken off by a messenger. We drank endless cups of tea with the sergeant, congratulated him on the station's admirable record of solved crimes (including bicycle theft) as shown on a painted wallchart, and joined him in the station mess for a *thali*, a tray of rice with *dhal* and a selection of curried vegetables. As the hours drifted by, we got worried and I came out in a mysterious and furiously itching rash. But the sergeant kept smiling and saying, 'No problem.'

Permission finally came and we were escorted down the platform to a dirty room with two rumpled beds, which were obviously used by the station personnel. The mosquito nets were in holes and the dust-covered dressing table was littered with shaving gear, hair oil, sparsely bristled toothbrushes, candle stubs and paraffin for the lamp. At the back was a concrete shower and a fetid hole in the ground. But at least we could lock ourselves in with our bicycles, and we were under police protection. We pushed the two beds together and slept across them, like a row of sardines, cocooned in our sleeping bags.

The next night we found quite a pleasant roadside hotel, but then we ran out of rupees and the banks in Muzafarpur were on strike. We gave up. We had just about enough money for the bus to Patna and a pair of teenaged brothers adopted us and led us to the stop – but not before they had taken us to a professional photographer, so that we could all be photographed together, 'for memory'.

As might be expected of the capital of Bihar, Patna was filthy, garbage-strewn, ill lit, rat-infested and dangerous at night. Shirley was thrilled to see the Dalai Lama at a fundraising meeting for Tibetan refugees; and we were all glad to be able to stock up on Indian rupees. But we left as soon as we could get a booking on the train to Faisabad. We set out from our hotel in the dark, just before dawn, and I nearly ended up as a jammy blob on the station road. A truck came roaring along, headlights blazing, on the wrong side of a roundabout. Blinded, I swerved out of the way and threw myself off my bicycle. The truck missed me by inches. It was my closest call ever in all my thousands of miles of cycling. When I close my eyes, I can still see those terrifying headlights and the menacing black bulk of the truck speeding towards me.

In Bihar the corruption continues. The politicians grow rich, the robbers and gangsters prosper, the police kill and maim the citizens they are supposed to serve, and armies of *goondas* wage caste wars which lead to the massacre of thousands of innocent villagers every year. The government in Delhi must know all about it, as Bihar's turpitude features almost daily in India's admirably free press, but it seems powerless to intervene – possibly because Bihar has fifty-four seats in Parliament and its politicians have to be courted in times of shifting coalitions. I should have left the state in utter despair, had it not been for the smiling, helpful schoolboys of Motihari and Muzafarpur. They were the one ray of hope in an otherwise desperate situation.

## C3 80

### The Birth and Boyhood of Rama

*King Dasaratha was a mighty warrior, who could trace his ancestry back to the Sun God himself. He was the ruler of Kosala, a north Indian kingdom on the banks of the River Sarayu, where his capital was the splendid city of Ayodhya. He was wise, just, learned in the scriptures and devoted to the gods. Under his illustrious rule, the land was bountiful and his loving people prospered.*

*King Dasaratha had three beautiful wives, the Queens Kausalya, Kaikeyi and Sumitra. But, to his great sadness, he had no heir to the throne. When he was nine thousand years old and beginning to tire of his kingly burden, he decided to make one last appeal to the gods. He prepared the Ashvamedha, the elaborate and costly horse sacrifice, which only a monarch could perform.*

*Meanwhile, in heaven, there was despair among the Immortals. Ravana, the ten-headed king of the demon Rakshasas, was terrorising the universe. Even the gods were powerless to control him. Not only was he King of Lanka, but he was a Brahmin, a member of the priestly caste, and a Vedic scholar. By performing the extraordinary ascetic feat of standing on his head for ten thousand years between five fires, he had so impressed the God of Creation, Brahma, that Brahma had made him invincible.*

*The gods went in a body to Brahma to plead for his help. Ravana was insufferable in his pride, they said. He was so evil, that 'in his presence the sun ceases to shine, the wind fails to blow and the ocean, garlanded with waves, is still'. Brahma comforted them. When Ravana had asked for the boon of invincibility, he had asked for power against the gods, demons and other spirits, but he had been too conceited to think that he might be overcome by men or beasts, so he had not asked for protection against them.*

*At this point in the discussion, Vishnu, the Preserver of the Universe, arrived on Garuda, his vehicle which was half man, half eagle. Vishnu had already become incarnate in the world on six occasions, in six different forms, to save it from the forces of evil. Now the other gods prostrated themselves at his feet, begging him to go down to earth again, this time as a human being, to destroy the Demon King. Vishnu agreed. 'For eleven thousand years,' he promised, 'I shall dwell in the world of men and protect the earth.'*

*Brahma then persuaded the other gods to support Vishnu by producing earthly sons. He himself yawned, and out of his mouth sprang Jambavan, the King of the Bears. Then Indra, the God of the Thunderbolt, produced Bali, the Monkey King, while the other major gods produced his advisers and generals. Surya, the God of the Sun, created the monkey chieftain, Sugriva. And finally, Vayu, the Wind God, produced the gigantic monkey, Hanuman, who could fly through the air with the speed of Garuda, tear up mountains and change his form at will. When the gods had produced the forest leaders, they went on to create millions of monkeys and bears to be their foot soldiers. All these animals assembled in Kishkindha, in what is now Karnataka, to await Vishnu's call.*

*These events took place in heaven just as King Dasaratha's horse sacrifice was reaching its climax. The onlookers stood* amazed as a splendid being, covered in celestial jewels, 'tall as the peak of a mountain, fierce as a raging tiger, resembling the sun', rose from the sacrificial flames and offered King Dasaratha a golden bowl with a silver lid. It contained pasaya, a mixture of rice and milk, specially prepared by the gods, which the King was told to serve to his wives. They would then present him with the sons, for whose sake he had undertaken the sacrifice.

King Dasaratha hurried to the Queens' apartments. He gave half of the pasaya to his first queen, Kausalya, and a quarter each to Queens Kaikeyi and Sumitra. Some months later, Queen Kausalya gave birth to Rama, a baby of immeasurable glory, as might be expected of a child who was half Vishnu. His body was the blue of the firmament, he had slightly red eyes, a golden navel, long arms, a voice like a kettledrum, and he carried the imprints of Vishnu's conch and discus on the palms of his hands. Bharata, a baby of great strength and grace, was born to Kaikeyi and was a quarter Vishnu; and Sumitra produced twin boys, Lakshmana and Satrughna, each one-eighth of Vishnu and destined to become great warriors. They were all born at the most auspicious conjunction of the stars and, at their birth, the heavenly spirits danced and sang, celestial gongs sounded and the gods showered the babies with flowers. King Dasaratha and all the citizens of Ayodhya were delighted.

The four boys were perfect. They were obedient, modest, prudent and well versed in the scriptures. When they went hunting in the forest, there was no one to compare with them in the skills of archery and horsemanship. Rama was their standard bearer, 'dear to all and brilliant as the moon', and his younger brother, Lakshmana, was his devoted follower. The pair were inseparable. Lakshmana would never eat until Rama had been served and, wherever Rama went, Lakshmana went too, bow in hand, to protect him.

When they were fifteen years old, the great sage Vishvamitra came to Ayodhya. He told King Dasaratha that demons, sent by Ravana, were polluting his altar with blood and flesh, whenever he tried to perform a sacrifice. He asked for Rama's help in destroying them. In return, he would pass on to Rama the secrets of his divine weapons. Reluctantly, King Dasaratha agreed and Vishvamitra led Rama, with Lakshmana in attendance, to the banks of the River Sarayu. There he gave them two mantras, which would protect them and free them from hunger, fatigue, fever and old age. On their way to Vishvamitra's ashram, Rama killed a demoness, who was terrorising the people of the forest, and the sage rewarded him for his bravery by giving him Vishnu's discus, Shiva's spear and a clutch of celestial arrows and javelins, together with the mantras which controlled them. As Rama spoke their names, the forest was filled with shadowy figures, some like blazing fires, others like columns of smoke and others as bright as the rays of the sun and moon. Rama greeted them respectfully. 'When I call you to mind,' he said, 'come and serve me.' The weapons bowed low, circumambulated their master and faded into the air.

Rama put them to good use in Vishvamitra's ashram. When the demons Maricha and Subahu came screeching through the air and tried to defile the sacrificial flames with lumps of raw flesh, Rama released Brahma's mighty Manava weapon, struck Maricha and hurled him a hundred miles into the sea. The weapon of Agni, the God of Fire, despatched Subahu and the rest of the demon army was destroyed by the swift arrows of Vayu, the God of the Wind. The sacrifice complete, Vishvamitra led Rama to the court of King Janaka, where he bent Shiva's bow and married Sita.

This account of Rama's birth, boyhood and marriage appears in the Bala Kanda, the first book of The Ramayana. It is generally agreed to be later than Valmiki. Its purpose is to demonstrate the divine nature of Rama as an incarnation of Vishnu.

# 4 Ayodhya

(1996 and 1998)

THE DISTINGUISHED ECONOMIST JK Galbraith, who spent three years of his long and varied career as American Ambassador to India, once described the country as 'a functioning anarchy'. He must have been thinking of the station parcels office in Patna.

It was a scene of utter chaos that winter morning. Porters milled about among the mountains of packing cases and bursting produce baskets, while mobs of customers brandished documents under the noses of barking officials, screaming for attention. The manager, swathed in a woollen headscarf, shawl and mittens, crouched over a one-bar electric fire inside a kind of tiger's cage, and it was there that we had to fill in our forms and pay our despatch fee. We had to describe our bicycles as 'old and damaged', pay for a porter to make a crude cardboard label to dangle on the handlebars, then leave them to the mercies of the system. My friends were convinced that they were seeing the last of their gleaming machines, but I knew better. My Condor had made many Indian rail journeys and had always arrived unscathed at the other end. I was quite sure that we should find our bicycles smiling at us in the Faisabad parcels office, which is exactly what happened.

Faisabad is the place to stay if you want to visit Ayodhya. It has one or two reasonable hotels and we were badly in need of a mouse-free room and a functioning shower after crossing Nepal and Bihar. But even in Faisabad, things were not perfect. I was shown to a room, which was quite acceptable, but the Indian-style lavatory was filthy.

'I'll take the room,' I said to the manager, 'but will you please have the lavatory cleaned first?'

He rang down to reception, and soon a little boy of perhaps eight or nine appeared, wearing a woolly hat and carrying a twig brush. The manager dragged him by the ear to the lavatory, roared at him and beat him about the head. The little boy started to cry. I couldn't stand it. I rushed into the bathroom.

'Stop hitting him! Show him how you expect to have the job done and supervise him properly. He's only a child. You can't expect him to clean thoroughly, unless you tell him how to do it and provide him with some lavatory cleaner. That little twig brush is useless.'

The manager stormed out of the room, greatly offended. He belonged to a higher caste, and lavatories and their supervision were not jobs for the likes of him. When the porter brought up my panniers, I showed him the handle, which had just dropped off the bathroom door. He grinned, opened my wardrobe and shut the offending handle inside. Door furniture was not his responsibility. In a complex organisation like a hotel, the strict job-demarcations of caste make it extremely difficult to get anything done efficiently.

Meanwhile, down at reception, the clerk pointed to our baggage and said to the porter, 'Two men, one lady.' Two men, one lady? Which of us, we wondered, was the lady? We were all tall and we were all wearing trousers. The same sort of thing was said about us in many hotels. Then one day, the light dawned. Shirley and Suzanna had crossbars on their bicycles, whereas mine had a mixte frame. I was the lady! Indians find it quite difficult to determine the sex of Westerners, when we all dress alike. Even our hair-length is no guide, as men often wear it long, while their girlfriends are close cropped. Failing any other yardstick, the hotels were relying on our cycle-frames.

Faisabad was once the capital of the wealthy princely state of Oudh, or Avadh, until the Nawab Asaf-ud-Daula moved it to Lucknow in 1775. It remained a garrison town under the Nawabs and later under the British, who planted trees and laid out their spacious Civil Lines around the barracks, well away from the Indians and their noisy, crowded bazaar. Now the Dogra Regiment has its headquarters in the Cambridge Barracks, but the lawns of the officers' bungalows are still manicured and dotted with rose-beds, the stones are still whitewashed and the sentries at the gates still salute smartly. If it weren't for the sunshine and the turbans, it could be Camberley.

We rode our bicycles through the gardens and parks of the Civil Lines, past schools where the neatly uniformed tots of 'Blooming Buds' and 'The Rainbow Nursery' were standing in orderly rows, singing to the beat of a drum, and came to the River Sarayu. Here, a small temple marks the spot where Rama ascended to heaven after his eleven thousand years on earth, to assume once more the divine form of Vishnu. The shallow grey water with its sandbanks was very peaceful. Blue-hulled boats dotted the nearer shore, while the further shore was veiled in mist. Along the bank, between the temple and the Company Gardens, stood a row of thatched shacks, where sadhus in yellow robes, their faces and upper bodies smeared in ash, were hanging out their washing. These wandering holy men were devotees of Rama, on pilgrimage to this sacred spot. A herd of cows gazed at us from the bathing ghats. They looked uncomfortable, lying on the concrete steps, but centuries of sacredness had given them a supremely confident air.

We were made welcome in the small temple. Its central courtyard was a busy place. Women were doing their washing, small children were playing ball and an old man, who looked exactly like Mahatma Gandhi, was sitting cross-legged on the floor, reading a newspaper. Many old people in India retire to temples, where they live in monkish cells and are fed by the temple authorities. They find both companionship and spiritual comfort in their later years. It seems like 'care in the community' at its best. On this visit, we were simply shown the shrine, where Rama, Sita and Lakshmana stood in a row, splendid in red and gold, with a little Hanuman kneeling modestly at their feet. In 1996, perhaps because I was with a Hindu rickshaw wallah, the priest appeared and gave us both *prasad*, sweets which had been offered to Rama and were therefore sanctified. Afterwards, he ladled some holy water out of a brass pot. My driver drank his with enthusiasm, but I was more cautious. I raised my two palmsful of what I guessed was untreated river water to my forehead and chin, then rubbed it on my face and into my hands, hoping that this would look reverent enough. My donation of five rupees was certainly considered reverent, as the priest beamed and gave me a red tilak mark on my forehead, blessing me in the name of Lakshmi, Sita's heavenly Original. Once outside the temple, I gave my *prasad* to the bony rickshaw wallah, who looked as if he needed the sustenance more than I did. In any case, the small snails of fudge were so sweet that they set my teeth on edge.

After the disappointment of Janakpur, Rama's small temple in Faisabad was a delight. It was not crowded, but it was alive, it was cherished, and it had acquired a kind of spiritual charge over the centuries. It was a deeply significant holy place, because it was truly a *tirtha.* The Sanskrit word for a pilgrim site actually means 'ford', as these sites are the crossing places between the human and the divine. At the end of his reign, Rama waded into the River Sarayu to make the transition between earth and heaven. It is therefore a *tirtha* in the literal as well as the spiritual sense. It has a special quality, which I could feel, even though I was there as a sympathetic observer, rather than a worshipper. Away from the sectarian tensions of the more politicised pilgrim destinations, it was a peaceful place where Hinduism, which is in essence the world's most tolerant religion, could flourish uncorrupted. I was grateful to Hanuman and *The Ramayana* for leading me there.

Ayodhya itself is altogether different. As Rama's birthplace, it is one of India's seven holy cities, but in recent years it has been ravaged by fanaticism and sectarian violence.

The problem centres around the Babri Masjid, the mosque built by Babur, the first of the great Moghul Emperors (1504–1530). It is claimed that he tore down a Hindu temple on that site, the very spot where Rama was born. The Muslim population in Ayodhya is relatively subdued, so the mosque gradually fell into disuse and for years it was locked up. Then, in December 1949, a miracle occurred – an image of Rama materialised in the night in the central hall of the mosque. Sceptics said that it had been smuggled inside with the connivance of the predominantly Hindu police and the local politicians, but this did nothing to deter the faithful, who crept in to worship. In 1984, the Vishwa Hindu Parishad, a militant Hindu organisation, announced their intention of 'liberating Lord Rama from his Muslim jail', and the following year, a court order gave Hindus the right to worship openly in the disputed building. This led to widespread agitation between Hindus and Muslims throughout north India, but it was a popular measure with Hindus and it helped the political allies of the VHP, the nationalist Hindu BJP (Bharatiya Janata Party), to jump from two seats in the Lok Sabha to eighty-six in the 1989 elections. As part of the election campaign, the VHP encouraged Hindus to bring bricks to Ayodhya from all parts of India, to build a new Rama temple. The secular Congress Government intervened and serious communal rioting broke out, claiming many lives, especially in Bihar.

The Hindu fundamentalists continued to fan the communal flames for political advantage. In 1990, they announced their intention of taking over the Babri Masjid and constructing the Ram Janambhumi (Rama's birthplace) temple on the site. At the same time, Mr L K Advani of the BJP staged the most spectacular stunt. Harking back to the glorious days of the Hindu epics, he rode a *rath yatra*, a temple chariot (mechanised for comfort and convenience), 10,000 kilometres across India, from Somnath to Ayodhya, whipping up frenzy and leaving a trail of communal riots in his wake. Finally, on 6 December 1992, Ayodhya was invaded by 300,000 extremists of the VHP, the Shiv Sena and other nationalist Hindu organisations. Armed with crowbars and axes, they utterly destroyed the mosque. The ensuing riots across India resulted in the massacre of some 2,500 people, mostly Muslims, while Hindus were set upon in Pakistan and Bangladesh.

The future of the site is such a political hot potato that no government has dared to come to a decision about it. The problem was referred to the judiciary, who decided in 1994 in favour of preserving the status quo. Meanwhile, the Vishwa Hindu Parishad, ignoring the decision of the court, began to prepare a splendid temple for the Ram Janambhumi. Flagstones and pillars are even now being carved in workshops in Rajasthan, ready to be transported to Ayodhya. The dream of the VHP is a new temple for the new millennium.

The popularity of the BJP continued to grow until, in early 1998, it finally won enough seats in the Lok Sabha to form a coalition government, under the leadership of the relatively moderate Atal Behari Vajpayee. Contrary to the vision of Nehru, Gandhi and the Congress Party, who established a secular state at Independence, the BJP are working towards a Hindu nation. But they have been something of a disappointment to their militant allies. It is one thing to be vociferously Hindu in opposition. Once in power, they are reliant on the support of a fragile coalition and hope to attract at least some of the country's 120 million Muslim votes, so they have to tone down the rhetoric. On 6 December, the anniversary of the destruction of the Babri Masjid, it is always a tense day in India. Sectarian violence erupts into annual killings and there are often unseemly skirmishes in both Houses of Parliament, with calls from the Congress Party for the punishment of the destroyers.

The end of the conflict gets no nearer. An illiterate mass, exposed to glorious mythology on television (the serialisation of *The Ramayana* and *The Mahabharata* were both enormously popular and carried no warning to simple people that the epics were not historical fact) and cynical gimmicks such as Mr Advani's *rath yatra*, are matchwood waiting for the match. The sad thing is that all this feuding has nothing to do with true Hinduism. The Hindu scriptures teach tolerance and due regard for all human beings. As the respected journalist Khushwant Singh wrote in *The Indian Express* in 1990, 'Mahatma Gandhi, perhaps the greatest Hindu of our times and the most ardent worshipper of Shri Rama, if alive today, would have undoubtedly undertaken a fast unto death to prevent this impious and anti-Hindu design to destroy a mosque.'

I have visited Ayodhya twice. The first time, in 1996, I found it a very tense place. A high wall with a barbed-wire topping surrounds the area which was once the Babri Masjid and a roadblock bars the approach. I waited behind the barrier with a crowd of curious, but friendly, Indians. 'What is your name? What is your profession? How much do you earn? How many children have you got? Why aren't they with you? Where is your husband? Why do you come here, when it's so different from England? How old are you? You are in good condition for your age, madam.' The usual catechism and comments which plague any traveller in the East.

At 1.50 p.m. a khaki platoon marched smartly on to the scene and at 2.00 p.m. precisely the barrier was lifted and the mob surged up the hill towards the temple site with cries of 'Sri Ramaji ki jai!' (Glory to Lord Rama!). I was searched at the main gate and sent away because I was carrying a camera. A shy, giggly young sergeant, who saw what was happening, came up the road to meet me and volunteered to look after it for me. With his small, neat moustache, he was tremendously handsome in a 1930s kind of way, like a pale-brown version of Errol Flynn. Back at the entrance, I had a handbag search, then a body search behind a screen by two policewomen. I walked with the pilgrims down a long corridor to a row of thatched booths. There, my passport and visa details were laboriously copied out into a ledger by a chatty clerk, who put me through the catechism again. Then we were divided by sex for another, more thorough body search. I presented the usual puzzle. I was barred from following the ladies and directed by a bossy corporal into the men's queue, where the poor young policeman nearly died of embarrassment when he started to run his hands over my body. The policewomen sniggered as he bundled me hastily into their queue. My handbag and passport were then taken from me and I emerged into the great flat field which was once the Babri Masjid.

In single file, we zigzagged through steel cattle pens, about ten feet high, set out like a Hampton Court maze. Back and forth, round and round, up a small rise and down again, we bustled along under a battery of pointed rifles until we reached the makeshift shrine. Rama and Sita in their gold crowns sat in a box under a faded awning. There was much fervent praying. I had only two rupees in my pocket, a paltry offering from a foreigner, but the priest gave me *prasad* and blessed me with the red tilak on my forehead just the same. Then we all trooped out through more steel pens into a back alley. My handbag was waiting at the front entrance and the smiling young sergeant came up with my camera, then whisked me off to a nearby stall for a delicious glass of tea with ginger.

That was in 1996. In 1998, the atmosphere seemed less tense, perhaps because 6 December had just passed without bloodshed. But the military presence at the disputed site was even stronger and they were more wary of foreigners; we might be journalists who were planning to file a sensational report. The Commanding Officer interrogated us.

'Why do you want to visit the Ram Janambhumi?'

'I am writing a book about *The Ramayana* and I need to visit all the sites connected with the epic.'

'What is so special about Ayodhya?'

'It is the birthplace of the Lord Rama.'

'Where have you come from?'

'From Janakpur, where Sri Sita was born.'

'And where are you going next?'

'To Allahabad, then to Chitrakut, where Lord Rama began his exile.'

'Have you read *The Ramayana*?'

'Yes. I have read Valmiki all the way through, but in an English translation. I'm afraid I can't read Sanskrit.'

It took me a quarter of an hour to convince him of our honourable intentions, a quarter of an hour of close questioning about Hindu religion in general as well as the plot of *The Ramayana*. Apparently satisfied with my answers, he asked to see our passports. That was almost our downfall. Shirley, who has dual British and Turkish nationality, had chosen to travel in India on her Turkish passport. The crescent of Islam emblazoned on its green cover (the colour of the Prophet) nearly produced apoplexy in our Hindu interrogator. We protested that Shirley was an Englishwoman, born and brought up in England, who just happened to be married to a Turk. She swore that she was not, and never had been, a Muslim, and the CO finally let us through.

To visit the other pilgrim sites in Ayodhya, I hired a cycle-rickshaw and a neat young man with some English as my guide. He was a BA student, who said that he was an accredited guide, but was reluctant to tell me his name. 'It would be too difficult for you. Just call me PK' he said.

We started our tour on the banks of the Sarayu River, at another pilgrim *tirtha*, the crossing place hallowed by Rama when he went over the river into exile. There I had a river and cow *puja* from a brahmin. He first poured river water over my hands, then marked my forehead with a gold tilak. Then we both held a calf's tail, while the brahmin chanted in Sanskrit, introducing my name and my parents' names. After that, I walked clockwise round his two calves and he touched my forehead with their tails. In the middle of all this holiness, with PK acting as interpreter, he asked:

'How much are you going to give me?'

'Five rupees.'

'Two hundred.'

'Ten.'

'One hundred.'

Between Sanskrit *slokas*, we bargained. He finally settled for twenty rupees and a photo of himself grinning toothlessly at me over the backs of his calves.

Everywhere I went in Ayodhya, the sight of me arriving in a rickshaw sent financial hopes, like rockets, zooming into the stratosphere. At Sita's Kitchen, I was told that food is cooked daily and provided, free of charge, to the one thousand holy men and women in residence in the compound. I was taken to meet their teacher, a grey-bearded, bespectacled scholar dressed in yellow, who was sitting impassively before the main shrine. PK made obeisance, forehead to the ground, and I did the same. Then a ledger was produced, in which donors had entered their names and addresses and the amount of their donations. All the amounts ended with the figure 1. Some people say that it is luckier to end a sum in a 1 rather than a 0, but I'm a bit too sceptical to believe that. It looked to me as if the entries had been doctored afterwards to encourage, or shame, others. For instance, 20 rupees had become 201 rupees, and 100 rupees had been converted by a deft hand to 1001 rupees. I declined to become a 'life member' of the shrine and my gift of 50 rupees, to help feed the *sanyasis*, was accepted by the teacher with a steely glare.

'The Master says that much more generous gifts are usually given by wealthy Hindus such as yourself,' said PK.

'But I'm not a Hindu.'

'What are you then?'

'I'm a Christian.'

'It's all the same. Here you are Hindu. Hindus and Christians same. Muslims other.'

As we sped away to the Hanuman shrine, I laid into PK. I had now spent 50 rupees on the *sanyasis'* food and 20 rupees on the cow *puja* – 70 rupees on just two visits. I was not made of money. That was my lot! I had many, many temples still to visit, and I couldn't afford *pujas* at all of them. I didn't mind giving a few rupees more than the local people, but I hated the constant pressure to give outrageous sums which were out of all proportion to the needs and running expenses of the temples. So no more *pujas*! PK sat in offended silence for a while, then began to prepare the ground for his eventual tip.

'I have five sisters, which is such a problem for me and my parents. Girls are so expensive. It will cost us at least 2,000 rupees for each of their weddings, not to mention their dowries.'

I was the only foreigner that day in Ayodhya. I could afford to travel there from England, hire a guide and pay for a rickshaw, so I was obviously wealthy beyond the aspirations of anyone in the town. I couldn't blame them for trying to prise money out of me on any pretext. But I couldn't help getting annoyed, all the same. Here I was, in one of India's seven holy cities, trying to do serious research on one of India's holiest books, and I was being distracted from start to finish by demands for money. I took off my shoes and stamped up the flight of steps to Hanuman's temple, which was thronged with devotees. With them, I circumambulated the shrine and peered inside at Hanuman in a silver tiara, swathed in marigold garlands. But I sped away from the priest, who was beckoning me to *puja*, his finger already scarlet with kumkum powder.

The day went downhill after that. I paid off PK, whose knowledge of sacred Ayodhya was too limited, and went to the Tourist Office. None of the priests had a word of anything but Hindi, so I hoped to pick up a well-informed, English-speaking guide there. I was unlucky. The man on duty had two words of English. He pointed at the biro, with which I was signing the visitors' book, and said 'one pen', indicating that he wished to have it. There was no lunch at the adjacent Tourist Bungalow, as they were catering for a party of 95; and the lavatories there were closed, as the tanks had run out of water. So I crouched behind a bush in true Indian style, then bought a bunch of bananas and a Fanta at a stall on the main road. I was just peeling my second banana, when the other three were snatched off the table by one of Hanuman's living relatives. I realised then why all the stallholders were armed with big sticks. The town was swarming with monkeys, who thieved everything in sight. Fortunately for the stallholders, they could be chased off – unlike the sacred cows, who could munch as much of the produce as they liked, and no one was allowed to touch them.

On the way back to my Faisabad hotel, I felt mean and ungenerous. I was riding along in a cycle-rickshaw, when a chorus of shouts in the street caused the rickshaw wallah to brake. A ragged man came panting up with my handbag, which had slid from the seat as the rickshaw jolted over a pothole. I hadn't noticed. But for his honesty, I should have lost my money and my notebooks. Such shining selflessness in the midst of blatant rapacity is one of India's paradoxes. They will badger, bully and importune until you could scream with exasperation. Then they will melt your heart with a simple act of kindness.

There are well over a hundred temples in Ayodhya and I have still not visited all of them. The city is described in the Vedas, the Hindu scriptures, as 'a city built by Gods, as prosperous as paradise itself', a description hardly merited by today's jumble of gimcrack pilgrim stalls and run-down temples, all under the watchful eye of the military. Yet, despite its tensions and its poverty, it still has the spiritual charge of a true pilgrim centre. The devotion at the shrines was almost palpable. Despite the fact that I rarely buy souvenirs, in Ayodhya I was moved to buy a hand-woven saffron shawl, block-printed in red with the names of Rama and Sita. I wore it often that winter in the chill of early morning and was greeted by the breakfast waiters with delighted cries of 'Sita Ram, Sita Ram'. I shall go back again one day to finish my tour, and perhaps even to view the new Ram Janambhumi Temple, if the Vishwa Hindu Parishad is successful in its millennium project.

CB 80

## Palace Intrigue

*King Dasaratha watched his sons grow up in strength, wisdom and virtue. Rama, in particular, was the delight of the people of Ayodhya. He was so dear to everyone, and so gifted in all the arts of kingship, that his father decided to install him without delay as prince regent. He consulted the astrologers and fixed an auspicious day for the enthronement. In their happiness, the people began to decorate the city with flags and banners. They scattered flowers along the highways and filled the air with incense and costly perfumes.*

*But disaster struck on the eve of the enthronement. The three Queens, who all loved Rama, were at first equally delighted at the news. But Queen Kaikeyi, the mother of Bharata, had a mischievous hunch-backed servant, Manthara. This scheming creature poured venom into her ear. She convinced her mistress that when Rama ascended the throne, he would attack Bharata, as his greatest rival, and Kaikeyi would become a slave to Rama's mother, Queen Kausalya. It was all part of King Dasaratha's plot against her and her son that he had sent Bharata away at the critical time on a visit to his grandfather. Kaikeyi had the power to protect herself and make Bharata king, if only she would use it.*

*Queen Kaikeyi was King Dasaratha's favourite wife. He had once taken her on a campaign and been wounded in battle.*

Queen Kaikeyi had rescued him from the battlefield and saved him from certain death. In his gratitude, the King had granted her two wishes, which he vowed to honour, whatever they might be. She had saved them up and now, at Manthara's prompting, she demanded the fulfilment of the promise. Her two wishes were that Bharata should be enthroned as prince regent and Rama be banished to the forest for fourteen years.

King Dasaratha pleaded in vain. Kaikeyi was obdurate and the aged King was a man of his word. He was 'caught in the net of duty'. Rama was equally dutiful. When Queen Kaikeyi told him about the two wishes, he immediately agreed to honour his father's promise. He gave up the kingdom without a murmur and retained his composure, though everyone around him was weeping and fainting with grief. Lakshmana, always quick to anger on Rama's behalf, had to be restrained from killing his father, whose infatuation with Kaikeyi had caused such a disaster. And though he tried to dissuade her, the faithful Sita insisted on accompanying Rama into the Dandaka Forest: 'I shall remain sinless by following piously in the steps of my consort, for a husband is a God.' There was never any doubt that Lakshmana would go too. He would walk before them, bow in hand, to protect them, and would gather the roots, herbs and fruits on which the three hermits would live.

When they had given away all their possessions and clothed themselves in tree bark, they went to pay their last visit to King Dasaratha and his Queens. The King made one final attempt to overthrow destiny. 'Since the boons I bestowed on Kaikeyi have made me lose my wits,' he cried to Rama, 'you must become King of Ayodhya and have me confined!' But Rama disclaimed all ambition. 'I shall never renounce what is right for a mere kingdom.' He embraced his grieving parents, then summoned his charioteer.

Ayodhya was in turmoil. When the three exiles drove towards the gates, the whole population, even the elephants and horses, surged after them, crying out to the charioteer to slow down, so that they could gaze once more into Rama's face. Their tears fell in torrents 'as water falls from the lotuses when fishes leap'. The sacred fires in the temples died, the sun went into eclipse, a tempest arose and earthquakes shook the city. King Dasaratha *was overwhelmed with grief at his own folly and fell into a mortal decline.*

*By evening, Rama, Sita and Lakshmana had reached the Tamasa river. The crowds from Ayodhya were still with them, but they managed to escape the next morning by crossing the river before the sleeping citizens awoke. They travelled for days across King Dasaratha's Kingdom of Kosala, until they reached the lands of the friendly monarch, King Guha, and the holy River Ganges. Near the city of Shringavera, Rama and Sita lay down under a sacred fig tree and slept, while Lakshmana and King Guha watched over them. Then Rama sent his faithful charioteer, Sumantra, back to Ayodhya and the three exiles crossed the Ganges in a boat provided by King Guha.*

*They were alone now in the forest. They walked along the south bank of the Ganges until they reached its confluence with the River Yamuna at Prayag, where they spent the night at the hermitage of the great rishi, Bharadvaja. The rishi had heard of their misfortune and begged them to stay with him in Prayag for the fourteen years of their exile. But Prayag was still quite near to Ayodhya and Rama was afraid that his people would discover his hiding place and flock to visit him. So Bharadvaja directed him to the Chitrakuta mountain. 'Those who behold the peaks of Chitrakuta obtain felicity and the mind is free from illusion there.'*

*Rama and Lakshmana constructed a raft, placed Sita, 'who was unimaginably lovely and somewhat apprehensive', on a throne of reeds, and ferried her across the River Yamuna in safety. Then they followed the winding paths through delightful woodlands, where peacocks called and monkeys and elephants roamed, until they reached holy Chitrakuta.*

# 5 Across the Sacred Rivers

*Faisabad – Lucknow – Allahabad – Chitrakut*

F ROM FAISABAD WE SPENT two days cycling to Lucknow. This was a diversion from Rama's route, but Lucknow, formerly the capital of Oudh and the scene of the famous siege, is an interesting city, and Shirley and Suzanna were keen to see it. From there we had to take the train to Allahabad, as it was already 23 December and we had made an advance booking at a smart hotel for the Christmas period. On blacked-out nights in dismal, mouse-ridden quarters, it was the gleaming prospect of dinners in an elegant restaurant, breakfasts in a flowering garden and a television with some world news which had kept up our spirits.

As for *The Ramayana*, I was really in luck in Allahabad. The Tourist Office was run by a most knowledgeable young man, who had gained an MA in English at Allahabad University, despite being blind from birth in a country where help for disabled people is limited. He knew the modern names of the places mentioned in Valmiki and told me how to reach them.

Allahabad is a spacious city with flat, wide boulevards – perfect for cycling. We shopped on our bicycles for Christmas treats of plum cake, tangerines and Indian gin and whisky, known as IMFL (Indian Manufactured Foreign Liquor). And on Christmas Eve, we cycled in the dark to Midnight Mass at the Anglican Cathedral of All Saints. There we were dazzled by the spectacle. As we turned from Mahatma Gandhi Road into the cathedral roundabout, we found the whole bulk of the mighty building, from its foundations up to its roof, picked out in hectic neon lights and surmounted by a flashing green cross. We approached the west door through trees swathed in flickering fairy lights, under an arcade of blinding red and green neon. Inside, the cathedral was packed with Indian Christians. We were the only white faces in sight, but we were made extremely welcome. The service itself was less impressive than the lighting. There was no choir and the congregation's rendering of the sung Communion service was very hesitant, especially as the tinny piano was out of tune and was played by a struggling learner. The sermon was long, but the taking of Communion was short. So many hopeful communicants surged up to the altar, that the clergy were overwhelmed and could do no more than bless them and send them back smartly to their seats. We read accounts in the newspapers of Hindus going on the rampage and setting fire to Christian missions in different parts of the country, but in Allahabad both the Anglican and Catholic churches were crowded over Christmas and no one interfered. Tolerance reigned in this holy Hindu city.

Rama passed through Allahabad, Valmiki's Prayag, which is specially sacred because it stands at the confluence of three holy rivers, the Ganges, the Yamuna (sometimes spelt Jumna), and the mystical, invisible River Saraswati. In the scriptures, it is known as *Tirth Raj*, the king of all pilgrim centres. All rivers have particular purifying powers at the places where they merge, and pilgrims bathe throughout the year in Allahabad. But there is a special festival in January, the Magh Mela, which draws in two or three million pilgrims from all over India. And at the Kumbh Mela, which takes place in Allahabad every twelve years, when Jupiter is in Taurus, the city has to cope (according to the Tourist Office literature) with no fewer than 35 million Hindus who pour in for the biggest pilgrim fair in the world.

I cycled across the city to the site of Bharadvaja's 'ravishing hermitage', where the great Rishi had tried in vain to persuade the three exiles to stay with him for the whole fourteen years of their banishment. A notice behind a crumbling wall read BHARADWAJ ASHRAM but the gate was locked. I peered through a gap in the fence and saw mouldering buildings with broken windows and an over-grown garden. Such dereliction doesn't necessarily mean that a building in India is abandoned. Maintenance is not their strong point. But I saw no sign of life in the ashram, and none of the locals seemed to know anything about it, so I cycled back to the hotel.

Christmas Day dawned warm and sunny, so we followed Rama down to the *sangam*, the spit of sand where the holy rivers actually merge. A huge township of tents was under construction for the coming Mela, and the worshippers were already congregating in advance of the great processions of holy men which open the proceedings. These sadhus from all over India are the stars of the show. A hundred thousand of them, many stark naked, parade into the Mela ground garlanded with marigolds, while the pilgrims shower them with flowers and brass bands play. The leaders of the various sects precede the rank and file on richly caparisoned eleph-ants, shaded from the sun by tasselled, bejewelled umbrellas. It is one of India's greatest spectacles – and one of the noisiest, as amplifiers follow the brass bands. The event may be holy, but it's an organisational nightmare for the adminis-tration of Allahabad. Despite security, hundreds of pilgrims are sometimes trampled to death in the stampede for a sacred dip, and epidemics in such overcrowded quarters are only a rainstorm away. But on Christmas morning, the *sangam* was tranquil and we enjoyed our walk along the sandy shore. Even Hanuman was at peace there. Instead of standing in his usual warlike posture, mace in hand, he was reclining at his ease on a sunken bed. It is said that when the Ganges floods, the waters rise just far enough to touch his feet in reverence before they begin to recede. We circumambulated his sleep-ing vermilion figure and watched his worshippers sprinkling him with marigolds and rose petals.

The *tirtha* where Rama's party crossed the Ganges was not on any of my maps, but my useful friend in the Tourist Office identified Valmiki's Shringavera with Shringverpur, forty kilometres from Allahabad, and gave me the directions for a taxi – which was as well, as neither the hotel staff nor the manager of the taxi firm had ever heard of the place! We set out on a cold foggy morning, following the Ganges northwest out of the city along a country road. The fog was so thick that we heard the camel bells long before we saw the lumbering caravans. We turned off the road down a narrow track, where the sand was so deeply rutted that we got no further than the first village. From there we went on foot to the Ganges, with a horde of giggling children for company. Foreigners are rarities in Shringverpur.

The sacred crossing place was deserted on that bleak winter morning, but it was obviously much frequented at other times. The wide sandy shore which sloped down into the river was a forest of wooden beds, where the devout spent the night, to be sure of their sunrise dip in the holy waters. We climbed the rock to the temple overlooking the beach and saw the usual dazzling white porcelain images of Rama, Sita and Lakshmana, but this time they were peering at us over the side of a delightful little boat. Then we were led across the fields by our gaggle of village children to the Ramchaura, a platform beneath a peepul tree, which is said to be the exact spot where Rama and Sita slept on the night before their embarkation. Here the faithful Lakshmana bathed their feet, then spent the night watching over them, together with Guha, the King of the Boatmen.

Taking a break from cycling in a good hotel is always a treat, eagerly anticipated. But after a few days, I can't wait to be back on the road again. We breakfasted for the last time on the Hotel Yatrik's scrambled eggs, which must be the best in the whole of India, then made our way from the Civil Lines through the pandemonium of the bazaar to the one bridge over the Yamuna. India's 'functioning anarchy' was in full swing there. The bridge is a two-tier miracle of Victorian engineering. The top tier carries deafening trains. The bottom is a nightmare road, where lorries and cars thunder across the iron plates of the centre lanes, blowing their horns to no purpose. To the sides, separated by the cast-iron struts of the bridge's structure, there are narrow passageways for unmechanised transport. Here herds of cattle, bullock carts, horses and traps, laden camels, pedestrians and cyclists fight for their few inches of space. The bridge shudders and rattles, while the black diesel smoke belched out by the lorries has nowhere to escape and fills the confined space with choking fumes. It was a real struggle to cycle across and I envied Rama his raft of reeds. We burst out into the sunshine at the far end like prisoners escaping from a dungeon.

Over the Yamuna the landscape changed. Though it was no longer Valmiki's deep forest of flowering trees, where monkeys, peacocks and elephants roamed, it was more wooded than the country to the north and there were streams where kingfishers dived in a flash of blue. There were even hills with rocky outcrops, which made a change from the endless flatlands of the Gangetic Plain. It was delightful cycling along quiet roads.

Chitrakut was 120 kilometres from Allahabad and there were few places marked on the map. We were banking on Mau, about halfway along the road, to provide us with overnight accommodation, but it turned out to be a tiny place with no facilities whatsoever. Then Shirley got a puncture, which meant that we had to stop at a wayside teastall with a very convenient cycle repairer next door.

In the teastall, we started chatting to a student with good English, who told us about a *dharamshala*, guest accommodation attached to a college at Shankargarh. We found the place after a long search through Shankargarh's bazaar and were greeted by a group of enthusiastic students. They took us inside a large open-sided hall, brought us chairs and plied us with cups of tea, while a messenger was sent to find the official in charge of accommodation. Night fell, the mosquitos came out in swarms, village children played tag in the echoing hall, and still we waited. It was an agricultural college consisting of the hall, a few classrooms round an open yard ('courtyard' is too grand a term for the area of broken concrete and weeds), with dormitories above for the boarders, and basic lavatories and showers behind a low wall. As always in Indian villages, we were hemmed in by crowds of locals, who came in droves to stare at us. Finally, the official arrived and led us to a windowless box, which he proudly called 'the VIP room'. He supplied us with one small candle, by whose dim light we could pick out the shapes of three wooden plank beds and three steel and plastic wickerwork chairs full of holes. But at least the bare concrete was well swept and we were grateful for a roof over our heads. Dinner that night consisted of samosas and sweets, the only edible items to be found in the bazaar. But we did manage to buy some more candles to cheer up our lodgings. We spread our mats and sleeping bags on the wooden planks and slept surprisingly well. We might have lacked home comforts, but at least we had a door that bolted, and we knew that we and our bicycles were safe inside. The next evening we cycled into the holy city of Chitrakut, which stands on the border between Uttar Pradesh and Madhya Pradesh. There Lakshmana built Rama and Sita a charming leafy hut; but we three repaired thankfully to the UP Tourist Lodge with its restaurant and hot showers.

೧೩ ೮೦

## Rama and Bharata

*The three exiles were delighted with Chitrakuta. Lakshmana built them a spacious hut, roofed it with branches of flowering trees and carpeted it with springy grass. Inside he hung their gold-plated bows, their swords in golden scabbards and their shields of chased silver. Then, facing the east, he built an altar for the sacrificial fire.*

*The countryside was idyllic. The mountain shimmered with precious metals and provided an abundance of fruit, roots, honey and sparkling water; and the limpid River Mandakini, with its blue and white lotus flowers, was the perfect place to bathe. They were surrounded by the creatures of the forest, but even the tigers, panthers and bears were as tame as the herds of deer and the playful monkeys. Rama would sit for hours with Sita on a rocky ledge overhanging the river, exulting in the natural beauties which surrounded them. He was so content in the wilderness that he gave no thought to the loss of his kingdom. He had done his duty by obeying his father and he had, or so he thought, brought happiness to his brother, Bharata.*

*But Bharata was far from happy. He was staying with his maternal grandfather when a messenger arrived from Ayodhya,* summoning him home with all speed. He found the city in mourning. King Dasaratha, overcome with grief at the loss of Rama and his own folly, had died of a broken heart. Kaikeyi was jubilant, because her son was to be crowned king.

To her surprise, Bharata was horrified when he heard how she had plotted on his behalf. He performed the funeral rites for his father, then announced his intention of going into the forest to find Rama, who was the rightful king, and bring him back in state to Ayodhya.

As soon as a special highway had been laid from the city to the Ganges, Bharata set out with nine thousand elephants, six thousand chariots and a hundred thousand cavalry, an escort fit for a king. He was accompanied by his brother Satrughna and the three Queens in a splendid chariot. All the citizens of Ayodhya dressed up in their finest clothes and rushed along behind, overjoyed at the prospect of seeing Rama again.

Guha, the King of the Boatmen, helped them all across the Ganges and the Rishi Bharadvaja produced a miraculous entertainment for the whole contingent. Rivers of pure water were made to flow at their feet, trees were transformed into dancing girls, who bathed them and served them with exquisite wines and dishes of goat, venison, boar and peacock, all in delicious sauces. Even the animals were pampered, with pasture as green as emeralds, sugar cane and ponds of crystal water. The next morning, the Rishi directed Bharata to the Chitrakuta mountain. In his wisdom, he told Bharata that he should not reproach his mother, Kaikeyi, for what had happened, but should accept it as the working of a higher destiny. 'Rama's exile will prove a source of great felicity,' he prophesied, 'and his banishment will be productive of great good to the gods, the Danavas and the pure-souled Rishis here.'

Bharata's vast army marched along the south bank of the Yamuna with a noise like thunder, scattering the wild animals and raising such a cloud of dust that it blotted out the heavens. When he heard the tumult, Lakshmana climbed a tree to report. He saw King Dasaratha's faithful elephant, Shatrumjaya, leading the procession, but he was not carrying the white canopy of the worlds. This was the first inkling the brothers had of their father's death. Lakshmana, always spoiling for a fight, declared that

Bharata had ascended the throne and had come to kill Rama, to secure his position. Rama, as always, knew better and calmed him down.

Bharata left his army behind and came forward on foot with Satrughna to greet his brothers. He was grief-stricken to find Rama, the prince who had always lived a life of the greatest luxury, sitting on the floor of his hut dressed in bark and antelope skins, with a long beard and matted hair. He pleaded with him to return to Ayodhya and, as King Dasaratha's eldest son, take his rightful place on the throne. The three Queens and the senior courtiers wept and added their arguments. But Rama was immovable in his determination to carry out his father's wishes. He advised Bharata to resign himself to his fate and ascend the throne. 'Man is not able to do what he wills on this earth. He is not the master. Fate drives him hither and thither.'

They argued long into the night, until Rama finally persuaded his brother to return to Ayodhya as its ruler. But Bharata refused to be crowned king; he would act only as regent until the fourteen years of Rama's exile were over. He asked for Rama's sandals, circumambulated them with great reverence and placed them on his head. Then, with great sadness, he marched his army back to Ayodhya. He escorted the Queens to their palaces in the grieving capital, but he would not stay there himself. He carried Rama's sandals to nearby Nandigrama, where he placed them on the royal throne under the white canopy of the Kingdom of Kosala and made a vow to the people: 'Till Rama's return, I shall preserve the trust he has lovingly reposed in me. When he comes once more to Ayodhya, I shall myself fasten these sandals on his feet and, making over the kingdom to him, I shall serve him like a son. So shall I wash away the dishonour brought upon me by my mother.' True to his vow, Bharata laid all matters of state first before the sandals and the seals of office. Dressed in bark and leading the life of an ascetic, he waited in Nandigrama for Rama's return.

Left behind in Chitrakuta, Rama, Sita and Lakshmana grieved over King Dasaratha's death and the departure of all their friends. Then a new danger presented itself. The Rishis in the area came to Rama in great distress and told him that the disturbance caused by Bharata's army had lured man-eating demons to their ashrams. Led by Ravana's brother, Khara, they were defiling the altars and extinguishing the sacred fires. Hatred of Rama was driving them to ever more hideous excesses and all the Rishis feared for their lives. So Rama resolved to leave Chitrakuta.

The three wanderers spent the first night in the ashram of the aged saint Atri and his even saintlier wife, Anasuya. There Anasuya expounded to Sita the duties of a good Hindu wife:

'Those women, who are devoted to their husbands, whether it be in the city or the forest, or whether their husbands be well disposed towards them or not, attain the highest bliss. Whether he be a sinner, or a slave to desire, or poor, the husband is a god to the woman of noble sentiments.'

Sita agreed wholeheartedly, and Anasuya rewarded her for her pious observations by giving her enchanted ornaments and celestial balm, to enhance her beauty and ensure that it would never fade. Decked in this new finery, she left the ashram early next morning with Rama and Lakshmana, to penetrate deeper into the demon-haunted Dandaka Forest.

# **6** The Guru of Chitrakut

HITRAKUT WAS RECOVERING from a huge pilgrim fair which had spread over three adjacent fields. The stalls were being dismantled and the fairground lights, which had dazzled us on our entry into the town, were being disconnected and loaded on to trucks. The fair had drawn large numbers of pilgrims, many of them from Rajasthan, who lit up the streets with their brilliant red, yellow and orange saris and turbans. Most of them were poor country people. They cooked their own meals on open fires and slept on the dusty footpath beside their coaches. In the bazaar, they crowded the stalls, shopping for little images of Rama, Sita and Hanuman, and rejecting the beautiful hand-carved wooden toys in favour of hideous green plastic cameras and fake Barbie dolls to take home to their grandchildren.

They were obviously enjoying their break from everyday life. The majority were elderly and they shuffled around in groups, like village Darby and Joan clubs, shepherded by professional guides. Chitrakut was a well-organised place, where the coachloads of new arrivals were briskly sorted into caste and language groups. The pilgrims may have been a bit doddery, but they were happy and excited. They had come to place their naked feet on the very earth which Rama had trodden and to bathe, like Rama and Sita, in the River Mandakini. Songbirds, wild flowers, clear streams and the spreading shade of mature trees created a landscape which seemed almost too soft for a pilgrim destination. No wonder it was particularly attractive to villagers from the burning sands of Rajasthan.

India is a spider's web of pilgrim paths. *The Mahabharata* lists hundreds of sacred sites in an order which follows the movement of the sun. The majority are in north India, the cradle of Indo-Aryan civilisation, with a few in other areas to complete the circle. There are seven sacred cities (Varanasi, Ayodhya, Mathura, Haridwar, Ujjain, Kanchi and Dwarka); seven sacred rivers (Ganges, Yamuna, Cauvery, Narmada, Godavari, Saraswati and Indus); four sacred abodes of Vishnu and his incarnations at the four cardinal points (Badrinath in the north, the home of Vishnu himself; Puri in the east, the home of his avatar Krishna in Jagannath, or Juggernaut, form; Rameshwaram in the south, where his avatar Rama stayed and worshipped Shiva; and Dwarka in the west, another home of Krishna). Then there are holy mountains and holy forests; sacred sites associated with each of the Hindu deities; and places where saints and great religious teachers have lived and built their ashrams. And these are only the Indo-Aryan sites. In addition, there are all the sacred places of the southern Dravidian tradition, where Shiva and his family of gods are supreme. The whole of India can in fact be seen as one great pilgrim site, sanctified now in the modern cult of Mother India, Bharata Mata, who has a temple in Varanasi where a map of India serves as the deity. The sacred geography of pilgrimage has helped knit together a people that has only in the last 150 years of its long history been unified under a single rule.

With so many sacred places to visit, it is easy to see how sadhus can spend their whole lives as holy mendicants. And it is not uncommon for retired people, whose families are established in the world, to leave their homes and their wealth behind them and set out, staff and begging-bowl in hand, to devote their remaining years to wandering in search of spiritual purity. A favourite destination for the aged is Varanasi. To die there, where the holy Ganges flows north in the direction of enlightenment, away from the south and death, and to have one's ashes scattered on the water, can bring *moksha*, the release of the soul from the cycle of birth and rebirth. Even a few drops of Ganges water on the tongue of the dying can bring salvation, no matter where death occurs.

The concept of pilgrimage is common to all religions. A true pilgrimage is a long, arduous journey across difficult and dangerous terrain. The laboured, mechanical setting of one foot in front of the other, day after day, with blisters, sunburn and rough beds, becomes such an all-absorbing effort that our minds are emptied of the trivia with which we normally fill our days; and when the sheltering structures of habit are swept away, we have nowhere to hide from the eternal questions. No wonder the Vedas, the earliest Sanskrit hymns, describe the feet of the pilgrim as 'flowerlike'. His sins disappear, 'slain by the toil of his journeying'. The more modern Swami Vivekenanda expresses it crisply:

The water is pure that flows,
The monk is pure who goes.

Pilgrimage is, in fact, such a powerful element in all religions, that it has come to stand as a metaphor for human life itself, life's journey, with all its hardships and temptations.

In the old days, pilgrimages took such a long time that only holy men, the wealthy and those who had renounced everything had the leisure to undertake them. But times have changed, and it is no longer just the monk who goes. The building of the railways and the current availability of cheap coach travel along reasonable roads have opened the floodgates of Hindu pilgrimage. Every farm labourer who has a few spare rupees and a few spare days between harvest and planting can make a quick trip to a sacred place. For a few brief hours, he can immerse himself in sacred time and space and attempt the crossing between the earthly and the spiritual. And no one, however lowly his caste, is barred from pilgrimage. It is closely associated with *bhakti*, the path of devotion, and even an outcaste can gain merit and consolation from visiting a sacred place.

Pilgrimage, in India as elsewhere, obviously means different things to different people. The simplest go to make offerings to a deity because they need help with specific problems: they need a good harvest, a child, a cure for their rheumatism. For the more sophisticated, going on pilgrimage is a form of religious retreat, or at least an opportunity for reflection. While for the mystic, there may be no point in pilgrimage at all: Varanasi or the New Jerusalem is in the heart, not at the end of a journey.

The pilgrims who were swarming around Chitrakut were mostly of the simpler sort. They may not have struggled to their destination on foot but, once there, they were determined to go through all the prescribed rituals in all the sacred spots and these involved a great deal of barefoot walking.

Their first duty was a dawn bathe, to greet the rising sun from the waters of the Mandakini at Chitrakut Ghat in the town centre. This was a lively stretch of the river, dotted with pleasure boats and lined with souvenir stalls. The steps down to the water were always busy with bathing pilgrims and others who were there for less sacred purposes, like doing their laundry, cleaning their bicycles or washing their cattle. A herd of black goats seemed to live there permanently, eating the remains of the pilgrims' marigolds and reclining on the embankment benches. The Ghat was dominated by a giant statue of Hanuman in scarlet and green shorts, kneeling on his left knee with his great mace in his right hand. He was not associated in *The Ramayana* with the events which took place in Chitrakut, but so great is his popularity these days that his presence is everywhere.

Having taken their holy dip in the River Mandakini, the pilgrims changed into clean saris and dhotis and went off in their coaches, with their wet clothes flapping out of the windows to dry. They did a tour of the Chardham, the four holy places in the vicinity. First, there was the Jankikund (Janki or Janaki is the patronymic of Sita), the spot where Sita herself bathed every morning. It was a deep pool in the fast-flowing river, shaded by overhanging trees, and now the haunt of ash-smeared sadhus and troops of monkeys. Here the pilgrims took another sacred bathe, changed back into their first set of clothes, which had already dried in the wind and the sun, then sat outside to enjoy the warmth of the morning on the Sphatikshila, the very ledge overhanging the river where Rama and Sita used to pass their days in joyful contemplation of Nature.

Then their coaches took a winding road deep into the forest, to visit the ashram of the Rishi Atri and his saintly wife Anasuya, who by her meditations had produced the River Mandakini to water the drought-stricken land. These two saints had befriended Rama and Sita in their exile. Now a dreary whitewashed concrete building, the ashram contained large statues of the sages sitting in glass cases and some naïve Hindu religious propaganda. There was a large mural of the Crucifixion, with an amazingly gory Christ on the Cross. Beside it was a mural of Mecca, with soldiers chopping off the hands of a bunch of thieves, in accordance with Islamic shariah law. Blood was spouting up from their wrists in fountains. Pollution is a major preoccupation of the Hindus, and blood is one of the worst pollutants. The main reason why Christianity has never prospered in India is that the very idea of communicants consuming the body and blood of Christ is repellant to vegetarian Hindus, as also is the notion that a god (who would be all-powerful if he were a proper god) should allow himself to be sacrificed, and in such a gory way. So the propaganda in the ashram was really hitting the mark. The pilgrims were gazing in horrified fascination at the murals, amazed that so much blood should be shed in the name of religion.

With their Hindu faith suitably bolstered, they went off to their final site, the Gupt-Godavari caves. Climbing up a long flight of steps, they reached a network of caverns, in whose heart was a spring known as the Sitakund. Its stream gushed out of the caves and fell in a cascade to form tanks in the garden below. Inside the caves, the water was waist high and the pilgrims had a fine time wading through it to see the two thronelike rocks on which Rama and Lakshmana used to hold court. Pilgrimage in India is quite a jolly affair, with a lot of splashing and laughter. Everyone beamed at us, and patted us on the arm, as we stumbled out into the daylight again in a crush of white dhotis and brilliant saris.

Our New Year's Day was truly memorable. The Chitrakut mountain, Kamadgiri, is steep and thickly forested. Around its base lies a chain of 56 small temples and shrines, all associated with *The Ramayana* story; and there are some believers who claim that the whole mountain is an embodiment of Rama. Early that morning, in brilliant sunshine, we set off for the mountain in a scooter-rickshaw, to join the pilgrims who were making the holy *parikrama*, the ritual clockwise circuit of the base. We took off our shoes at the bottom of a flight of stone steps and climbed barefoot up to the small temple of Hanuman, which was crowded with pilgrims praying and cracking auspicious coconuts before the idol. Then we joined them on the walk.

The *parikrama* is three miles round and is paved with smooth flagstones – which is fortunate for those of us who are not used to walking barefoot. We soon overtook a young man in well-pressed grey trousers and a gleaming white shirt, who was performing the whole circuit in prostration. He lay on his stomach on the path and stretched out to deposit a coconut as far ahead of himself as he could. Then he rose up on his knees and shuffled forward until he knelt on the spot where he had placed the coconut. There he prostrated himself again and edged the coconut forward by another body-length. He must have had some great sin on his conscience, or perhaps he was asking an enormous boon. But he was the exception. The other pilgrims were marching along gaily, calling in at teashops and buying trinkets from stalls between offering prayers at each of the shrines. Three small areas of the path were covered with little thatched roofs, to shelter the footprints of Rama. One had a confused batch of prints and we were told that this was Bharata Milap, the very spot where Rama embraced his younger brother, Bharata, when he came to offer him the throne. A flight of 150 rough, gritty steps led up to the vantage point where Lakshmana stood guard over Rama and Sita. Our feet were grateful that we could follow the example of the other pilgrims and put on our shoes for the climb.

At a number of the shrines along the way, we coincided with a particularly large group of pilgrims, who seemed more prosperous than the rest. They had musicians with them, and they chanted and clapped with fervour. Their leader was a portly, saffron-clad guru, with a splendid white beard and flowing locks. At noon, as we were sitting on a low wall, taking a rest from our walk, a young woman came across the path from the group and invited us, in English, to join them for lunch. We went over and sat with the cross-legged ranks on the ground.

The guru himself was reclining on a rock, where his disciples had spread a comfortable mat. Two of them held a long white awning over his extended frame, while a third fanned him. Containers of delicious food were produced, and he was served first with dishes of the daintiest morsels. The rest of us ate, in traditional fashion, off banana leaves. Scooping up curry with fingers and a chapatti is not an easy thing to do elegantly when you are used to cutlery and a table, so more of the sloppy vegetable stews landed on our shirt-fronts than in our mouths, to the amusement of our hosts. A number of them were professional people, who spoke good English, and they did their best to entertain us. But it was extremely hot under the noonday sun and we wondered how soon we could politely take our leave.

The guru finished eating and closed his eyes for a nap. This seemed the right moment to make a move. But as soon as we started to scramble to our feet, his eyes snapped open and he began to address us directly. We found his English difficult to understand, but the girl who had invited us came to the rescue as interpreter, while the guru told us his remarkable story.

Some years ago, he had developed a brain tumour. It was malignant and the specialists had told him that it was too far advanced for surgery. As death seemed imminent, he decided to come to Chitrakut, to spend his last days on the holy Kamadgiri mountain. He lived, unsheltered, on the mountainside and devoted all his waking hours to repeating the name of Rama. One night, he dreamed that Rama came and smiled on him. The next morning, he had a terrific nasal haemorrhage and fell down unconscious. When he came to, he felt better than he had felt for years. He went for a scan and the hospital confirmed that the tumour had completely disappeared. 'That is the power of God's name,' he said. 'It doesn't matter which god you believe in. Just keep in contact with Him by repeating His name. That's all you need do. He will be satisfied with that.' The disciples, who had listened intently, chorused, 'Rama, Rama, Rama', and our interpreter said, 'Isn't he wonderful? Everything he has told you is true, which is why we revere him.'

At that point, the women in the party collected up the empty food containers and we all moved on to complete the *parikrama*. We managed to detach ourselves from the group, though we came across them at intervals during the afternoon. Near one shrine, we found the guru sitting on a wall, while two devoted followers massaged his feet. And there was one wonderful occasion, when the musicians struck up a tune and some of his male disciples began to dance in his honour. The guru was helped up on to a wall, where he sat looking benign. Shirley, as a ballerina, couldn't resist the dance. She joined in, leaping and twirling around with the dancing men. The guru called her over, patted her on the head and gave her two rupees. She was delighted with the gift, but I was a bit uncertain about it myself. It seemed somehow patronising. But Shirley was obviously so thrilled, that I put aside my scepticism and smiled on her two rupees.

We completed our leisurely *parikrama* as dusk was falling and agreed that it was the most delightful day we had spent in India and one of the best New Year's Days ever. We had enjoyed a sunlit walk through a smiling landscape and, though we were not believers, we had been embraced in the joy of those who were. Hinduism, which is in essence the most inclusive of all religions, had been pleased to share its holy mountain with us.

Chitrakut was altogether our favourite place and there was so much to see there that we stayed for a whole week. There were pilgrim *dharamshalas* dotted about the town, but the UP Tourist Lodge was the only proper hotel, so we met all the better-off Indian visitors and had quite a sociable time. Two Australian cyclists made an overnight stop, but they were the only other Westerners. We took our breakfast and lunch on the lawn, but dinner was a gloomy affair, as the dining room was a huge barracks of a place, where a few shabby formica-topped tables were lost in the gloom, and the service was painfully slow. One evening, a family from Kanpur, who found the dining room as depressing as we did, invited us to go with them to a *dharamshala* which accepted outside visitors for meals. It took quite a lot of sweet talking on the part of our host before the management would admit three English non-Hindus, but perhaps a little extra money changed hands, and we were eventually allowed in. We sat cross-legged in a circle round the walls, nursing our stainless steel trays, while barefoot serving boys kept circulating with generous helpings of rice, assorted vegetable curries and pickles. The food was greatly superior to the drab fare in the Tourist Lodge but, despite our friends' kindness, we did find it rather an ordeal to be stared at unblinkingly by a hundred pairs of Indian eyes. We fidgeted to ease the cramp in our legs and fought the runny food with awkward fingers. We didn't go back there, as our friends left for Kanpur the next morning. Instead, we took to room service in the hotel. Shirley was terrified that the food would attract rats, but it didn't.

Apart from one little mouse in the hotel lobby, we saw no rodents at all in Chitrakut. But we were plagued by monkeys. We had a small private balcony at the back of our room and hung some washing there. Suddenly, there was thundering on the roof as a troop of monkeys descended. We rushed out to drive them away, but one was too quick for us. He scampered up a tree and sat watching us, with a pair of knickers draped jauntily over his head. After that, we dried our underwear in the bathroom and aired it off in the morning on the front verandah, with one of us sitting guard by the open door. These town monkeys were stocky brown rhesus macaques, while the ones who thieved around the Hanuman Dhara, his shrine in a cave on a mountain-top, were elegant black-faced langurs, with long curly tails – which was very appropriate, as the langur is thought by some to have been the original Hanuman.

The main problems of our Chitrakut life were the food and drink. It was such a holy city that the diet was totally vegetarian. Even eggs were banned. As for alcohol, that was right out of the question. We used up our private supply, drinking it furtively in our bedroom, and then New Year's

Eve dawned. We couldn't see in the New Year with nothing at all for a toast, so we took a scooter-rickshaw to Karwi, the nearest non-holy town. There we tramped the bazaar, looking in vain for a liquor store. Just as we were getting desperate, we saw a man weaving his way unsteadily along the street. He was just the person to help us. 'Where can we buy some whisky?' we asked. He looked most offended. Swaying slightly on his feet, he muttered, 'I don't drink', in a cloud of rum-soaked breath. But he did tell us where to find the one and only licensed outlet. It was so far out of Karwi, right on the other side of the railway tracks, that we had to take a couple of cycle-rickshaws to get there. When we found it, the 'English Wine Stores' was no more than a tin shack, but it was a well-stocked one. To avoid another trip into Karwi, we decided to get in a good supply. A crowd gathered and watched in silence as we bought whisky, gin and twelve bottles of beer. We were so embarrassed under their aston-ished gaze that we said gaily, 'We're giving a party tonight. Lots of people! It's New Year's Eve. It's our custom to celebrate with a few drinks.' Then we loaded all the bottles on to one of the rickshaws, transferred them to a Chitrakut taxi and crept like criminals into our hotel, clutching the brown paper bags to stop the bottles clinking. Dinner that night was the inevitable vegetable mess, but at least we had a bottle of Kingfisher beer to help it down and a whisky or two for our midnight toast.

Chitrakut was the parting of our ways. Suzanna and Shirley left for Agra and Jaipur, while I rode the buses to Varanasi, with my bicycle roped to the roof. I particularly wanted to see the modern temple to Tulsi Das, who wrote *Ram Carit Manas*, the first Hindi version of *The Ramayana*. His epic was engraved in its entirety on marble panels inside the temple and there was a series of precious bas reliefs, which told *The Ramayana* story in pictures of gold, silver and bronze. But the really amazing part of the temple was the hall of clockwork scenes. Upstairs, inside glass cases, hundreds of tiny figures enacted the most significant episodes. Rama and Sita danced at their wedding, Rama and Hanuman fought the ten-headed Ravana, and Rama returned to Ayodhya for his coronation.

Hindus up from the country pressed their noses against the glass in a state of utter enchantment.

I had intended to spend a month in Varanasi, drafting the first chapters of this book. But it was an unusually cold winter. Fog rolled in from the Ganges morning and night, leaving only a couple of hours' sunshine in the middle of the day. Indian hotels are designed to keep out the summer sun, which means that in winter the bedrooms are exceedingly gloomy. They need constant electric light, which they don't get because there are frequent power cuts. So I could write neither indoors nor out. I decided to go home early.

On my last day, I crossed the Ganges on a seasonal bridge of planks and steel drums to visit Ramnagar, the palace of the Maharajah of Varanasi, where one of the most splendid of India's Ramlilas is performed at the October/November festival of Dassehra. The story of Rama is acted out with music, dance, mime and poetry in the great palace courtyard, attended by the Maharajah himself, who arrives in full regalia on his elephant. Dassehra means in Sanskrit 'taking away the ten sins'. Ravana was the ten-headed king of the demons and each head represented one of the sins. By killing Ravana, Rama destroyed those sins and Good triumphed over Evil. One day I shall go back to India at Dassehra to see this brilliant spectacle.

On that misty January morning, the courtyard was draped with laundry, but otherwise empty. I wandered round the depressing dust-covered collection of elephant howdahs, sedan chairs and palanquins in the old stable block. They were lit by the occasional 25-watt bulb, so the custodian first came to me as a disembodied voice. When my eyes got used to the gloom, I saw an old retainer.

'Coming from, madam?'

'From England,' I said. 'I live in London.'

'Like the Queen. Queen Elizabeth came here. She came to this museum and I showed her round,' he told me proudly. I hoped they had found some stronger light bulbs for her.

There was one state room open to the public, its walls covered from floor to ceiling with photographs of past Maharajahs driving Rolls-Royces and shooting tiger. As I left the room, I was preceded downstairs by a young man in beautifully cut grey flannel trousers and a beige cashmere sweater. He passed through an archway into the courtyard and two guards leapt to attention with a smart salute. As I passed through myself, one of them whispered reverently, 'That is our king.' India may be a republic and it may be the politicians in Delhi who wield the power, but feudal loyalties are still strong. The Indians, like other people who have got rid of their monarchies, are still enthralled by a title and avid for gossip. You have only to look at the French and 'France Dimanche'.

The Maharajah of Varanasi crossed the courtyard, climbed a flight of steps and emerged on a verandah, where a liveried attendant bowed so low that his red turban almost hit the flagstones. He took the proffered newspaper and retired to an armchair in a shady corner to read it. He seemed oblivious to the dilapidated buildings, the untended grounds and the laundry draped in full view along the fences. No doubt his main home was elsewhere and was far better maintained, but I did wonder how such an elegant young man could bear to stay, even for a week, in such mouldering surroundings. He and his aged servants must have lost all hope for the Palace of Ramnagar.

My encounter gave me food for thought, but what interested me most that morning was a small shrine by the river. It was devoted to a very special Hanuman – Hanuman as the God of Grammar. Although Hanuman almost always appears in a macho stance, as the great fighter with his mace in one hand and a whole mountain from the Himalayas on the palm of the other, he is in fact a very learned monkey, eloquent in the exposition of the Scriptures and a fine Sanskrit scholar. As a linguist, I was delighted to stumble upon this rare representation. I scrambled out of my rickshaw and took a whole series of photographs, while the puzzled driver stared. Why on earth was I taking photos of such an unimposing little shrine? Another crazy foreigner!

My favourite god was sitting cross-legged against a sky-blue background, with his long tail dangling down beside his very human feet. He was studying one great tome and had piles of others stacked on both sides. His face was a picture of concentrated piety. He was not wearing his crown, but was modestly dressed in a monk's robes, with the vertical sign of Vishnu painted on his forehead. Vishnu's vehicle, the Garuda, a bird with a man's head, was sheltering him under his outspread wings, and the name of Rama was daubed around him in auspicious red paint. It was an utterly delightful little shrine. And finding such a rare representation of Hanuman was the culmination of my week in Varanasi. My perseverance in the foggy chill had brought its reward.

CB EO

## The Abduction of Sita

*The Dandaka Forest once covered the whole of the Deccan, the high plateau which stretches right across central India from the Eastern to the Western Ghats. It was inhabited by ascetics. 'There were those who lived on the moon's rays; those who did penance by standing in water; those who never sought the shade; those who dwelt on the summit of high mountains; and those who lived between five fires', to describe but a few. They all begged Rama to rid the forest of the demons who tormented and sometimes devoured them.*

*The three exiles moved steadily south-westwards, staying with the holy men in their ashrams. Rama was true to his promise and destroyed forest demons whenever they crossed his path. After nine years of constant wandering, they came to the ashram of the powerful Sage Agastya, whose austerities had made him invincible. He had been waiting many years for Rama and when the hero arrived, he armed him with the panoply of the great Protector of the Universe himself, the God Vishnu – his bow, encrusted with gold and diamonds, his quivers, arrows and sword. Rama asked for advice on a safe place with abundant fruit and water, where he could live happily with Sita and Lakshmana, and Agastya directed them to delightful Panchavati on the banks of the sacred Godavari River. There the ever-useful Lakshmana built them a thatched cottage, in whose shade they could sit and admire the flowering landscape, and watch the teeming wildlife come down to the lotus-covered river to drink.*

*But it was all too idyllic to last. One day, Ravana's sister, Surpanakha, a hideous demon, half woman, half monster, passed their cottage as Rama stood outside reciting the scriptures. She immediately fell in love with him. Consumed with passion, she proposed marriage:*

*'I am endowed with power and able to range at will by thought alone. I should prove a well-matched partner, my beauty equal to your own.'*

*When Rama protested that he was already married, Surpanakha offered to rid him of the ugly Sita, and also of Lakshmana, by devouring them. Rama decided to tease her. He offered his brother instead.*

*'He is youthful and attractive and would be a fitting husband.'*

*So Surpanakha turned her amorous attentions on Lakshmana.*

*'My beauty renders me a worthy wife,' she tempted. 'Therefore come, and we will range the Dandaka Forest and mountains happily together.'*

*Lakshmana continued the teasing. He pointed out that he was only Rama's slave and not worthy of the love of such a paragon of beauty. Only Rama was worthy and he was bound to surrender to her charms eventually.*

*'O lady of ravishing complexion and lovely limbs, what sensible man would sacrifice your unrivalled beauty for an ordinary woman?' he exclaimed.*

*Incited by these words, the Rakshasa hurled herself upon Sita, to tear her limb from limb. Lakshmana sprang to the rescue and cut off the monster's nose and ears. Howling in agony and streaming blood, Surpanakha rushed into the forest and threw herself at the feet of her formidable brother Khara.*

*Khara first sent fourteen demons from his personal bodyguard to avenge his sister, but they were no match for Rama. So, together with his brother Dusana, he mounted his golden chariot and led an army of fourteen thousand demons to Rama's hermitage. Single-handed that mighty hero slaughtered them all with the aid of Vishnu's weapons. In one battle, he rid the Dandaka Forest of all its remaining demons, to the great delight of the holy men.*

*Surpanakha then flew in a fury to Lanka. Her brother Ravana, the ten-headed King of the Rakshasas, sat on his golden throne, 'blazing like a flame, resembling Time at the destruction of the* worlds'. He had already heard of his brothers' death and now the sight of his sister's mutilations drove him to frenzy. Surpanakha craftily goaded him on by describing Sita's amazing beauty and amiable temperament. If he did his duty by his sister and killed Rama, Sita would be his.

Ravana mounted his jewelled chariot drawn by mules with goblins' heads and drove across the straits from Lanka to seek help from the demon Maricha. He found him in his ashram, dressed in the skin of a black antelope, leading the life of an ascetic. His extreme austerities had gained him magical powers. When he heard Ravana's plans, he was appalled. Maricha was the very demon whom Rama, as a child, had flung a hundred miles into the sea to protect Vishvamitra's altars, and he knew his prowess only too well.

'O King of the Demons,' he cried. 'Do not hurl yourself into that dreadful and bottomless ocean called Rama, whose bow is the crocodile, the strength of whose arm is the quagmire, whose shafts are the rising waves.'

Ravana was persuaded not to attack Rama himself, but he would not give up the idea of capturing Sita. If she was as wonderful as her description, Rama would undoubtedly die of grief at her loss. Though he was terrified, Maricha reluctantly agreed to take part in a plot.

By his magical powers, he transformed himself into a gazelle of surpassing beauty, with jewelled antlers and hooves of emerald. Shining with iridescent light, he grazed in the forest near Rama's cottage until he caught Sita's eye. She was captivated and longed to keep the gazelle as a pet, so Rama rushed out to catch it for her. The gazelle lured him deeper and deeper into the forest. Being a magic creature, it proved impossible to capture, and Rama, in frustration, finally shot it in the heart with one of Brahma's arrows. In its death throes, the gazelle turned itself back into Maricha and called out the names of Sita and Lakshmana, mimicking Rama's voice. Lakshmana suspected treachery, but Sita was so distraught when she heard Rama's agonised cry that, against his better judgement, he went into the forest to find him, leaving Sita alone in the cottage.

This was Ravana's chance. He came to the gate, disguised as a holy man, so that it was Sita's duty to admit him and offer him refreshment. Once inside, he resumed his own gigantic, ten-headed form and dragged Sita by the hair into his aerial chariot. Jatayu, the King of the Vultures, who had been a childhood friend of King Dasaratha, attacked Ravana in a desperate bid to rescue her. He smashed his chariot and killed the charioteer, but every time he tore off one of the demon's twenty arms, he grew another, until the aged vulture had no more strength to fight. Then Ravana cut off his wings and he plunged mortally wounded to the ground, prophesying disaster. Ravana laughed and flew off with Sita to his palace in Lanka, 'carrying his own destruction in his arms'.

When the two brothers returned to the cottage and found it deserted, they searched in vain for Sita. The deer, full of pity for Rama in his distress, lifted their eyes to heaven and ran towards the south, indicating the direction in which Sita had vanished. Then Rama found the dying Jatayu, who told him of his fight with Ravana and Sita's abduction. Rama performed the funeral rites for the noble bird, then he and Lakshmana took their weapons and followed the deer southwards.

On the way, they received the piece of advice which was to lead to Sita's recovery. They met a revolting monster, a headless creature with one eye and a lolling tongue protruding from its hairy breast. When Rama shot it, it introduced itself as Kabandha, told of the curse which had transformed it and begged to be burned, so that it could revert to its previous beautiful form. Rama obliged, and a celestial being rose from the ashes and ascended to heaven, where a chariot drawn by swans awaited him. Before he drove away, he told Rama to go to Mount Rishyamuka, near Lake Pampa, where he would find a wise and powerful monkey named Sugriva. Rama should win his friendship, because Sugriva knew all the haunts of the Rakshasas. He was the ally who could track Sita down and help him destroy Ravana.

# 7 Bandit Country. The Badlands of Madhya Pradesh

[1991–92]

*Delhi – Agra – Gwalior – Jhansi – Ujjain – Jalna – Aurangabad – Nasik*

LAKSHMANA CHOPPED OFF Surpanakha's nose in a place which Valmiki calls Panchavati, near the source of the sacred River Godavari. This is commonly identified with modern Nasik, a name which means 'nose' in Sanskrit. To reach Panchavati, the three exiles left Chitrakut, on the edge of modern Uttar Pradesh, and wandered through the forest for nine years, across the entire breadth of Madhya Pradesh, plus a bit of eastern Maharashtra. It was a journey of about 1,400 kilometres.

And this is where my bit of artistic licence comes in. I did cycle that route, but I cycled it in the winter of 1991–1992, as part of a solo ride from the north to the south of India, from Chandigarh in the Punjab to Kanniyakumari, which used to be called Cape Comorin, at the very southern tip. When I embarked on that journey, I was not thinking of Rama at all. I chose the route simply because it seemed an interesting and convenient way to get down from Delhi to Bombay. But it was a providential choice. It took me through the city of Ujjain, and it was there, in the dust of the morning rush hour, that I saw the barefoot man in the check scarf praying to the monkey god, Hanuman. And Hanuman led me to *The Ramayana*. That morning in Ujjain, my travels in India acquired a focus, a purpose beyond getting miles under my bicycle wheels. As a change from my usual historical routes, I decided that day to travel a mythological road – an appropriate decision in India, where myth and religion are woven into every aspect of life.

I knew a little about Rama at the time, but not very much. The previous winter, (1990–1991) I had flown out to Delhi in December to begin my north to south ride and had found India in a state of emergency. It was the month when Mr L K Advani of the fundamentalist Hindu BJP drove to Ayodhya in his motorised temple chariot, leaving 10,000 kilometres of communal killings in his wake. As I cycled in the early morning from the airport to the centre of Delhi, I was overtaken by army lorries full of children, who were being escorted to school by armed guards. Squadrons of cavalry pranced by, looking very smart in their maroon *pukrees*, and I overtook small groups of infantry in white puttees, green cockades in their caps, cycling towards their camp to start the day's duties. There were armed guards at the airport and troops at every intersection. I was moving in a sea of soldiery. The television news was predicting the collapse of Mr V P Singh's government, amid scenes of mayhem in Parliament. So I went to a bookshop in Connaught Place and bought an illustrated children's version of *The Ramayana*. It seemed a painless way to learn a bit more about this god, Rama, who was the cause of all the trouble.

That particular visit to India came to an abrupt end, not because of the political situation, but because I became too ill to cycle. My neck and shoulders seized up, and I had such terrifying pains in my head that I was convinced I had a brain tumour. I struggled on my bicycle from Chandigarh back to Delhi and took the first flight home. The pains turned out to be nothing more serious than an attack of polymyalgia rheumatica, which responded immediately to treatment with corticosteroids, and the next winter I was back in Delhi, as nimble as ever I am, ready to pick up my north–south ride where I had left off.

Had I followed Rama along his route from Chitrakut, I should have travelled east for something like 250 kilometres, crossing and recrossing the wavy boundary between Uttar Pradesh and Madhya Pradesh, to the city of Jhansi. As it was, I cycled about 400 kilometres south from Delhi, through Agra and Gwalior, to reach that point. There our paths met and I began my travels with Rama.

This explanation is not a flashback. It is the start of the narrative proper. Henceforward, my journey goes in chronological order, and is easy to follow. The stretch from Nepal to Chitrakut was for me a 'flashforward'. It was the first leg of Rama's journey, so I wrote it up first, even though it was the last leg of my own. Soon, I'm pleased to say, our legs will be synchronised and we shall be marching across India to the same drum.

When I left Delhi at 9 a.m. on New Year's Eve, 1991, it was a cold, misty morning and most people were still in bed. The shops were closed and the traffic thin. As I cycled down the Rajpath, Delhi's ceremonial parade ground, I was a solitary, muffled figure in an empty landscape. The India Gate loomed out of the fog. There was a marigold wreath in the shape of the chakra, the Buddhist wheel of the law and Vishnu's discus, on the Tomb of the Unknown Warrior. I stopped for a quiet look at the 85,000 names engraved there and marvelled again, as I always do at the Gate, that so many thousands of men, all volunteers, had died for King and Empire in the trenches of Flanders and the dust of Mesopotamia, fighting a war that they probably didn't understand. In some ways, Lutyens' Gate is even more distressing than the military cemeteries of northern France. At least the Europeans knew what they were fighting for and had grown up with mud and rain.

I cheered up a little when the sun broke through. The poor bundles of rags, who were brewing up their morning tea on the pavements, waved, grinned and shouted, 'Hello Auntie!' to me as I cycled by. On foot, in Connaught Place, I had been just another rich tourist, beseiged by beggars. Now, the perception was totally different. I must be almost as poor as they were, because I was riding a bicycle! One pavement family even invited me to share their breakfast of tea and chapattis.

It was chilly and when I got out into the country, I saw the bullocks in their winter coats. One pair was particularly smart. They were stepping out, pulling their cart in matching sky-blue quilted coats, lovingly made, with little quilted excrescences to cover their brahmin humps. They were a fine sight. The roadside safety posters cheered me up too. In India, they're always catchy:

Do not zoom
To your doom.

Impatient on the road
Patient in the hospital.

Better be called Mr Late
than the Late Mr.

I had cycled along the Grand Trunk Road from Delhi to Agra in 1988, on my first ride round the world, and I knew that the tarmac was good, if crowded, and that Haryana prided itself on its string of tourist complexes, all named after Indian birds. So I cruised along in the shade of the trees with no worries about accommodation, looking forward to the gardens and comfortable chalets of the Magpie or the Dabchick. I never train before my rides, so I took it easy along the highway and spent four very pleasant days covering the 200 kilometres to Agra.

Agra is one of the ugliest, busiest, crookedest cities I know, with the world's most beautiful buildings. To give me the strength to grapple with it, I stopped at a roadside teastall on the way in, and was just beginning to sip my sweet, milky Indian tea, when I was accosted by a scruffy individual with a harelip and one central tooth. To my amazement, he opened the conversation with:

'You are coming from England, madam? You are knowing Bertrand Russell? I have read three of his books. I have also read the complete works of both Sigmund and Anna Freud. Have you read our *Bhagavad Gita*? It's superior to all that Freudian stuff. You see, the Gita teaches that people have the potential for goodness, whereas those Freuds have a very low conception of the springs of human behaviour.'

Typically of India, we were soon deep into philosophy. It's the only country I know where a chance meeting with a stranger in a teastall can lead immediately to a discussion of ethics. He ordered more cups of tea for the two of us and for his companion, who obviously didn't understand English.

'I'm afraid your friend is getting very bored,' I said. I still had a long way to cycle through Agra's traffic and I was looking for a tactful way to end this profound conversation.

'I don't care. Let him be bored! I'm an elected member of Agra Council and I'm very kindly taking him back to a camera shop, where he's been tricked over a film. I'm giving up two hours of my time for him, so he can jolly well give up a few minutes of his time for me. I'm very interested in human behaviour, and you and I are speaking most importantly.'

Night was already falling by the time I persuaded him to leave for the camera shop. He hitched up his rather grubby *lunghi* and swept off on his motorscooter, with his silent constituent riding pillion. I cycled into Agra in the dark, so late that my usual hotel was full. India was less tense that winter, but the Hindu fundamentalists were on a march from Kanniyakumari to Delhi and trouble could erupt at any time, especially in a city like Agra with a large Muslim population. I didn't like the idea of cruising round the city streets on my own at night, looking for another Western-style hotel, so I went next door, to a cheap little Indian lodge, where they were thrilled to have a real live tourist. The manager himself rushed along to my room with a top sheet (not usually supplied in local hotels), and proudly presented me with one coat hanger, labelled 'Made in England'. I had a sparkling clean washbasin and lavatory, but the plumbing wasn't connected, so I took an auto-shower with a bucket of hot water and a ladle. Later, as there was no restaurant, a boy was sent out for an excellent takeaway, which he served in my room. Altogether, it was a charming little hotel, in its simple way, and much more obliging than the tourist palace where I'd failed to get a room. And it was extremely respectable. A notice in the hall informed us, in both Hindi and English, that there was a 10 p.m. deadline for visitors and 'Homely lady guests can be entertained in common hall or open lawn.' No improper behaviour there!

I'd already 'done' Agra on three previous occasions, so my only sightseeing was the Taj Mahal, that ethereal dream of a building which never loses its magic. To take me there, I hired Mr Ban Wari Lal and his rickshaw. I chose him because he was such a poor, skinny old man that I felt sorry for him.

He turned out to speak very good English. He had ten years' high school education, but couldn't get a proper job, so he rode a cycle-rickshaw. It wasn't his; he hired it for fifteen rupees a day. Agra was swarming with cycle-rickshaws and the going rate for taking a tourist to the Taj Mahal was only one rupee, so he needed fifteen fares a day, just to pay the rickshaw rent, before he even started to maintain himself and his family. When we came to a gentle slope up the road from the Jamuna River, Mr Lal found it quite beyond him and had to get off and push. 'I'm sorry,' he said. 'I'm not as young as I used to be. I'm 47 now.' I was shocked. He looked at least 65.

After the Taj, he offered to take me shopping. At first I refused, as there was nothing I wanted to buy. 'But it's only for looking,' he pleaded. 'Not for buying. I get five rupees, sometimes even ten, just for taking a tourist into a shop. And if they buy anything, I get 2 per cent of the purchase price.' I had nothing special to do that afternoon, and the fifteen rupees rent he had to pay for his rickshaw was preying on my mind. So I said, 'Right. Let's go! We'll do a tour.'

And we did a grand tour of Agra's tourist traps. I swept into shop after shop, inspecting jewellery, pietra dura boxes, silk shirts, saris and stoles. Whenever I was offered a cup of tea, I accepted it, adding grandly, 'And a cup of tea please for my friend, Mr Lal', to the great annoyance of the shopkeepers. I'm extremely sales-resistant, and I watched with great satisfaction as Mr Lal stacked up his pile of 10-rupee notes, at no expense whatsoever to me. I did in the end succumb to a beautifully carved little coral Ganesh, which now sits on top of my microwave, so Mr Lal got a bit of commission too. It was a profitable afternoon.

I like solitary travel. If I'd been sitting in that rickshaw with a friend, we would have chattered together all the way to the Taj Mahal. I should not have got into conversation with Mr Lal and I should have had no idea of the financial hardship of his life, or the fortitude with which he endured it. He was old before his time and there was I, a pampered Westerner, fatter and healthier by far than he was, sitting back in his rickshaw, while he struggled to pull me around. I was ashamed. But at least, by talking to him, I had found a way of helping which didn't damage his pride. When we shook hands outside my hotel, he cycled away, a slightly more prosperous man, while I felt a little less guilty. If only the world were a fairer place!

I left the Grand Trunk Road at Agra and turned on to Highway 3, which runs from Agra to Bombay. (Needless to say, the Indians with their love of initials refer to it as 'the AB Road'.) It was much less crowded than the GT, with more shade-trees. In the morning, I cycled under a brilliant blue sky across farmland rich with sugar cane, winter wheat, rape seed and what looked like the first rice paddies of my ride south. It was the tomato season, and thousands of them were being sorted into shallow baskets, covered with newspaper and left by the roadside for collection. It seemed to be hunting country, as I kept passing men with rifles. The afternoon was, if possible, even more idyllic. I climbed from the Jamuna valley into a landscape of low hills, where the road dipped down to blue-green rivers flowing through golden sand, and hawks hovered overhead. I spent a pleasant half-hour on a country railway station, drinking tea with two Sikh guards, who were armed to the teeth with rifles and bandoliers of bullets.

But the idyll came to an abrupt end in Morena, where I had to spend the night. As I hadn't at the time travelled through rural Nepal, I was still an innocent with regard to truly dire accommodation. 'The Laxshmi Lodge' was my worst to date, and I viewed it with horror.

It was upstairs, over a row of shops, and it took the local policeman quite a long time to persuade the owner to give me a room. It was not a suitable lodge for a tourist, and he knew it. But there was no alternative in the town, so he finally showed me to a windowless box with a wooden plank bed. It gave on to a central courtyard, where the cook was preparing our fiery vegetable curry on an open-air stove. There was a communal latrine and one cold water tap. I rinsed my hands and face under the gaze of all the residents and staff, and smiled at my Roger et Gallet soap, my one travelling luxury. It had cost more than my room and dinner combined.

At first, I wondered how I could endure a night there. But then I warmed to the place. The owner, who called me 'boss', came bustling along with a cup of tea and hung a mirror on my wall. Then a dapper young fellow guest knocked on my door and offered, most ceremoniously, to escort me to the bazaar for shopping. His shirt was gleaming white and his trousers had knife-edge creases. I padded along beside him in my dusty cycling outfit, wondering how Indians managed to stay immaculate in dumps like Morena. In the morning, a group of men took it in turns to watch me dressing through the crack in my door, until they were chased off by the proprietor. I drank two cups of his 'bed tea' with a biscuit, then made my escape into the privacy of the open country. It was the day when I reached the palm-tree belt and shed my long johns.

My next stop was Gwalior, dominated by its gigantic fortress, which the first Moghul Emperor, Babur, described as 'the pearl among the fortresses of Hind', and Warren Hastings, less poetically, as 'the key to Hindustan'. In the days of the Raj, the Maharajah of Gwalior was one of only five Maharajahs to be accorded a twenty-one-gun salute by the British – a sure sign of the strategic importance of his fortress. Today's Maharajah is a politician, a member of the Congress (I) Party, representing in Parliament the people he no longer rules. His mother is also an MP, for the fundamentalist BJP, which must make for interesting conversation over the dinner table.

As I was a governor of Cobham Hall, I was invited to stay at the Scindia School, founded by one of those Maharajahs (family name Scindia) to educate his son and a few other hand-picked boys. It is now one of India's leading independent schools and is, like Cobham Hall, a member of the Round Square Conference of schools run on the principles of Dr Kurt Hahn. The school is part of the fortress complex, so I had the tremendous good fortune to stay in a guest house commanding what must be the most dramatic view in the whole of India.

My attendant there, Narayan, was a delightful old man, who cooked my breakfast and lunch, and devoted himself between meals to cleaning and polishing my bicycle. He spent hours on it every day, until it shone so brightly that I had to put my sunglasses on to look at it.

'What do you do about caste in a boarding school?' I asked Mr Mukherji, the deputy head.

'We discourage it,' he said. 'What do you think of Narayan?'

A little surprised at what I took to be an abrupt change of subject, I said, 'He's charming, and so attentive.'

'He was a dhobi wallah, a washerman, a member of one of the lowest castes, but he was so honest and conscientious that we promoted him. We put him in charge of the guest quarters. Of course, there are some visitors who refuse to be looked after by a member of such a low caste. But that's up to them. If they don't like it, there are plenty of hotels in Gwalior. One of our sweepers – and sweepers really are the lowest of the low – is captain of a local football team. They have regular fixtures up here against the boys, and after the match they all have refreshments together. The next morning, the sweeper's back at work, cleaning the lavatories with his twig brush, and the boys are back in their classrooms. But now that they know him in a different context, he's become a person to them – and I hope that awareness will stay with them for the rest of their lives.'

The restrictions and degradations of the caste system are being broken down deliberately in enlightened multi-faith schools like Scindia, and they are crumbling naturally in the new high-tech professions, where there are no traditions of employment. But to the outsider, it seems that considerations of caste are still far too dominant in India and are at the root of many of the country's problems.

Originally, there were only four castes, or ranks in society. They were probably set up by the invading Indo-Aryans, who wished to absorb the indigenous inhabitants without allowing too much competition. At the top of the hierarchy were the Brahmins, or priestly caste. Then came the Kshatriyas, or warriors. Then the Vaishyas, or Banyas, who raised grain and livestock, and engaged in trade. And finally, the Sudras, who performed the manual work. In the Scriptures, they are said to be the head, arms, thighs and feet of Brahma. It is probable that admission to a caste was at one time based on aptitude, but later it came to be determined by birth.

In the course of time, these castes were divided into separate *jati*, one for each of the individual trades. They were like the mediaeval guilds, formed to protect the interests of their members and to promote the skills of the craft. Their number has increased over the centuries until there are now something like five thousand of them, each with its own exclusive role in society. They perpetuate a sort of trade unionism gone mad. Job demarcation is so strict that it stifles all initiative and innovation. If your job is to wash the clothes, you can't mop the floor. If your job is to mow the lawn, you can't pick up the litter. If your job is to be a custodian in a museum, you preside vacantly over showcases so dusty that visitors can scarcely see the exhibits, yet it never occurs to you to while away a few of those long, empty hours by wielding a duster. You are born into a *jati*, you learn the work of the *jati* from your father, and that is the work you do. Socially too, the *jati* is your straightjacket. It dictates your marriage partner, the way you dress, what you eat and drink, where you live, who your friends are. The villages of India are little self-contained kingdoms, where the stratification is still rigid. In the cities, everyone mingles in offices, buses and shops, but even there, the members of different *jati* rarely visit one another – and if they do, they often take their own food with them in tiffin-boxes.

All these divisions and sub-divisions are difficult to eradicate, because they have the sanction of religion. The Hindus believe in reincarnation. If they are born into a lowly station in life, it is because they have sinned in a previous existence. So they must accept their lot and try to be good in this life. Then they may be reborn next time into a higher caste. Conversely, if they behave badly, they might be reborn as dogs or mosquitos, or even as women. To the cynical, it seems an excellent system for keeping the proletariat in order.

Beneath the members of the castes come the outcastes or 'untouchables.' There is no religious sanction in Hinduism for the concept of untouchability, though passages were later interpolated into the scriptures to justify it. Untouchability is a social practice introduced by the upper castes to provide menials for the repulsive tasks which they themselves had no wish to perform – such as cleaning the lavatories, scavenging, working in tanneries and looking after the cremation grounds. Even the shadow of an untouchable, cast over a brahmin, could at one time pollute him, so that he had to rush home and go through lengthy cleansing rituals. The untouchables are necessary to take society's impurities upon themselves as, without them, the higher castes would be polluted. The advent of the railways in the nineteenth century did as much as anything to cure the worst excesses of untouchability, as the British refused to divide up the trains by caste. They divided them, as in England, by class and people of all castes, or none, paid the appropriate fare and rode together in the same carriages. But even now, there are many refreshment stalls where tea is served in unfired clay cups, which are broken after one use, so that there is no danger of one of the higher castes drinking from the same vessel as an outcaste. And often in shops, the shopkeeper will place the change on the counter, rather than hand it to the customer, who might be a member of a lower caste, if not an outcaste.

The British never interfered with caste, as they considered it to be an integral part of Hinduism. But when India became independent, the democratic socialism of Nehru and Gandhi left no room for such a divisive system. Nehru was a brahmin, Gandhi a vaishya, yet both were equally determined to outlaw the most degrading practices. The Constitution of 1950 refused to recognise caste distinctions and forbade 'untouchability'. Gandhi gave the untouchables the new title of Harijans, 'Children of God', though they now prefer to be called Dalits, 'the Oppressed', since the term Harijan is based on Hindu religious beliefs, which many have rejected. Legislation has also been passed to reserve quotas of jobs and university places for the lower castes and tribal peoples. Yet change has been slow. The poorer northern states of Bihar, Uttar Pradesh and Haryana are notorious for caste injustice, and block voting by caste distorts election results. Even when members of a caste have migrated to the city, their whereabouts can now be tracked electronically. The computer may have offered new freedoms, but it has also made it possible for politicians to maintain their caste blocs. Legislation in favour of the lower castes is resented by the higher ones and there are incidents of brahmins setting themselves alight to demonstrate against their loss of privileges. For all brahmins are not prosperous. Wealth these days bears little relationship to caste and caste rivalry often leads to caste warfare. Bihar, in particular, is a lawless state, where caste wars result in the slaughter of entire villages. It is not easy for a democratic government to fight against two millennia of tradition. The majority of Indians can see nothing wrong with caste and find it difficult to visualise a social system without it. Even Muslims, Christians and Parsees are affected by pollution taboos, though they don't subscribe to the beliefs on which the taboos are founded. Change, if it ever comes, will come through increased social mobility and a greater social awareness, rather than through legislation.

Meanwhile, the caste system leads to some peculiar situations. For instance, because flesh, blood and other bodily substances are considered to be polluting, brahmins from orthodox families can be excommunicated – become outcastes – if they take up medicine. But a highly acceptable trade is that of restaurateur. A brahmin may not eat food touched by a member of a lower caste, but all the other castes may eat food prepared by a brahmin. Many restaurants, particularly in holy pilgrimage cities, have signs saying 'Brahmin Establishment', so that other brahmins know they can dine there without fear of pollution. Foreigners, being outcastes, are automatically polluting, which causes conflicts of interest in the tourist trade. And some brahmins who have studied abroad have to submit to purification rites on their return home. The most efficacious purification is to drink a mixture of the five products of the sacred cow: milk, ghee, curds, urine and dung!

VS. Naipaul has said that 'cleaning is unclean'. The Hindus look at it from their own special angle. We view the end result, the cleanliness, with satisfaction; they are obsessed with the polluting aspect of the dirt. Some regular domestic cleaners in the big cities will now wash both floors and clothes, but they will not clean the lavatories. So foreigners who live in India often clean their lavatories themselves, rather than have the complication of employing a special 'sweeper' for this one particular job.

I once spent a couple of weeks in an ashram not far from Bombay. There were two ashrams in the village, one patronised by a healthy mix of Indians and Westerners, the other exclusively Indian. I was met off the bus by a little boy who spoke good English and was anxious to be my guide. I asked him to take me to the Gurudev Siddhu Peeth, the mixed ashram, as that was the one which had been recommended to me by my devout Hindu friend in Jhansi, Anuradha.

'You can't go there!' cried the little boy in horror. 'It's a terrible place. It's a sort of cage, a prison. The people there have to work in the kitchens and clean their own rooms – even their own lavatories!'

'Don't they do that in the other ashram? I thought ashrams were for people who wanted to lead the simple religious life.'

'They are. They're for prayer and meditation – not for cleaning lavatories! Go to the Indian ashram. They have sweepers there.'

Caste is a most complex web of regulations, where there is no room at all for the ambitious spider. Western-style self-improvement is unknown. Past deeds predetermine the Hindu's place in society. He must therefore acquiesce and hope, by being good (not necessarily by doing good), to rise higher up the scale in the next life, and the next, until he finally escapes from the tyranny of space, time and action altogether and merges with the Absolute.

Each caste has its dharma, its religious and social obligations. The dharma of the Brahmins is to memorise the Vedic texts and hand them down to the next generation. The Kshatriyas have to learn weaponry and the rules of good government. It is the dharma of the Vaishyas to follow their inherited agricultural or commercial path. The Sudras' dharma is to serve the other castes; and like the Outcastes, the Sudras cannot participate in any of the Vedic rites. Krishna states in the *Bhagavad Gita* that it is better to fulfil your own dharma badly than to achieve success in another. It is the disinterested performance of your duty which is important, not its outcome. When he goes on to say, 'Giving up or carrying on one's work both lead to salvation,' he does little to encourage the pursuit of a career. And when this world is simply *maya*, or illusion, earthly life is of little importance anyway, so what is the point in trying to improve one's own lot, or that of the world's people? *Maya* is a consolation, but it is also a recipe for apathy. In other societies, people are born into higher and lower stations in life, but they still have a chance to better themselves, through their own enterprise, determination, education, an advantageous marriage or sheer good luck. For the Hindu, the only way to escape from the straitjacket of his *jati* is by converting to another religion – unless he has the education to equip him for one of the new high-tech industries, or he manages to get hold of every young person's dream, a visa to work abroad.

I could write a book about my stay in Gwalior, but it would be a book on education and philosophy, with some history thrown in. It would not be relevant to Rama, and I need to hurry on to Jhansi to meet him.

When I discussed my onward journey with Mr Mukherji, he was concerned at the lack of hotels along the road. He wrote me a letter of recommendation and sent me into town with a driver, a peon and Mitul, a housemaster's son, to request permission from the District Commissioner to stay in Government Rest Houses. In the DC's compound, Mitul pointed to a hefty character with long, curling mustachios, a rifle and a double bandolier of bullets. He was Malkhan Singh, once a leading dacoit, who controlled a gang of five hundred men. He had surrendered to the police and served his time, and was now a famous national figure, about whom books had been written. It began to dawn on me then that all those armed men I kept passing on the road might not be innocent huntsmen!

On the way out of the compound, we had to negotiate a narrow corridor, in which a bicycle had fallen over, blocking the way. The crowds of Indians hitched up their *lunghis* and clambered over it with the greatest difficulty. It never occurred to any of them to move it, because that was a peon's job and the bicycle might belong to an outcaste and be polluting! It would have stayed there all afternoon, had I not suggested to Mitul that we pick it up and lean it against the wall.

When I was invited the next day to address the graduate business students at the Maharani Lakshmibai College, I said what a good thing it was that Mr Rao's government was now encouraging wealthy expatriate Indians to set up businesses in India. The principal agreed, but added, 'What we really need, even more than the capital, is training in initiative. Lack of initiative is our downfall. It runs through Indian society, from top to bottom.' To support his argument, I told the sad tale of the bicycle. I didn't wish to get myself embroiled in religious controversy, so I said nothing about the evils of the caste system, but I'm sure that the rigid demarcation of caste has a lot to answer for.

The Business School was in very poor shape. It had old desks, crumbling concrete stairs and only two computers, one of which was obsolete. Students in the West would drop out, rather than work in such grim surroundings. Yet the MBA students of the Maharani Lakshmibai College were eager and alert, quizzing me on the future of the EEC, the prospects for a single European currency and my views on India's economic performance. They deserved better.

Before I left Scindia, Mr Mukherji arranged for me to stay in Jhansi with an important Scindia family. The father was an old boy of the school and two of his sons were current pupils. I had great difficulty in convincing them all that I would rather cycle to Jhansi than travel there in one of my host's cars, but I won in the end and swooped down from the towering fortress on my own two whirling wheels.

When I cycled into Datia that evening, I was astonished to be met on the outskirts by a reception committee of four men, sent to escort me to the Judge's quarters in the Circuit House. An attendant was on hand to serve my dinner and while I was enjoying it in the solitary splendour of my dining room, two policemen arrived to check on my welfare. They were followed by an elegant young man in a car, who explained everything. Ramesh, my host, had a large pharmaceutical factory in Datia, one of a chain of such factories throughout India, and he was also Mayor of Jhansi.

The next morning, I was eating my scrambled eggs, when I heard a terrible clanking. I looked out of the dining-room window and saw a workman in his best suit wheeling a rusty Hero bicycle up the Circuit House path. Ramesh had sent him to escort me into Jhansi. It was an escort I could well have managed without. I'm not a speedy cyclist, but my Condor is light and makes easy work of hills. I could have got into Jhansi in half the time, had I not had to wait on every hilltop for the poor toiling lad on his unoiled, gearless machine. To add to the delay, his boss had given him tea money, so we stopped for refreshments at every roadside stall.

My journey from Gwalior to Jhansi put me in mind of something I once read about Gandhi, who always insisted on eating the simplest food and travelling third class: that it cost a fortune in time and money to enable him to live in poverty. Had I travelled in style in a company limo, I should have saved everyone an enormous amount of trouble.

When I arrived at the house, I walked straight into the sort of conversation which makes India such a delight. A government minister (another old boy of Scindia, and a Raja to boot) had just dropped in for a chat on his way home from a political meeting.

'Whereabouts in London do you live?' he asked.

'Don't tell us!' cried Ramesh. 'We'll guess. I don't think it's the Old Kent Road or Whitechapel. They're too cheap.'

The minister cottoned on immediately. 'On the other hand,' he grinned, 'I don't think you could afford Mayfair. That costs £400.'

'Perhaps Piccadilly, or Regent Street? Somewhere green or yellow anyway.'

We were, of course, playing Monopoly. Indian and English, we were bound together in our childhood memories. Ramesh told us that he had visited London only once, to attend a conference on homoeopathic medicine. In the evenings, when all the other delegates were socialising in the bar, he had gone out and walked the streets of London. 'Fleet Street, Trafalgar Square. Red. Leicester Square. Now I'm on yellow.' The highlight was when he reached purple, and saw all those hotels he had once schemed to buy.

The family were devout Hindus and it was the many conversations I had with Anuradha which sparked off my interest in their religion and, I suppose, added to my fascination when I saw the man in Ujjain praying to Hanuman.

Their house was laid out on strictly orthodox lines. First, there was a large hall with chairs and a golden swing, where clients, employees and constituents waited on Ramesh. A few steps led up to a second hall, where there was a glass table resting on two white and gold swans. My bedroom and bathroom led off from this hall and my meals were served on the swan table. Orthodox Hindus will not share food with members of another caste. Although I was made extremely welcome, I was a foreigner and therefore an 'outcaste', lower in the system than even the lowliest Hindu, so I couldn't possibly eat with the family. Beyond the second hall lay the family rooms. Then came the magnificent marble *puja* room, where Anuradha and her guru prayed. Both Ramesh and Anuradha spent two to three hours first thing in the morning telling their beads and reciting their mantras. At 9 o'clock, Anuradha did what she called her 'second shift', this time in the *puja* room, and there was a third shift there in the evening, when a Brahmin blew a conch and waved oil lamps before the images of the gods. Despite all this holiness, Anuradha told me that she still didn't have as much time as she would like for meditation, so she had not yet reached self-realisation. She was looking forward to the stage when her household duties were lighter, and she and Ramesh could go on pilgrimage and devote their lives to the gods. Of course, she never addressed him as Ramesh or referred to him in that way, as Hindu wives never speak their husbands' names, for fear of bringing misfortune down on their heads.

Everything Anuradha did had its rationale in religion, even down to the colour of her saris. She told me that every day of the week had its special god and its special colour. On Sundays she wore red, in honour of Surya, the Sun God. Monday was white for Shiva; Tuesday orange and red for Hanuman; Wednesday green for Ganesh; Thursday yellow for Vishnu and her own guru; Friday pink and red for the goddess; and Saturday, black, purple or dark blue (ill-omened colours) to propitiate Saturn and the planets. She regarded herself as a devotee of Durga, a female form of Shiva, the 'great goddess' who rides on a tiger and slays demons. (Durga is popular today with strong, purposeful Indian women.)

On Tuesday morning, she was doing her *puja* to a Hanuman tape, with a servant sitting behind her and a sweeper sweeping around her with his little twig brush. She waved to me through a cloud of incense as I left with a driver for my rendezvous with Rama.

There is only one temple in India where Rama is worshipped as King, the sixteenth-century Ram Raj Temple in the fortress of Orchha, just nine kilometres from Jhansi. Unfortunately, we arrived there on Sankranti, the day when the sun moves into the northern hemisphere and signals the end of winter – an auspicious day for a holy dip in the Betwa River. The mobs in the temple were so great, and so frantic, that the army had been called in to help the priests control them. I couldn't get anywhere near King Rama's shrine, so I did a tour of the elegant Moghul palaces, then spent an hour in what was for me the jewel of the complex, the Lakshminarayan Temple. Frescoes of the most astonishing colour and freshness covered the whole interior, both walls and ceiling. There were sacred murals of Krishna and the gopis, hunting scenes, wrestling matches and wonderful caricatures of East India Company officers. The largest and most detailed mural depicted the Siege of Jhansi by the British. The Indian defenders were blasting their cannon from the battlements, British cavalry were prancing around on their horses, infantry were firing flaming rifles, and the gory British wounded were littering the field. Leading the Indian troops was the heroine of the Mutiny, the valiant young Rani of Jhansi, Lakshmibai. When the Raja of Jhansi died in 1853 without a male heir, the kingdom 'lapsed' to the British, in accordance with a recent law introduced by Lord Dalhousie. The Rani refused to accept the transfer of power and waged war on the British until she fell in the battle of Kotah-ki-sarai in 1858, dressed as a man and holding her horse's reins in her teeth, to leave both hands free for the fight. Her splendid equestan statue rears up over the site of her cremation in the centre of Gwalior.

I had one more day of luxury. Ramesh would not allow me to cycle along the route I had chosen, through Lalitpur and Bina-Etawah. He insisted on sending me by car to Shivpuri, to rejoin the AB Road. It was more frequented and therefore safer. As I was beginning to suspect, northern Madhya Pradesh was dacoit country, where bandit castes made their living from armed robbery. It was one of the most notorious regions in the whole of India, which is why Ramesh had organised police protection for me in Datia and a cycle escort to Jhansi. The badlands had evidently started on the Agra–Gwalior road. No one in Agra had warned me, and I had cycled innocently across the Chambal river, the State boundary, marvelling at its beauty and giving cheery waves to 'countrymen' with guns.

I have never felt threatened in India. The people are so gentle. Occasionally, they go on the rampage, butchering one another in the name of religion. But that has nothing to do with foreigners. Although there was tension over the Babri Mosque in Ayodhya, the British Consulate had assured me that I had nothing to worry about, provided I kept away from excited mobs and stayed in at night. In Madhya Pradesh, there was not a mob to be seen and I was cruising along in bright sunshine, so I felt completely at ease. I suppose I have my Condor to thank for my safety. No one with money could possibly be riding a bicycle! I obviously wasn't worth robbing, so the dacoits had allowed me to pedal my charmed way across open scrubland where no Indian of any importance would have ventured without an armed guard.

I was waved off to Shivpuri in a Maruti jeep, with a soldier as my driver. He raced along the hideously potholed road, dodging past ox-carts with his horn blaring. He had been told to take me through the Madhav National Park, which we toured at such speed that any wandering wildlife would have been mown down. There was a tigress in an enclosure with three small cubs. My driver did imitations of them later, taking both hands off the steering wheel to claw and hiss while travelling at top speed along the highway. It was an eighty-kilometre nightmare. When we arrived at the Shivpuri Circuit House, which Ramesh had reserved for me, I felt so sick that I couldn't eat my elegant picnic lunch. The driver polished it off in no time and sped away in a cloud of red dust.

When Rama, Sita and Lakshmana crossed Madhya Pradesh, they had demons to contend with, not dacoits. And they wandered through dense forest, where tigers and leopards roamed. Today, the state is still more wooded than the Gangetic Plain, but much of the forest has been chopped down to make way for cotton. Where the land was too hilly for agriculture, men were busy chopping down the few trees which remained and goats were demolishing the under-growth. It was a sandy, eroded moonscape.

I crossed two mountain ranges, the Vindhya and the Satpura. They were not particularly high, as their peaks rarely exceeded 1,000 metres, but they were gruelling work. It was growing hotter by the day. There was little shade, and the road surface was appalling. Mostly, it consisted of stones held together with a dribble of tar. Sometimes it was just loose stones, sharp enough to puncture tyres, so I had to push my bicycle along the sandy verge, keeping an eye open for piercing thorns. When I did manage to cycle, the bumps in the road made my teeth rattle in my skull and I got pins and needles in my arms. What the Paris–Dakkar Race is to cars, Madhya Pradesh was to bicycles.

I passed teams of roadmenders. Whole families, from grannies down to toddlers, crouched by the roadside breaking rocks. When they had reduced them to fist-sized stones, the women carried them on their heads in little baskets and scattered them along the carriageway. It seemed such inap-propriate work for women who walked so gracefully in their colourful saris. When the surface was fairly even, a boy would come along on a bicycle, with a bucket of tar hanging from his handlebars. He ladled a trickle over the stones and the road repair was complete!

One day I caused amazement by doing a road-mender's job myself. I cycled over a narrow bridge, took a tight corner and just missed a boulder which was lying in my path. When truck drivers in India have mechanical problems, they usually surround their vehicles with a warning ring of stones. Once the truck is repaired, they drive off, leaving the stones in the road. Presumably, they are not of the road-mending caste, so it's not their job to see that the roads are kept clear. Nor is it the job of passers-by. I usually cycled past these rings of stones myself, but on this blind corner, they were such a traffic hazard that I felt obliged to move them. I leaned my bike against a wall and started hauling them to the roadside. I was soon surrounded by an astonished group of village men, who just stood and stared. I completed the job single-handed, thinking back with some amusement to Gwalior and the Professor's remarks about Indian lack of initiative. Or is it slavery to caste?

I often had company on the road. I would hear the desperate clank of unoiled chains and a group of boys would catch up and cycle alongside. Many of them just gawped, but a few had some schoolboy English and subjected me to the usual boring catechism: 'What is your name? You are coming from? What is your profession? Where is your husband?' It was hard to be patient in the heat, on a gruelling climb, but I did my best. I was really out in the sticks and none of the boys had so much as seen a foreigner before, let alone had the chance to talk to one. I was the event of their year, perhaps even of their lives. When I cycled through villages and stopped for tea, the whole place came to a standstill. I was mobbed by men and boys. One day I got irritable. 'What are you all staring at? Don't you have any work to do?' A long silence. Then a sad voice said, 'No work. No jobs.'

It was desolate country and life was hard, even for me. There were few hotels so, clutching Mr Mukherji's letter of recommendation, I cycled from Rest House to Circuit House.

These buildings were always in pleasant situations, usually on a hillside, with a verandah overlooking the town. They must at one time have been very agreeable places to stay, but the Indians are not strong on maintenance, and little work had been done on them since Independence in 1947. Beds with broken springs, no blankets, plastic bags stuffed with foam rubber off-cuts to serve as pillows, worn haircord carpets, peeling paint, spent light bulbs, no running water – these lofty, once gracious buildings were depressing in the extreme. They usually had a caretaker who cooked, and I was dependent on his meals, as the town centre was too far to walk in the dark.

I always carried a packet of sweet biscuits and, if I could find it in the local grocer's, a wrapped, sliced cake of some highly artificial flavour. Water for my journey came out of the tap and I treated it with Puritabs, as bottled water was nowhere to be found. When the daily wage of an agricultural worker was sixteen rupees, there was obviously no market for fancy mineral waters or soft drinks at fourteen rupees a time. A typical day's menu would be:

Breakfast: Chapattis and tea.
Lunch: Bananas and tangerines, if I was lucky in the market. Half a dozen of my sweet biscuits and a cup of tea if I wasn't.
Dinner: Eggs, chapattis and tea.

One evening I ordered a two-egg omelette and it came, together with two hard-boiled eggs in masala sauce. Plenty of protein that night! I started to dream of chicken curry.

I'm not keen on the country, even when it's at its most lovely. Ten days of it and I'm pining for company and culture. My journey across the wilds of Madhya Pradesh was lightened only by my visits to the palaces of Indore and the temples of the holy city of Ujjain.

Ujjain is usually a nondescript provincial town on the River Shipra, but every twelve years it has its moment of glory. Then it becomes a major pilgrimage centre, swarming with bathers at the Kumbh Mela, the triennial festival which circulates round the four riverside cities of Allahabad, Hari-dwar, Ujjain and Nasik. This festival celebrates a divine victory. Before the universe took shape, the gods and demons churned the formless waters for the nectar of immortality. It arose in a pot (kumbh) and a terrible battle ensued for its possession. The gods won. Vishnu seized the pot and ran off with it. As he was running, four drops of the precious nectar spilled on India. On one auspicious day in January, pilgrims flock in their millions to one of those four spots, to bathe away their sins and gain release from the cycle of birth and death.

Fortunately, it was not Kumbh Mela year, so I was able to find a room in the appropriately named Rama Krishna Hotel. The waiters were so fascinated with this rare foreign tourist on 'a cykel', that they sat with me at my table while I ate my vegetarian biryani. (Ujjain is such a holy city that meat is not allowed.) I could have done without their attention after a hard day's cycling, but they were keen to oblige, and I actually managed to get a pot of tea with separate milk and sugar. 'Ek teapot' seemed to be the local term for this. 'One teapot'.

Ujjain's other claim to holy fame was the Mahakaleshwar Temple, dedicated to Shiva and housing one of India's twelve *jyotirlingas*, phallic symbols whose power arises from within themselves, rather than being invested in them by priestly ritual. This temple was said to be closed to non-Hindus, but I walked along there to look at the outside and was immediately swept in by cheerful Sunday crowds. They queued up with their flowers, coconuts and little wicker baskets of sweets, until the priests appeared, naked to the waist, but decked in the most gorgeous saffron and orange dhotis. When they opened the gates to the shrine, the worshippers surged forward like a football mob, and had to be controlled by a policeman. I was caught up in the swell and found myself in the holy of holies, circumambulating the linga with everyone else. Wherever I went in the temple complex, I was greeted with beaming smiles, handshakes and *namastes,* even by the brahmins. I couldn't have been made more welcome.

The next morning I had a very satisfactory breakfast of 'ek teapot' and 'tosbutterjam', which is Indian waiterspeak for toast, butter and the judicious blend of saccharine, additives and cochineal, with a hint of onion flavour, that passes for jam. Then I set off on my bicycle for Indore. My splendid reception in the Shiva Temple had left me feeling well disposed towards Hinduism and I was thinking back to it with pleasure, when I saw the barefoot man in the middle of the swirling crowds, praying to Hanuman, and decided there and then to research *The Ramayana*. It made no difference to my immediate plans, as I was intending to stay in the holy city of Nasik anyway, on my route to Bombay. But the fact that Nasik was Rama's next stop gave me a compelling reason for my visit.

When I crossed the Satpura Range into the prosperous state of Maharashtra, my life became much easier. I found better roads (they even had steamrollers!), decent hotels and interesting conversation. The tourist trail, which we all scorn in theory, has many practical advantages.

Most of the tourists I met were European or Australasian, as Americans are nervous of unhygienic India. But in Phardapur, where I was staying to visit the Ajanta Caves, I did come across two brave souls from Texas.

'What medication are you on?' they enquired, as they peered suspiciously at the menu.

'I'm not on any.'

'Not for your stomach? You must be taking something.'

'I'm not. There's nothing wrong with my stomach. And if I get a touch of the runs, I just rest for a day and drink plenty of safe black tea.'

They expressed horror at my rashness.

'Well, we're on antibiotics, the sort they give to people who've had bowel surgery. They're real powerful. Guaranteed to kill off anything.'

'Even the benign bacteria. That can be dangerous.'

'We know that. We'll have to go on a special rehab diet when we get back home. But it's worth it not to get sick.'

They sipped their boiled water with sliced ginger and waited for their custard, while I tucked into my delicious *thali* with a Kingfisher beer.

There were two German cyclists camping in the hotel garden and I was fascinated by their luggage. Instead of the usual canvas panniers, they were carrying two plastic rafting containers, like large, old fashioned sweet jars, which they hooked on to their rear carriers and padlocked together across the top with a horizontal steel bar. It was the perfect arrangement for campers, as the containers were light, yet totally thief-proof. I told them to patent their invention.

After my days of solitude, I enjoyed all my conversations in the hotel there, but perhaps the best was one I only overheard. It was breakfast-time and the table next to mine was occupied by two elderly Indian gentlemen, both engrossed in their copies of *The Times of India*. They had the look of retired army officers. They both ordered coffee with their scrambled eggs.

'I thought you always took tea in the mornings, Buffy.'

'I do – when I'm at home. But I'm very particular about my tea, so I generally order coffee in hotels. Coffee is more difficult to ruin.'

(long pause)

'One can ruin anything, if one has the art.'

Phardapur was only about 200 kilometres from Nasik and I could have reached Rama's hermitage in two or three days, but I had a detour to make. I'd promised to visit the Christian Mission Hospital at Jalna, to see if it would be a suitable gap year placement for an English student. I cycled under a blazing sun through fields of sunflowers and checked into the aptly named Surya Hotel (Surya is the Sun God). The obliging young manager ran me to the hospital on the back of his Suzuki.

The hospital was founded in 1896 by the Presbyterian Church of Scotland and is now run by Indian Christian doctors. It is self-supporting and fees are charged on what Dr Mojis called 'a Robin Hood basis'. The payments of the richer patients subsidised the free clinic, so that no one, however poor, had to be turned away untreated. In 1978, a Dutch charity gave the money for new buildings, including a new suite of operating theatres, but they were not in use, as there were not enough nurses to staff them. The Government had shut down the Mission Hospital's own nursing school; and recruitment from elsewhere was difficult, as Indian nurses would rather work in the Gulf States, where the pay was better.

There was no doubting the dedication of the doctors and nurses, or the standard of medical hygiene. The nurse in the premature baby unit was gowned and masked, and we had to take our shoes off before we went inside. The old operating theatre was shabby, but spotlessly clean, and the eye clinic was immaculate. But the wards and corridors were disgusting. They get a fresh coat of whitewash every year, but the villagers spit their red betel juice on the walls and camp out in the wards, cooking meals for the patients over open fires. They are poor people, in a depressed corner of Maharashtra, and they are just not used to being in a building. The patients were cowering in their beds, wrapped in their own tatty blankets. They were frightened of the hospital and salaamed humbly to Dr Alexander. I was so distressed by my tour, that I didn't see how any teenager could possibly cope with a gap placement there. In any case, the Indian Government was not keen on help from abroad and discouraged it with bureaucracy. Volunteers had to submit their applications six months in advance, then some Government department took a few more months to consider them. By the time permission came through, the volunteers had already fixed themselves up elsewhere. Dr Mojis said he had given up asking for help.

That evening, he and his wife, who was the chief gynaecologist at the hospital, took me to dinner at the home of two ancient Parsee sisters-in-law, Mrs and Miss Jalnawallah. Their bungalow was full of tigers' heads and old photos, and they had a calendar of the Queen and other members of our Royal Family. They presided over the dining table in their Parsee saris, which have strange bunched-up shoulders, while their servants produced chicken fricassee, potato fritters and baked beans, followed by blancmange and a dish of toffees. The British Raj was alive and well in that household.

The Mojis told me afterwards that the Jalnawallahs had for generations been great benefactors to the town. They had paid for the construction of its water supply, founded the

Science Department at Jalna College and still subsidised the work of the Mission Hospital – all without plaques or any wish for recognition. The Parsees were invariably wealthy and successful, but they were not resented by other Indians, because they were so generous. The biggest Parsee firm, Tata, was a worker-oriented company and consequently strike-free. Unfortunately, they were a small community who were obliged by their Zoroastrian faith to intermarry, and that was causing infertility and congenital abnormalities. The Parsees were dying out – to India's great loss.

To cheer myself up after my depressing visit to the hospital, I spent a few days in Aurangabad on the way to Nasik. It was a city I'd wanted to visit for a long time, not for its own industrial sake, but because it was near to Khuldabad, where the last great Moghul Emperor, Aurangzeb (1658–1707), was buried. His predecessors had all built themselves magnificent tombs: Babur in Kabul, Humayun in Delhi, Akbar on the outskirts of Agra, Jehangir in Lahore and, most notably, Shah Jehan, who was buried in his Taj Mahal in Agra. I had seen them all (except Babur's in Afghanistan, which is out of bounds these days) and needed only Auran-gzeb's to complete the set.

Aurangzeb was different from his predecessors. He was an ascetic, a strict Muslim, who despised extravagance and courtly pursuits. He deposed his father, Shah Jehan, when his building projects threatened to bankrupt the state, and devoted his life to consolidating the Empire and extending it southwards. When he died at the age of 89, he was buried in a simple grave, open to the sky, next to the much more elaborate tomb which he had constructed for his religious teacher. As a woman, I was not allowed through the silver doors of the teacher's tomb, but I could see the gold cloth and the string of ostrich eggs hanging round it. Aurangzeb's own tomb was of clay, covered with a plain white sheet. A small rectangle of earth in the centre held a pot of basil (which in India is the plant of humility) and visitors had scattered rose petals. Aurangzeb would not have approved of Lord Curzon's marble screen, but at least it kept out the goats which were clambering over all the other tombs in the cemetery.

Nearby, on a volcanic lava rock 250 metres high, stood the amazing Deogiri Fort. Computer games, where the knight has to rescue a damsel from an impregnable castle, are simplicity itself compared with the real thing in Daulatabad. First, it is girdled by three massive concentric walls and a moat, which used to have crocodiles. If invaders managed to force their way through all that and broke into the fortress through the main Elephant Gate, they found themselves in a courtyard with three exits. While they hesitated, trying to decide which one to use, archers rained arrows on them from the battlements above. If they found the right inner door and broke it down, they were faced with the first fork in the corridor. There followed blind alleys, circular passages and false exits leading to drops down into the moat. We were taken by a guide with a flare up the correct corridor, an enormously long, dark, uphill climb, with yet another fork at the top. Then came an iron walkway, which was heated by a furnace underneath, to roast the invaders. A final tunnel led to the heart of the fortress. Needless to say, the Deogiri Fort had never been taken, except by bribery.

The stunning Ellora Caves, with their temples carved out of the living rock, completed my Aurangabad holiday. Back on the road to Nasik, I was held up at a level crossing, because the Minister of Railways was inaugurating the new broad-gauge track between Aurangabad and Manmad. This would enable a much-needed direct service to be run between Aurangabad and Bombay. The celebration of the new line was endless. Bands played, and the minister and local dignitaries made speech after long-winded speech. Then the inaugural train pulled into Manmad Station. The engine was garlanded with marigolds and hung around with little shiny brass elephants. A painting of the Goddess Lakshmi, Sita's heavenly Original, adorned its side, and there were Lakshmis on all the newly painted carriages. Most of the train was empty and shuttered. There was one carriage full of soldiers, and another had sundry officials in their best suits, who were too busy staring at me and my bike to take much notice of the proceedings. The only other passengers were joyriding urchins. They clung on to every step, ledge and buffer, and even rode cheekily on top. The station master chased them off with a stick, when he escorted the minister on board, but the moment his back was turned, they jumped on again, grinning gleefully. They were the only people who were having any fun. I certainly wasn't, stuck at the barrier for two full hours, in a convoy of fuming motorists. Rama had demons to contend with, but at least he was spared a Minister of Railways and his toadies in all their pomp.

# 8 Nasik to Karnataka

*Nasik – Bombay – Pune – Hubli*

WITH BOMBAY BURSTING at the seams, Nasik has become an industrial overspill town. It is only 150 kilometres away from Bombay's sprawl, with reasonable road and rail connections, so what used to be a quiet market town is now a buzzing dusty giant, ringed with factories and expanding by the day. Despite these developments, it is still one of India's holiest pilgrimage cities, on the banks of the sacred River Godavari. It is not a holy city because Rama lived there. Rama built his hermitage there because it was a holy place.

Nasik stands near Trimbak, where the Godavari rises to begin its journey across the entire breadth of the Deccan to its delta in Andhra Pradesh, on the Bay of Bengal. Its spring on a hilltop, 690 steps up, flows into a tank which is called Gangasagar, reflecting the belief that the Godavari has the same underground source as the holy Ganga. Together with Ujjain, Allahabad and Haridwar, it is one of the four Kumbh Mela cities.

For some reason which I couldn't understand, Sita's Nasik home was not a thatched cottage like the one which Lakshmana built, but a series of four interconnected caves. I was told that Sita hid underground, when she was trying to avoid capture. She was obviously a very small person. The cave mouth, which opened on to a steep flight of steps, was so low that I didn't see how I could possibly get my large frame through it. I was on the verge of giving up, when the resident brahmin poked his head out and encouraged me. I managed to get in by sitting on the top step and shuffling down to the caves on my bottom. Once inside, I could just stand up, but I had to struggle against claustrophobia. The heat of the oil lamps and the clouds of incense didn't help. There was an antechamber, where Ganesh, the elephant-headed god of auspicious beginnings, looked down benignly from a blue-tiled ledge. Then came the main shrine with the usual three idols, but this shrine was unusual in that Sita was the central figure, flanked by Rama and Lakshmana. The third room had splodges of vermilion paint all over the walls, but was otherwise empty. The fourth had a garlanded linga, the phallic symbol of Shiva as god of creation. Five men ahead of me were taking it in turns to photograph one another, crouching over the lingam with happy holiday smiles on their faces. I was slightly annoyed that the brahmin allowed those frivolous photographs, but wouldn't let me take a picture of Sita's shrine. Was it because I was a non-Hindu? Or was he Sita's priest and jealous of her sanctity, while he cared less about Shiva's? It was one of those little mysteries which I couldn't resolve without speaking fluent Marathi.

I crawled up the steps and out of the cave mouth into the fresh air with an enormous sense of relief. Across the road was a less daunting building. It was guarded by a hectic orange Hanuman in a green hat, to whom a little boy was making an offering as I approached. A most dramatic mural of Lakshmana cutting off Surpanakha's nose covered the outside wall. Blood gushed down the front of the unfortunate demoness and spattered the stones at her feet, while Lakshmana brandished his sabre, watched by Sita, the blue-skinned Rama and some startled swans on the river. Inside were waxwork tableaux of the three hermits in the forest and Rama shooting the magical deer.

A visit to the temple of Black Rama, Kala Ram, completed my mandatory sightseeing. Rama was indeed black, as were Lakshmana and Sita. All three wore gold crowns and Sita was dressed in a Schiaparelli pink organza creation under her marigold garlands. Their staring eyes peered out from among the flowers, offering darshan to their devotees.

Darshan in worship is a uniquely Hindu concept, meaning 'sight' or 'view'. It is important for the worshipper to view the deity. This is done at particular times of day, when the priest opens the ornamental gates to the shrine and reveals the idol. In some temples, the idol is processed along the corridors and round the courtyard, so that even more worshippers can have darshan. But it has to be a two-way traffic. The idol has to 'see' the worshipper. This is possible, because the idol is one of the forms which a god can take to show grace to his devotees. Contrary to popular belief in the West, a Hindu idol is not itself a god. The god takes up temporary residence in the idol and views the worshipper. Hence the importance of the staring eyes, which must always be visible, however many garlands may obscure the rest of the body. The one exception is Sri Venkatesvara, the idol of Vishnu in the temple at Tirupati, India's most visited pilgrim shrine. Here Vishnu's eyes are shielded, because his gaze is so piercing that it would blind his devotees.

Gurus and national figures also give and receive darshan. Listening to what they say is less important than catching their eye, so disciples may read and chat at the feet of their guru; and country people often travel miles to attend political rallies, when they don't understand a word of the speaker's language.

In temples, the importance of darshan makes devotion easy for Hindus, as rituals are few and optional. The priests may chant and attend to the deity, but there are no sermons. Worshippers circumambulate the shrine, make an offering of fruit or sweets and give a small donation, for which the priest rewards them with a red tilak on the forehead. When the offerings have been 'seen' by the deity, they become *prasad*, sanctified food, and are eaten by the worshippers. But what really counts in the temple is the exchange of darshan. For the Hindu, *puja* (worship) is an individual responsibility, not a congregational event, and prayer to a deity or meditation on the Absolute can be offered just as effectively at home.

I walked down to the sacred Godavari River, where the bathing ghats were guarded by two Hanumen. It was market day and the vegetables had attracted a larger number than usual of holy cows, who were grazing unmolested on the heaps of fresh spinach. Weaving in and out of them, I found a stall selling delightful hand-carved animals and bought a little wheeled tiger for one of my small grandsons. It was delicate and wouldn't last two days, but for the equivalent of 12p it was a miniature bargain.

When Rama and Lakshmana set out from Nasik in search of Sita, they travelled 600 kilometres south, as the crow flies, to Mount Rishyamuka, near modern Hospet in Karnataka. Valmiki gives no details of their route, because he was a stranger to that part of the world. So I had a free choice. I could take any route I chose, as long as it took me down to Hospet. Legend, which often embellishes *The Ramayana*, connects the two wanderers with Bombay. I'd never visited the city and the AB Road was well maintained, so I thought I might as well cycle that way as any other.

To reach Bombay, I travelled south-east, climbing the Western Ghats. It was a ride to remember – three days when everything went well and I rediscovered the joys of cycling. The road surface was perfect and I had liana trees to shade me and a gentle breeze to cool me down. The wealthier end of Maharashtra reminded me of southern Spain. There were pleasant roadside restaurants set in gardens and I hit on my best hotel so far. A huge billboard of children's dream houses under a rainbow announced 'Paradise is only half a kilometre away'. I approached this paradise with some scepticism and was amazed to find the five-star Manas Hotel, a holiday resort complex where my spotlessly clean new bungalow with a cream marble bathroom cost me just £5 a night. Some of my fellow guests were Indian families on holiday. Others were attending courses in the meditation centre attached to a nearby Durga temple, but were sleeping in comfort in the hotel. All of them drove Mercedes and were astonished to see me arrive on a bicycle. In the evening, I sat under the stars in a sea of bougainvillea, dining on succulent lamb cooked in mint, with salad, onion and garlic bread, and a bottle of Kingfisher beer. The hardships of Madhya Pradesh seemed a lifetime away.

The Western Ghats, which form the mountain barrier between the Arabian Sea and the Deccan, turned out to be much less fearsome than I'd expected. Much of the grey shading on my map was steep downhill, not up, and I made excellent progress as far as Shahapur. There the balance of the hills shifted against me and it was hard work, especially in the afternoon, when I was cycling straight into the fiery sun. Although I was wearing total sun block, my face was ablaze and I had to cover it with my silk balaclava. The air was thick with diesel fumes and I had just run out of water when, miraculously, a lorry braked in a flash of gold tinsel, and the driver's mate reached out and handed me a bag of ripe tomatoes. I couldn't resist them. The cool juice poured down my chin as I gobbled them, skin and all. I was breaking the most basic traveller's rule, never to eat unwashed, unpeeled fruit, and I feared the worst. But there were no ill effects. I suppose I'd been in India long enough by that time to have built up a measure of immunity.

The final descent to Bombay was precipitous. The road cut down through eroded mountains in a tight corkscrew. I saw disasters at almost every turn – lorries which had taken the bends too fast and ended up at the bottom of gullies. At the most dangerous corners there were small shrines, many to Vishnu the Preserver and Hanuman, who bestows long life. In other places there were brahmins, sitting cross-legged, holding up pictures of these protective deities. The lorry drivers braked and threw coins at the shrines and brahmins out of their cab windows. This constant slowing down probably did as much to preserve them as their gods. One Hanuman was particularly striking. He was tearing open his breast to reveal Rama and Sita in his heart. At the time, I thought the idea had been copied from Catholicism, from the Sacred Heart of Jesus, but I later realised that it was an authentic part of the Rama myth. Mahatma Gandhi is quoted as saying:

Hanuman tore open his heart and showed there was nothing there but Ramanama. I have nothing of the power of Hanuman to tear open my heart, but if any of you feel inclined to do it, I assure you that you will find there nothing but love for Rama, whom I see face to face in the starving millions of India.

The starving millions of India overwhelmed me as I cycled through the outskirts of Bombay. As India's boom city, it draws the poor like a magnet from the countryside. Many of them end up sleeping on the streets in utter destitution, while others live in cardboard and sacking shacks on waste ground further out. The ones who succeed in scratching a living move into shantytowns. There they settle among the rubbish tips, by some fetid black stream, and build their hovels of mud or packing cases, roofed with corrugated iron. Until I cycled through them, I would never have believed that people could survive in such abject conditions. On the waste ground, they were filthy and bedraggled, starvelings without hope. But when I got to the shantytowns, I noticed a difference in the air. By some miracle of ingenuity, families emerged from their hovels looking neat and clean. There was faltering electricity and even a few television aerials. These people were on their way up in the world. As I approached the city from Thane, I passed through every gradation of poverty. People stared at me, but nowhere did I meet with hostility. I was not a voyeur. I was a cyclist. And I didn't take photographs.

To keep your sanity in India, you have to switch off from the poverty and squalor, because there's nothing you can do about it. Until the Indians control their population growth, and until their amazingly wealthy minority takes more responsibility for the welfare of the majority, they will never be able to raise their standard of living. The population has more than doubled since Independence and the infrastructure left by the British is crumbling under the weight of numbers. Government schemes for education and welfare drown in the sea of children. Although they educate more of them each year, the proportion of illiterates grows. Meanwhile, corruption in many states syphons off what little money is available.

So not through callousness, but as a kind of self-protection, I averted my eyes from the beggars and street-dwellers when I went for a stroll along Strand Road to Apollo Bunder. The evening air was balmy and there was a sliver of new moon. Peanut-vendors, snake-charmers and performing monkeys clustered round the Gateway of India and along the harbour walls. India's most famous hotel, the Taj Mahal, blazed with lights at one end of the promenade, while a dance at the Yacht Club lit up the other. Families were out enjoying the cool of the evening. Some were Indian, but they were almost outnumbered by the white-clad armies of Arabs, who flock to Bombay with their batches of wives and children for business, liquor and shopping. It was all very cosmopolitan, even Mediterranean, and I felt really at home there. To complete my enjoyment, I went to Leopold's, the tourist hang-out on Colaba Causeway, for a plate of fish and chips – a gastronomic delight after six weeks of curry!

Bombay was a good place to go in search of Rama, for it was overwhelmingly Hindu, the fiefdom of Bal Thackeray and his Shiv Sena. Fortunately, this was February 1992, some months before the series of riots which were to leave 1,400 dead. It was in December 1992 that the Shiv Sena and other Hindu fanatics destroyed the Babri Masjid in Ayodhya. One tenth of the population of Bombay is Muslim, and the destruction of the mosque led to street battles between Muslims and the police, who are mostly Hindu. In retaliation, the Shiv Sena systematically slaughtered the Muslims in the districts where they predominated, and burned and looted their property. The Muslims then blew up the Stock Exchange and the Air India building. That levelled the score and led to a fragile truce between the two communities. In a city of almost thirteen million (at the latest count), where half are homeless and a chasm yawns between rich and poor, all sorts of animosities bubble away. When these are exacerbated by hatred between rival religions, blood can be shed at any time.

Since that first visit in 1992, I have been to Bombay most years and have always seemed to pick the right time. I have missed the turbulence.

Rama takes me on some interesting excursions, which I would never otherwise make. One day, in the cool of the morning, I cycled along the beaches of Back Bay to Malabar Hill. At the foot of the hill was an area of modest middle-class houses and apartment blocks, where Condor and I were immediately mobbed by children. They were well dressed and spoke English, so when they started to beg, I told them it was naughty and they immediately stopped, with huge grins on their faces. I suppose a foreigner is always worth a try. I was there to visit the Walkeshwar (God of Sand) Temple and the Banganga Tank. Legend has it that Rama passed through Bombay in his search for Sita, to ask the blessings of Sage Gautama. The Sage advised him to worship Shiva daily, so the ever-dutiful Lakshmana took it upon himself to speed to Varanasi and back every morning for a fresh Shiva linga. One morning, when he was late returning, Rama went down to the beach and built a linga of sand, and that is where the temple stands today. Rama also shot an arrow into the ground and released Bhogavati, the underground Ganges, into the Banganga Tank. The place is popular with pilgrims and there were so many temples that it was difficult to see which one was Walkeshwar. But then I noticed a sacred cow tethered beside the tank. Devotees were queuing up to touch its forehead and pass its tail over their own foreheads, before going to pray through the grilles of a locked temple. It was obviously a place of great holiness and it did in fact turn out to be Walkeshwar.

After Bombay, I got into difficulties with my route. I had hoped to be able to cycle down the coast as far as Goa, then turn inland through Hubli to Hospet, but the coast road was not continuous and, according to the Tourist Office, there was nowhere to stay along there and food was scarce. The settlements marked on my map were no more than tiny fishing villages with no amenities. So I cycled back over the Western Ghats to Poona, now Pune, and another Bombay overspill. The fastest daily express train, the Deccan Queen, does the journey to Bombay in three and a half hours, bringing Pune just within commuter range for the thousands who work in Bombay and could never begin to afford Bombay rents. It is claimed that property in Bombay is now the most expensive in the world, beating even Tokyo and London.

In Pune, I was faced with two choices. I could cycle due south through the hill stations on the crest of the Ghats, which would be 400 kilometres of desperately arduous riding, down one mountain and up the next, all the way to Belgaum or Londa, where I could take a road running east across easier terrain; or I could attempt to cut directly across country to Hospet, along roads where acceptable accommodation would be hard to find. From a cycling point of view, that would be the easier route. But I had had my fill of wretched hotels and dilapidated Circuit Houses, and I didn't think I could stand another two weeks of the same. There was little of historical interest along either route and I had no idea which way Rama had wandered. I agonised for days over the two alternatives and in the end chose neither. I'd already circled the globe on my bicycle once, cycling every inch of the way, no matter how difficult or dangerous, as a matter of principle. I'd met that particular challenge and had nothing to prove, even to myself. So, faced with two such unattractive choices, I opted out altogether and bought a ticket to Hubli on the Bangalore express.

It should have been a twelve-hour journey, but the train from Bombay was over an hour late arriving in Pune. Then a lunatic built a fire in one of the lavatories on the train to cook his dinner. When smoke began to seep out into the corridor, the guard halted the train and the local fire brigade careered to the scene in a clanging of bells. They broke down the lavatory door, ejected the indignant culprit and threw his dinner, together with his pots and pans, out of the nearest window. Sensing trouble, the man jumped off the train – to the great annoyance of the railway police who arrived from the next station along the line to arrest him. The last we saw of him, he was haring across country, his skinny legs tangling in his *dhoti,* pursued by three puffing policemen. It was all such a diversion that no one minded losing another two hours.

The incident broke the ice in the compartment and we chatted amiably over our evening meal. There were two businessmen from Delhi, one from Nepal (the one who told me that Janakpur was Sita's birthplace) and a railway official with excellent English and heretical views. I told them I was going to Hospet, because that was supposed to be Valmiki's Kishkindha, to research *The Ramayana.* With a mischievous gleam in his eye, the railway official asked me an innocent question.

'Now you are a woman, so you will know about these things much better than I do. Can you explain to me how Rama was born?'

'He was born to King Dasaratha,' I said. 'Dasaratha had no children. He prayed to the gods and they gave him four, including Rama.'

'Yes. The gods gave him a bowl of *prasad*. He fed this *prasad* to his three wives and all three had children. But how can this be? How can you have children without sex?'

'You can these days. You can go to a clinic.'

'I knew you'd have the answer,' he crowed. 'This Rama was the first test-tube baby! But apart from that, what's so special about him? Now I like Krishna. Krishna and Radha were so close, they were the same person. Krishna Radha, Radha Krishna. But what about poor Sita? Rama threw her out when she was carrying twins. Just at the time when a wife really needs her husband's help, he said, "Out!" And out she went into the forest. Rama's no hero. Sita sacrificed everything for him. She gave up her comfortable palace and went to live in the wilderness with him for fourteen years. She sacrificed children for fourteen years, because how could she bring them up in a forest? She was snatched by a demon and suffered imprisonment. And at the end of all that, Rama said, "Out!" And what about Lakshmana? He left his wife, and for fourteen years the poor man never slept, because he was on permanent sentry duty for Rama and Sita. And then there's Bharata, who denied himself the kingdom. He put Rama's sandals on the throne and ruled in his name for fourteen years, living in a grass hut. These are the real heroes of *The Ramayana*, not that conceited Rama. Of course, the brothers were rewarded. But Sita was sent away. And then Rama had the cheek, years later, to offer to take her back if she passed a test. But Indian women have their pride. Once you send them away, that's the end of it. They won't come back. She prayed to mother earth and the earth swallowed her up. So I can't see that there's anything admirable about Rama.'

All this was too much for one of the businessmen from Delhi. He was obviously deeply shocked at this sacrilegious talk and put an end to it by asking me if I'd read the *Bhagavad Gita* and how I thought it compared with the Bible. The railway official smiled quietly to himself while I did my best to cope with this weighty topic.

But he was not as modern in his outlook as he liked to think. The next morning, he gave me a good ticking off for rattling about India on my own.

'A wife should always be with her husband.'

'But my husband doesn't travel,' I said. I didn't tell him I was a widow, because that often leads to problems.

'You and your husband are one. You must accept.'

'Like Sita?' I asked.

Everyone laughed. He told me then that I was very strong – like a boy in my boy's shoes.

At this point, a little boy of about eight jumped on to the train in a monkey mask. He wore a suit of red organdie edged with gold tinsel, and his gold crown was tied under his chin to keep it steady while he performed monkey acrobatics and sang. He was Hanuman, working the train for a few rupees. It was an inspired notion. Everyone loves Hanuman and he left the compartment with coins jingling.

'You didn't mention Hanuman,' I said, 'in your alternative *Ramayana*.'

'No. We were talking about Rama. But Hanuman is the greatest hero of them all. That goes without saying.'

On that final accolade, I left the train, collected my bicycle and rode off to Hospet, through fields of sugar cane and sunflowers. The sun shone and I felt elated. At long last, I was going to meet Hanuman, the inspiration for my journey.

## ☙ ❧

### The Kingdom of the Monkeys

*All the animals created by the gods to help Vishnu in his incarnation as Rama were waiting for him in the Kingdom of Kishkindha. Sugriva, the monkey chieftain, saw him approaching Mount Rishyamuka with Lakshmana and was afraid that the two heroes might be assassins in hermits' disguise, sent by his brother, King Bali, with whom he was on very bad terms. So he sent his trusted adviser, Hanuman, to find out who they were.*

Hanuman was a gigantic monkey, 'his body hard as a diamond and his face red as the brightest ruby, glowing like molten gold'. As he was the son of Vayu, the Wind God, he could fly through the air with the speed of Garuda, tear up mountains and change his form at will. To crown all, he was renowned for his wisdom , his knowledge of the scriptures and his eloquence.

So as not to alarm the brothers, Hanuman assumed the form of a holy man and charmed them with the felicity of his speech. They told him the story of Rama's exile and Sita's abduction, and asked for the help of Sugriva. When he heard their appeal, Hanuman reverted to his colossal monkey form and carried them up the mountain in giant bounds to meet his leader. Sugriva too was an exile, whose wife had been stolen by Bali, and Hanuman could see the wisdom of an alliance.

Rama and Sugriva made a pact. Rama would kill Bali, and in return Sugriva would find Sita and help defeat the Demon King. Sugriva told Rama that he had heard screams one day and, looking up, had seen a ravishingly beautiful woman wrestling with Ravana in his aerial car. She had thrown her cloak and jewels over the side and he had kept them hidden. He handed them now to Rama, who recognised them as Sita's and knew that he was travelling in the right direction.

His courage bolstered by Rama, Sugriva challenged Bali to a fight. As the two brothers looked alike, he wore a garland of flowers, so that Rama, who was hiding behind a tree, could distinguish him in the battle. It was a fierce struggle, 'like two thunderclouds clashing together', but Sugriva was the weaker of the two. When Bali's victory seemed imminent, Rama drew his mighty bow and shot him in the heart. The dying Bali committed his kingdom, together with his wife and son, Tara and Angada, to Sugriva's care; and Rama assured him that he had paid the penalty for his misdeeds and would gain immortality.

It was the start of the monsoon season. Rama was enchanted by the beauties of the awakening earth, but he pined for Sita and waited impatiently for the floods to subside. When the roads were passable again, Sugriva summoned his troops. All the monkeys of the world flooded into Kishkindha, 'covering the earth like locusts'. Sugriva divided them into four battalions and sent them out to the four corners of the earth, with instructions to search *everywhere until they found where Sita was hidden. He placed the greatest confidence in Hanuman, so Rama gave that heroic monkey a ring engraved with his name, to be a sign to Sita. Hanuman set out with his troops 'like the moon in a cloudless sky encircled by stars'.*

This episode causes considerable difficulty, because Rama appears in an unfavourable light. The dying Bali accuses him of treachery, of being outwardly virtuous, but at heart a scoundrel. He shot Bali from behind, when Bali was engaged in a fight with someone else and had done nothing to offend him. Rama was guilty of regicide, though he himself was the son of a king, who should have known his duty and been able to distinguish right from wrong. He should have controlled his passions, not acted irascibly, using his bow as his argument.

There is a great deal of strength in Bali's case, but Rama rails against him for his 'simian folly'. He argues that Bali stole Sugriva's wife and he, Rama, was acting as the agent of Bharata, the supreme ruler of the land, when he punished him. Also, he had pledged his support to Sugriva. He was therefore acting in accordance with his duties towards his king and his friend. He quotes the Laws of Manu: 'Those men who, having done wrong, submit to the penalty imposed by the king, are washed free from every stain and ascend to heaven like the good and those who do benevolent deeds. The king who does not put down vice himself assumes the guilt.' In conclusion, Rama states that attacking Bali from behind when he was fighting someone else was a matter of no significance, as Bali was only a monkey.

Bali is deeply mortified and begs Rama's forgiveness for addressing such an eminent person in disrespectful terms; the pain of his wound must have caused his mind to wander and he had insulted Rama without realising what he was saying. He acknowledges that Rama , in the serenity of his wisdom, knows the significance of all things and the working out of cause and effect. Rama, in words full of tenderness, forgives him and promises to protect his wife, Tara, and his son, Angada.

In the earliest versions of The Ramayana, Rama was almost certainly a human hero. As such, he could fall a little short of perfection. He may have been in the wrong when he shot Bali, *especially as he shot him from behind, but mortals are allowed to make the occasional mistake. The difficulty arises later, when Rama comes to be seen as an incarnation of one of the greatest Hindu gods. As Vishnu, he should be omniscient and incapable of error. There is only one way to resolve this dilemma, as it seems to me – to posit that when Vishnu took on human form, he took on human weaknesses too.*

*In Valmiki's Ramayana, Rama is both god and man. Sometimes he seems unaware of his divine nature; at other times, everyone recognises him. For instance, in their first conversation with Hanuman, Lakshmana variously refers to Rama as 'the defender of the whole universe', 'he, under whose compassion all things rest' and 'he who was formerly the guardian of the worlds'. Remarks of this kind are probably later interpolations, added to upgrade Valmiki's heroic tale to the status of a sacred text. They cause the most interesting confusion, and provide scholars and holy men with material for endless merry disputation.*

## The Adventures of Hanuman

*Hanuman and his monkey team searched everywhere for Sita, without success. When they came to the Vindhya mountain, they sat down to consider their next move. They were terrified of returning to Kishkindha to face Sugriva's anger. They spoke of Sita's abduction and praised the valour of Jatayu the vulture, who had died in his rescue attempt. How lucky they would be if they too could die in the service of the incomparable Rama!*

*By chance, Sampati, who was King of the Vultures and Jatayu's brother, overheard their lamentations. He loved Jatayu dearly and had lost his wings shielding him, when the two brothers had flown too close to the sun. The monkeys gave him a full account of Jatayu's fight with Ravana. He was comforted to hear that Rama himself had performed Jatayu's funeral rites and, in gratitude, he told the monkeys where Sita was hidden – four hundred miles across the southern ocean, in Ravana's kingdom of Lanka. When he rendered this service to Rama, Sampati's wings miraculously sprouted anew and he soared into the sky, restored to his youthful vigour.*

The monkeys hurried to the ocean and their hair stood on end in fright. They despaired of reaching Lanka across such dangerous waters. But Jambavan, the wise old King of the Bears, reminded Hanuman that he was the son of the Wind God and could easily jump four hundred miles if he summoned his divine powers. At this, Hanuman swelled to a gigantic size and 'like a winged mountain' leapt over the ocean to Lanka, defeating all the monsters in his path.

When he reached Ravana's kingdom, he shrank down to the size of a cat, so that he could explore the city unobserved. He crept around in the night, marvelling at the gold and emerald gates, the pavements studded with pearls, the crystal staircases and the diamond windows. Then he penetrated Ravana's dazzling palace and spied on him as he slept, surrounded by hundreds of beautiful women. As dawn broke, he discovered Sita. She was weeping under a shingshapa tree in a grove behind the palace, guarded by hideous demonesses.

Hanuman hid in the branches and heard the ten-headed King of the Rakshasas tempting Sita with jewels and kingdoms, if she would become his queen. But Sita thought only of Rama, 'her mind a chariot drawn by the steeds of resolution'. Ravana lost patience. He gave her another two months to accept his offer of marriage, at the end of which time, if she still refused, he would have her minced up and would eat her for breakfast.

Full of pity for her sufferings, Hanuman slid down from his branch and spoke to her most eloquently in Sanskrit. He finally gained her confidence by giving her Rama's ring. In his anxiety to free her from Ravana's clutches, he resumed his gigantic size and offered to fly to Rama immediately, carrying her on his shoulders. But Sita refused to escape in that way: she was wholly devoted to her husband and it was not right for her to touch the body of any other. More importantly, Rama must be given the opportunity to demonstrate his valour by defeating Ravana in battle. She gave Hanuman the pearl which she used to wear on her forehead, and dismissed him with loving messages for Rama.

Although his mission was now accomplished, Hanuman decided to make himself even more useful to Rama by surveying Ravana's forces. To test their strength, he went on the rampage. He uprooted all the trees in the grove and tore down Ravana's *temple, defeating eighty thousand demons single-handed. Then five generals led out their armies, and youthful champions attacked him from their aerial cars, but Hanuman deflected all their weapons and crushed his opponents, hurling mountains into their midst, until the paths were choked with fallen elephants, smashed chariots and mangled giants. Then he rested at Ravana's gate, 'like Time, pausing at the destruction of the worlds.'*

*Ravana finally despaired of killing Hanuman and sent his son Indrajit to capture him. Indrajit sped out in a chariot drawn by tigers and shot an arrow from the bow given to him by Brahma, the God of Creation. Hanuman fell, but he knew that he was under the protection of Brahma and would not be seriously injured. He pretended to be stunned, so that the demons would bind him and take him into the presence of Ravana.*

*Hanuman was amazed when he saw Ravana, seated on his jewelled throne, with golden diadems on his ten heads and his twenty arms gleaming with priceless bangles. He was 'like a blazing sun in his might and glory' and Hanuman thought, 'Were he not evil, this mighty monarch of the titans could be the protector of the celestial realm.' He introduced himself to Ravana, told his story and fearlessly demanded the return of Sita. He was saved from death only by the intervention of Ravana's brother, Vibhisana, who reminded Ravana that a messenger could be punished, but not killed.*

*Ravana was fascinated by the length of Hanuman's tail and thought of an appropriate punishment. He had it swathed in oily rags and set fire to it. Then Hanuman was led out into the city in disgrace, his splendid tail ablaze, but he felt no pain. Sita prayed to Agni, the God of Fire, to be gentle with him, and his own father, the Wind God, soothed him with cooling breezes. Once away from Ravana, he contracted his body until he could slip quite easily out of his bonds. Then he swelled again to a gigantic size, and ran along the rooftops, surveying the fortifications by daylight. When he had gathered enough information, he waved his flaming tail and started a conflagration which consumed the entire city. After which, he doused his tail in the sea and leapt across to the mainland 'like an arrow loosed from its bowstring'.*

*The monkeys heard his roars and climbed to the treetops, wearing their best clothes and waving their scarves in welcome. Jambavan and Angada went down to the seashore to meet him, and the monkeys brought rocks to form a circle of seats. Their faces shone with joy. With their palms together in a gesture of respect, they sat down and listened to Hanuman's adventures. The young Prince Angada was so inspired by Hanuman's prowess, that he wanted them all to rush to Lanka immediately to kill Ravana and rescue Sita, but the wise Jambavan restrained him: Rama had made a solemn vow that he would rid the world of the wicked tyrant and recover Sita, and it was their duty to help him keep his word.*

*On their way back to Kishkindha to give the good news to Rama and Sugriva, the monkeys came to a beautiful garden called Madhuvana, which was famous for its wild honey. The monkeys had been a long time in the wilderness, and they loved wild honey, so they stormed the garden to celebrate. They feasted on fruit and drank so much nectar from the honeycombs that they got themselves remarkably drunk and ran amok. When Sugriva heard that they were trampling down the garden with their wild dancing, he knew that Hanuman had been successful in his mission. He brought the monkeys before Rama and Lakshmana, and Hanuman delighted them with his account of Sita's discovery and the destruction of Ravana's capital. 'Hanuman alone could accomplish such a feat,' cried Sugriva. 'The success of that enterprise depended on the sagacity of that foremost of monkeys endowed with courage, strength and learning. Where Hanuman is the moving spirit, victory is assured.' Rama gazed on Hanuman with veneration and embraced him with tears of joy. The leaders then sat down together to plan the invasion of Lanka.*

There is a charming embellishment to this tale, which does not appear in Valmiki. When Hanuman was brought before Ravana, the fearsome King of the Rakshasas was sitting high up on his magnificent jewelled throne. Hanuman was thrown down on the floor and had to crane his neck to see Ravana's faces. But he was not a monkey to be humbled in this way. One of Hanuman's most useful attributes was the power to grow his tail to any length he wished. So he grew it and grew it, and wound it round, until it curled into a stool so high that he could sit on it and himself look down on Ravana. Ravana was incensed and sent for a pile of cushions, but every time he raised his seat, Hanuman calmly lengthened his tail, and still towered above him. That was the real motive behind Ravana's choice of punishment. He wanted to destroy that offending tail.

When Hanuman is carved or painted, his tremendously long tail is much in evidence. Sometimes it is so long that it sweeps up behind him and loops over to protect his head. As a minor deity, he often appears in temple sculpture as a bas-relief on a pillar. This allows his tail to be seen. When he is the chief god in his own shrine, his tail, like everything else apart from the staring eyes, is totally swamped in cloaks and garlands.

# **9** Kishkindha

*Hubli – Hospet – Vijayanagar – Goa – Kanniyakumari – Bombay*

AS I CYCLED TOWARDS KISHKINDHA, the Kingdom of the Monkeys, the sunflowers gradually gave way to scrub and then to a landscape of dramatic starkness. Huge rounded boulders were strewn over the empty countryside, rising in confused stacks from the red, iron-rich soil. There was not a tree to be seen, not a blade of grass. The grazing was too meagre to support even that survivor on stones, the omnivorous Indian goat. I passed no living creature, man or beast. The sun climbed higher and the road was shadeless. I cycled under one boulder massive enough to carry a crenelated fortress and saw in the distance whole mountains of them, boulder piled upon boulder, like giant building blocks. Stone-quarrying and opencast ore mining were the only possible occupations in this granite and iron world. There was not even wood for fence posts; they used granite blocks instead. And the meanest rural huts were granite built, strong enough to withstand centuries of monsoon rains.

In *The Ramayana*, the Kingdom of Kishkindha was still a verdant forest region, but erosion has reduced it to bare rocks. Without cattle, the women have no cowpats to dry for fuel. This means that they have to spend hours every day scavenging for firewood, ranging further and further afield to chop down the few twigs of scrub which manage to break through the arid soil. The problem is compounded by the Indian penchant for arson and self-immolation. It is a tradition which goes back a long way. The Greek geographer Strabo (64 BC–AD 20) gives astonished accounts of various

Indian holy men who burned themselves up in the presence of Alexander the Great and the Roman Emperor Augustus. These self-immolations were carried out for philosophical reasons. Today, arson and suicide by fire are more likely to be seen as a means of solving problems. Brides whose dowries are disappointing are set on fire by their husbands' families. Protesters against political measures set themselves or their local buses on fire. Hindus and Muslims set one another's houses on fire when sectarian violence erupts. And in Karnataka, the night sky was illuminated by a blaze which was sweeping out of control through the forests of the Western Ghats, started deliberately by a group of villagers who were angry with their local Forestry Officers. When all these criminal fires are added to the legitimate ones needed for cooking, temple worship and the cremation of the Hindu dead, erosion seems unstoppable. The poor multiply, and it is they who cook on open fires. You have only to take a night train and see the thousands of brightly burning wood fires beside the tracks to realise the enormous scale of the problem. Intermediate technology groups produce simple stoves which make more efficient use of available fuel, and send field workers into villages to break down traditional reluctance to try new methods of cooking. As far as India is concerned, such initiatives cannot come soon enough. But in India, as elsewhere, armaments are more attractive to politicians than humble cooking stoves; and the world aid organisations still seem dazzled by the glory of major projects such as dams, when what is really needed is help at ground level.

I got rather depressed, thinking about all this, and Hospet's dusty bazaar did little to raise my spirits when I cycled through it. But the Malligi Tourist Home provided a garden oasis beside a canal, where I avoided the clouds of mosquitos by treating myself to an air-conditioned room (inevitably known as AC in the country of initials). There was a verandah café for breakfast and vegetarian meals, and in a neighbouring garden was the non-vegetarian, licensed Eagle Restaurant. After days on the road, it was a good place to rest for a while and 'escape from India'. Travelling by bicycle, as

I do, brings full-time exposure to local people, their way of life and their beady-eyed curiosity. It's all extremely fascinating and rewarding, and it's grown on me to such an extent that I now feel weirdly disconnected when I travel in any other way. But I must admit that a few Western faces, and the chance of a chat in English or French, are very welcome from time to time.

The Malligi Tourist Home also seemed a good place to embark on a bit of research. I approached two English-speaking Indian women in the garden. After a few preliminaries to break the ice and get them talking, I asked:

'What do you think of Sita? Is she still your ideal today?'

'Yes. She is the perfect woman and we should all model ourselves on her.'

'Do you think your husband is a god then?'

There were embarrassed giggles at this bold question. For Indian women, it is not respectful to discuss your husband, or even mention him by name. He is 'he' in the polite form.

'Well, he's the chief breadwinner, so we should defer to him.'

'But supposing you don't agree with him? Supposing he's wrong? What happens then?'

'It depends. Women have ways.' They smiled knowingly at each other.

These replies were the same in essence as those I had received from all the educated Indian women with whom I had tried to discuss Sita. They might be high-flying lawyers or senior executives of large companies, who ran their households with ruthless efficiency, yet they still paid lip-service to the epic ideal of Sita. When discussing their work, they had a tendency to downplay their enthusiasm for their careers outside the home and to emphasise their domestic role. They felt it demeaning to both partners to defy or contradict their husband. They coped by softening him up, wheedling or tricking him into compliance. In the Independence struggle, Gandhi claimed that he had taken his policy of active non-cooperation from women. By observation, he had learned their techniques for getting their own way quietly, when the odds were stacked against them.

Sita represents the ideal woman, as portrayed in the Laws of Manu, the most influential of all Hindu codes, traditionally ascribed to one of the progenitors of mankind. Written down in Sanskrit somewhere between the first century BC and the first century AD, these Laws lay down the rules of dharma, the social and religious obligations of every person, based on his or her caste, sex and stage of life. They naturally give an elevated status to the brahmins, who compiled them. Here are some of Manu's rules for a woman:

She should do nothing independently
even in her own house.
In childhood subject to her father,
in youth to her husband,
And when her husband is dead to her sons,
she should never enjoy independence.
In season and out of season
her lord, who wed her with sacred rites,
Ever gives happiness to his wife,
both here and in the other world.
Though he be uncouth and prone to pleasure,
though he have no good points at all,
The virtuous wife should ever
worship her lord as a god.

(trans. *Basham*)

These laws were used by British officials in the eighteenth and nineteenth centuries as their primary guide to Hindu legal traditions. Even today, they are quoted in divorce suits by accused husbands to justify brutal behaviour towards their wives.

Women in India still get a very raw deal. Only an estimated 39 per cent of them are literate, as compared with 64 per cent of men. Unlike women in most other countries, their life expectancy is shorter than that of men. And there are only an estimated 935 women to every 1,000 Indian men, whereas the ratio in Europe and North America is 1,050 women to 1,000 men. Traditional Indian society has an overwhelming preference for boys. They stay in the parental home when they marry and look after their parents in their old age. They bring in a dowry (now against the law, but still a common practice) and they light their parents' funeral pyres, thus ensuring a successful departure from this world. Girls, on the other hand, are reared to go to someone else's home; they require a dowry; and they cannot perform the sacred funeral rites. They are expensive luxuries. No wonder many of them are aborted, or die of neglect and malnutrition in their early years. They are a liability to their family until they become mothers.

Yet the Indian woman is strong. She has to be. Even in the patriarchal, brahmin-dominated religion, the goddess is *shakti*, the dynamic force who motivates the somewhat dreamy god. She fulfils every role from that of compliant wife, like Sita or Parvati, through the Earth Mother and the moral force of Durga, to that of a gory demoness, like Kali, who dances on her husband Shiva's inert form. She is so powerful that she has to be held in check. And when she does succeed in rising to high office, as Indira Gandhi did, men cringe before her.

It may be that a Sita-like subservience enables many women to cope with brutal circumstances. If they are child-brides, if they are forced into unwelcome marriages, or marriages to abusive husbands, compelled to spend their days breaking stones on the road or toiling in the fields, as well as bringing up their children and managing their husband and home, they can go through their lives on auto-pilot, enduring everything with numb stoicism. But there are small stirrings of change. Rural and low-caste women are beginning, in some places, to form themselves into unionised self-help groups, to seek better wages and to establish their own banks for the modest loans which are denied them elsewhere. The many-armed Goddess Durga, brandishing her weapons, may at last be on the warpath.

One of my friends in Delhi told me that her modern career-following daughter sometimes disagrees openly with her husband. She comes round to see her mother, full of grievances, and when her mother says, 'But you should listen to him. He is your husband', her daughter replies impatiently, 'You sound just like Granny!'

For Indians, arguments are never as clear as they are in the West. We feel that we have to choose between alternatives: things are 'either . . . or'. Indians can choose both. So it is very difficult to get Indian women to adopt a position. In the cities, educated wives can still say (and truly believe) that Sita is their ideal, while behaving in quite a different way. If they feel hard done by, they often make a joke of it. 'I've been a proper little Sita this week!' Of course, in the countryside, the rules laid down for Sita still go unquestioned and unjoked about among the downtrodden masses of rural women.

One of the feminist solutions to this problem is to work with tradition, not against it. They emphasise Sita's virtues. She is fair-minded, courageous, intelligent, loyal, yet independent of spirit. She follows her own conscience and is a woman of moral stature, who does her best to be a compliant and dutiful wife. But in the end, Rama, for all his godlike attributes, is shown to be mistrustful, jealous and too much swayed by public opinion. He is emotionally more fragile than she is and she refuses to bend to his arbitrary authority. Sita remains the ideal woman, the ideal wife, but it is her strength of character which makes her admirable, not her subservience.

I found the position of women in the northern states, the patriarchal Hindu heartland, depressing in the extreme. They walked a few paces behind their husbands along the country roads and if there were burdens to be carried, it was usually the wives who were carrying them. I could only observe these women, as I had no interpreters to question them for me and, in any case, I knew what their answer would be. 'Sita is our ideal.' For an outsider like myself, meaningful dialogue was clearly out of the question. And I wondered how much real contact there could be between India's illiterate millions and the educated townswomen who were working towards social reform. They were centuries apart in their lifestyles and the road ahead would be long and hard. Fortunately, the women I met in the south seemed to fare much better. Down there, matriarchal traditions, communism, Christianity and a healthy Dravidian suspicion of Aryan brahmins combined to give them a much stronger role in society. My depression was due to lift as I cycled forther south.

*   *   *

Hospet is the place most people stay when they want to visit Hampi and the ruins of the great mediaeval Vijayanagar Kingdom. My own interest was in another more legendary kingdom, but it seemed a pity to be so near to Hampi and not to have a look at its extensive site. To save time and effort, I booked a day trip on a Karnataka State tourist bus.

When I went down to reception the next morning, I was told that the tour was cancelled, as it was Holi, the Spring Festival, when everyone squirts everyone else with coloured water. The cheeky little boys of Hospet were a menace at the best of times, chasing foreigners in gangs through the streets, demanding 'your country coins', rupees and 'one pen'. I dreaded to think how they would behave on Holi, so I stayed firmly in the Malligi gardens. I even stayed there in the evening for a vegetarian biryani washed down with a couple of hideously sweet Gold Spot orangeades, as the Indian Government bans the sale of alcohol on public holidays and the Eagle restaurant and bar were closed.

When I finally got to Hampi, I was the only Westerner on the coach, but I had an easier time than the other passengers, as the guide conducted the tour in English. When India has eighteen languages officially recognised in the constitution and a further estimated sixteen hundred local languages and dialects, English has retained its place as the pre-eminent means of communication. A Hindi-speaking businessman from Delhi and a Tamil-speaker from Madras can only negotiate terms if they do it in English. It was the same on the coach. I was wedged between a Punjabi family from Chandigarh, a family of Malayalam-speakers from the south and a party of friends from Ahmedabad, all talking to one another and to me in English.

I was fascinated by Vijayanagar, once the capital of a Hindu kingdom which stretched from Karnataka and Andhra Pradesh down to the southernmost tip of the subcontinent. Its wealth came from control of the spice trade and the cotton industry, which attracted merchants from Europe and Asia to swell its cosmopolitan population to half a million. It was, of course, a granite city, so that its striking temples, public buildings and domed elephant houses are still intact, their exquisite carvings scarcely worn at all, despite five or six centuries of weather. They tower in pristine splendour in the middle of that daunting, boulder-strewn landscape. The dwelling houses, even the palaces, have fared worse. They were wooden structures, which have not survived, though their granite foundations, carved around with friezes, show clearly where they stood. They reminded me of the black basalt platforms, which are all that remain of Darius' great palaces at Persepolis.

Today the bazaar flourishes again, but not with spices for wealthy merchants. In the shade of its granite monoliths, traders squat in raucous groups, selling straw hats, fizzy drinks and postcards to travellers. Vijayanagar has joined the tourist circuit, particularly for the backpacking young, who come on to Hampi from Goa. There are a few basic lodges in the bazaar, and more are being built to accommodate them. As for eateries, the number of cafés advertising pasta, omelettes and carrot cake says it all!

I am not writing a guide book, so I shall not attempt to describe the whole of this imposing site. My main interest there was the Hazara Rama Temple, the Temple of a Thousand Ramas. The Vijayanagar Kings had a special relationship with Rama and always prayed in this temple before attending to state business. The story of Rama is carved with delicacy and high drama on rows and rows of friezes round the walls of the temple and over the columns. I was particularly taken with the vigorous representations of Ravana and his ten heads. It seemed that the stonemasons had really enjoyed carving him, and I was reminded of our mediaeval cathedrals and the fun our stonemasons must have had with the gargoyles, demons and grotesques. Ravana and Hanuman were much more amusing to depict than the sober, pious Rama. It's little wonder that the cult of the follower, Hanuman, is flourishing today throughout India at the expense of his master, Rama.

Having paid my formal respects to the Kings of Vijayanagar, I was free to devote my full attention to the Kingdom of Kishkindha. And I was very lucky. The Malligi Tourist Home had its own little tourist office, which was manned by a retired archaeologist, a specialist epigrapher from the University of Madras. He knew exactly the guide for me, a man called Veeraiah, who was devoted to Rama and familiar with all the Ramayana sites in the area.

Early next morning, Veeraiah and I set off in style in an elderly chauffeur-driven black Ambassador. This chubby version of the Morris Oxford is still the standard Indian taxi and was, until the Mercedes took over, the official government car. We toured the seven hills of the Kingdom of Kishkindha, just north-east of the Tungabhadra river. As most of the Ramayana sites were new to our driver, he got out of the car when Veeraiah and I did, to join in the tour.

The seven hills were high mountains of bare boulders surrounding a plain. Each of them had a shrine perched on its pinnacle and I wondered how on earth worshippers managed to get up there. Fortunately, Veeraiah never suggested we should try it. He pointed out Mount Malevanta, where Hanuman came to meet Rama; Mount Angenadi, where Hanuman was born; Mount Rishyamuka, where Rama met Sugriva; and Bali's Mount Tarapavat. Mount Malevanta had the only example in India of Rama seated in the lotus position, to show that he was waiting for news of Sita. Beside the shrine was a tank, which Rama made by shooting an arrow into the ground and causing a spring to rise.

At Bali's tomb, I very nearly came to grief. The driver parked the car on a grass verge and the three of us entered a banana plantation. It was well watered and extremely muddy. As Bali was a giant monkey, he had a colossal funeral pyre. I dodged around in the plantation with my camera, looking for a spot from which I could get the whole mound into my viewfinder. Suddenly, my left foot sank right down to the shin in viscous mud. I nearly toppled over into a swamp, but I just managed to balance myself, with one foot firmly on dry ground. I tried to pull my foot clear, but it just kept sinking deeper and deeper. Veeraiah rushed over and grabbed my hand, but one of his own feet slid into the mud as well. We would both have been in grave danger had the driver not come into the plantation with us. He dragged the small, slender Veeraiah out of the morass, and together they heaved my much greater weight on to firm ground. Veeraiah fished out his flip-flop and washed it in an irrigation ditch, while the driver took care of my trainers.

Chastened, I crept gingerly back to the funeral mound in cold, wet shoes, and Veeraiah dug out a small chunk of Bali's cremated bone for me to take away as a souvenir. I had no idea what it was made of. It was certainly not a chip of local granite. It was reddish in colour and it felt slightly porous, like a fragment of volcanic lava. I later read that samples of what is claimed to be Bali's bone were analysed at the University of Bombay and found to be lumps of cow dung, ossified under extreme heat!

Travelling by bicycle, with two modest panniers, I have little room for the usual bought souvenirs, so I collect small stones from significant places on my journeys. For instance, I have pebbles from the Gobi Desert, a chip of red granite from Luxor, and a handful of gleaming little stones in a variety of colours, which I picked up at the watershed of the Andes. But my lump of 'Bali's bone' is without doubt the most exotic item in my collection.

To help us get over the scare in the banana plantation, I suggested a cup of tea. We pulled up at a teastall, but when I tried to get out of the car, I was told very firmly that I should stay where I was. I thought Veeraiah had decided that it was not a suitable place for a lady and was intending to make me go without. But, to my surprise, he came back promptly, bringing my tea and a plate of biscuits on a tray. We are not used to such service in the West and I felt very grand indeed, sitting in the back of my chauffeur-driven car, drinking my morning tea in solitary splendour.

Veeraiah was a great character. Short and skinny, he looked about sixty, but was probably fifteen years younger than that. His English was only just adequate, and I might not have understood him, had I not been so familiar with the plot. But his enthusiasm for his subject was infectious. He acted out every scene, miming as vividly as a trained ballet dancer what he couldn't express in words. He assumed a proud, austere expression when he was talking about Rama. At the spot where Rama stood to shoot Bali, he stood tall as a hero and drew his imaginary bow. He swayed and wiggled his hips seductively, when he told how Surpanakha tried to captivate Rama. When we visited the cave where Sugriva hid Sita's jewels, he became a monkey one moment and Sita the next, tying up her jewels in the end of her sari to throw them out of Ravana's chariot. He jumped high in the air to show Hanuman leaping across the sea to Lanka. Best of all was our visit to the Moduana orchard, where he danced about as Hanuman and his monkey army, reeling in drunken celebration and puffing out his cheeks to show them stuffing themselves with fruit and honey. What was the orchard is now the courtyard of an ashram, with an unusual image of Hanuman in its shrine. Not the threatening giant with a mace in one hand and a mountain in the other, this Hanuman is dancing, his long tail waving above his head and his face plump and benign under a silver crown. To Veeraiah he was still a hero. In fact, Veeraiah claimed that he was especially strong and bold, now that he had fortified himself with fruit and wild honey.

Veeraiah was living the epic and was so involved that I wondered if he believed it all really happened. Only once did he say, 'the local people believe . . .' and that was when he pointed to a long scrape on the granite approach to Sugriva's cave and told me that it was supposed to be the trail left by Sita's sari, when she leaned over the edge of Ravana's chariot. Did he really think *The Ramayana* was history, or did he know that it was a myth? As always in India, the distinction was unclear. Our tradition, based on Aristotelian logic, has trained us to take either one view or the other. We may acknowledge that a myth possibly has its origin in some historical event centuries ago, but to us it is still a myth. In Indian thought, a story can easily be accepted as both history and myth at the same time by the same person, because there are different levels of perception. Symbolic and literal meaning are not necessarily disparate.

The Moduana ashram was only one of many in Kishkindha. Ramdas Baba had his beside Lake Pampa, which was a pathetic, weedy little pond, not at all like Valmiki's 'jewel with its fresh and limpid waters, its lotuses and waterlilies lending it a coppery sheen'. But there was an interesting eleventh-century temple there, carved out of rock, on the spot where Rama is said to have worshipped Shiva. Ramdas Baba performed *puja* and put a red tilak mark on my forehead, in exchange for a donation to ashram funds. Then we went on to another ashram, another *puja* and another donation. After a Hanuman *puja* in the Moduana orchard, I called a halt. I doubt if they see many Western tourists in those holy places and I could almost hear the cash registers whirring in their heads as I walked through the gates. What was I worth? How big a donation could they exact for a tilak? Fortunately, I had Veeraiah to defend me and ward off unwanted *pujas* and extravagant demands.

I decided that I could become addicted to chauffeur-driven cars and personal guides. In Kishkindha, the guide was invaluable, as I should never have found all those Rama sites on my own. They were spread over a very wide area and some of them, like Ramdas Baba's ashram, might have been inaccessible without a Hindu to smooth my path. Veeraiah was a luxury well worth paying for. The chauffeur was a necessity, because it's impossible to hire a self-drive car in India outside the major cities and, in any case, I should not have felt at all confident, driving that ancient Ambassador through mountain passes and swampy plantations. The day was excellent value all round, as the whole excursion, car, driver and guide cost me less than £10.

Back at the Malligi Tourist Home, I discussed my onward journey with the archaeologist at the tourist desk. He confirmed that there was no known route, either in Valmiki or in local legend, for Rama's journey from Kishkindha to Rameshwaram, the coastal town from which he built the bridge over to Sri Lanka. So, once again, I had a free choice. There were 700 kilometres of India to cross, as Hanuman flies, and I had never been to the south before. I gazed at the map, and every route seemed equally tempting. Should I go by boat through the Kerala backwaters? Through Mysore? Or Madras and Mamallapuram? And what about Madurai, Trichy, Ooty, Bangalore, Tanjore . . .? The list of glittering possibilites was endless.

I couldn't make up my mind, so I decided to take a few days' holiday in Goa while I thought it over. I'd already cycled from Hubli to Hospet and saw no good reason for repeating that dreary cross-country journey in the opposite direction; and I'd already cycled twice over the Western Ghats, which I thought was enough for anybody. So I felt that I could take the train to Goa with a clear conscience.

I very nearly lost my trusty Condor on the first leg. When I'd bought my own ticket at Hospet Station, I registered my bicycle in the parcels office, then went out on to the platform to wait for the Hubli train. A porter came along. He said that he was the man responsible for seeing my 'cykel' on to the train and would I treat him to a coffee. I gave him two rupees. When I boarded the train, I saw Condor leaning against a pillar at the far end of the platform. The whistle blew, the stationmaster raised the green flag, and still Condor leaned against the pillar. I leapt off the train, screaming and waving my arms. The green flag was lowered and the stationmaster waited patiently while I wheeled my bike myself to the goods van and handed it up to the guard. These things happen in India.

I had to change trains and spend the night in Hubli. It was a dusty Deccan town, closed up for Sunday. Fortunately, the cricket World Cup semi-final between England and South Africa was on television and I spent a happy afternoon crammed with about a hundred young men in front of the Ajanta Hotel's small screen. Rain stopped play, but England won on a calculation of runs based on the overs played.

Awoken early by the dawn chorus of hawkers and spitters, I had plenty of time for my southern Indian breakfast of *idlis*, a sort of soggy, tastless rice dumpling, spiced up with fiery sambar. Usually, I buy buns at a baker's shop to take into breakfast, when I guess that 'tosbutterjam' will not be available. My taste buds are never alert enough first thing in the morning to cope with hot curry. But the bakeries had been closed for Sunday in Hospet, so I had to make do.

I boarded the daily express train for Goa and was soon joined in my compartment by six cheerful young men, all of whom spoke good English. They told me they were graduates preparing to take the entrance examinations for the Indian Civil Service. I had armed myself with newspapers, a book, my own travel notebook and a sheaf of *Times* crosswords, to keep me occupied during the day-long journey. The six boys, candidates for some of the most prestigious jobs in the land, had not one scrap of reading-matter between them. They chattered like magpies, first among themselves, then to me. I was subjected to the usual boring inquisition: 'What is your good name? You are coming from? What is your profession? Where did you take your degree? Are you married? Where is your husband?' Questions, questions, questions. After ten minutes of this interrogation, I started to get annoyed. I'm quite happy to respond in this way to simple people, who rarely see foreigners, but this group of well-educated boys should have behaved in a less intrusive manner and had better things to do with their time. The headmistress in me erupted.

'Haven't you brought anything to read on the train?' I asked.

'No,' they said, looking quite amazed at the question.

'So you're proposing to sit here gossiping for nine whole hours? Don't they expect you to know something about current affairs when you take the ICS exams? Don't they expect you at least to read the newspapers? They do in the British Civil Service.'

The boys looked crestfallen. 'You are so busy,' they said. 'Look at all the books and papers you've brought.'

'Well, I couldn't just sit here for nine hours doing nothing. I shall enjoy looking out of the window, but I like to have some occupations to fall back on.'

'I suppose that's why we lag so far behind,' said my neighbour sadly.

I felt a bit sad then for having shamed them. The people of India and many points east have an infinite capacity for doing nothing. But are we any wiser in the West? We make such a virtue of being busy that we work ourselves into nervous breakdowns. Perhaps we all have something to learn from one another. As a peace-offering, I shared my newspapers and tangerines with the contrite young men.

I arrived in Vasco da Gama Station, after a spectacular crossing of the Western Ghats and a beautiful train ride along the sunset shore. As soon as we left Karnataka and entered Goa, platform vendors rushed on to the train crying, 'Beer! Cole beer!' I didn't want any at 4 p.m., but it was good to know that I was in a liberal state, where the sale of beer was respectable enough to be carried out in the open, not at the end of dark, sleazy alleyways.

Apart from the smart international beach complexes, frequented by tourists on package holidays who wanted to be protected from the real India, Goa was disappointingly run down. I had expected something a bit more glamorous. My hotel had damp patches on the walls and was built around a central courtyard, probably intended as a garden, but now the hotel rubbish dump. The narrow strips of beach were kept clean enough, but ten metres behind them were thatched shacks and smelly tips where pigs and dogs rooted. Water was cut off in these villages for most of the day and the locals' gardens and fields were parched, so that we tourists in the hotels could take unlimited showers. The 'old Goans' complained bitterly. 'You should have seen Goa twenty years ago, before what the Indians choose to term its "liberation". It used to be a clean, enterprising, efficient state,' said a Goan English teacher. 'Since it became part of India, Indians have come flooding in, looking for work and, unfortunately, we have not been able to bring them up to our standard. There are too many of them for that. They are pulling us down to theirs. In a few more years, Goa will be indistinguishable from the rest of India.'

I made friends in my hotel with an Indian couple who worked in Saudi Arabia and were over in Goa for a holiday. They introduced me to feni, the local spirit distilled from coconut or cashew nuts. As we were enjoying a feni and cashew nuts one evening in their hotel room, the wife brought out all her jewellery and laid it on the bed for me to see. It was a dazzling collection of gold and gems. She draped the glittering necklaces and bangles all over herself and me. 'Now show us *your* jewels,' she said. Fortunately, I was not shamed by my comparative poverty. 'I never wear my jewels on my bicycle,' I said grandly. 'It's not safe.' They nodded approval at my wisdom.

*Left* Riding down the Pokhara Highway, Nepal

*Above* Marriage Pavilion, Janakpur, with custodian

*Left* Naubise Lodge with Shirley and Suzanna

*Left* Roadside cycle-repair shop

*Above* Guru and calf, Ayodhya

*Left* Dancing for the Guru, Chitrakuta

*Above* The apprentice barber

*Left* Traffic jam in Old Dehli

*Above* Mr. Ben Wari Lal and his rickshaw, Agra

*Right* Sorting the letters, Agra Post Office

*Above* The valiant Rani of Jhansi, Gwalior

*Right* Sacred calf at Walkeshwar Temple, Bombay

*Right* Condor at the Taj
Mahal Hotel, Bombay

*Below* Temple of Rama,
Vijayanagar

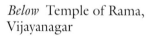

*Below left* Rama's footprints, Kishkindha

*Below right* Ramdas Baba and disciple,
Lake Pampa

*Left*  Beach Temples, Mamallapuram

*Below*  Thanjavur's granite Temple

*Above*  Fresco of praying duck, Thanjavur Temple

*Right*  Pilgrims at Rameshwaram

*Left* Rama's spring, Rameshwaram

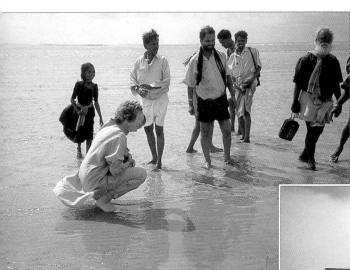

*Left* With the pilgrims at Dhanushkodi

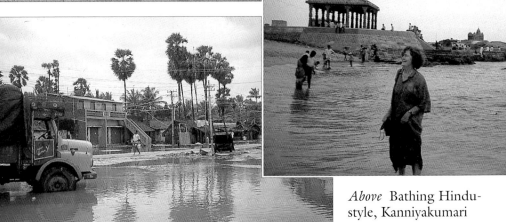

*Above* Bathing Hindu-style, Kanniyakumari

*Left* Monsoon weather, Rameshwaram

*Above left* A lonely level crossing

*Above right* "Vote bicycle!"

*Right* Roadside quilt-making

*Right* School children on an outing

*Above* Hanuman the God of Grammar

*Right* Hanuman the Hero

I visited Old Goa, where the body of St Francis Xavier lies in a silver casket in the Basilica of Bom Jesus and is exposed to view every ten years. He died in China, but Portuguese Goa was the place where he started his missionary work in 1541 (after a voyage of thirteen months!) and it remained his headquarters. It was appropriate that he should be brought back there for burial. In his short life, he garnered souls so tirelessly throughout the East that he became the patron saint of Catholic missionaries. As one of the first seven followers of St Ignatius Loyola, St Francis Xavier was a passionate Jesuit, and the Jesuits held on to their influence in Goa. This can be seen quite clearly in the Basilica. The lavishly gilded altar screen is dominated by a giant statue of St Ignatius, while Jesus is reduced in size to a tiny baby doll standing beneath his feet. The Jesuits were ever modest!

But they were not the first Christian missionaries to arrive in India. To their amazement, they found flourishing Christian communities in the south dating back to AD 52, when Doubting Thomas the Apostle is said to have landed on the Malabar Coast. He was followed in the sixth century by Syrian Christians on a missionary drive in Kerala. So Roman Catholicism is not so strong down there as St Francis Xavier might have wished. Although the Christians in the south of India constitute about one-third of the local population, many of them follow the Syriac order of service, an Eastern rather than a Western form of Christianity. They pray in church with their arms outstretched, palms upwards, like the early Christians in the catacomb murals, and their bushy-bearded priests are a familiar sight in the streets.

The earliest converts to Christianity were high-caste Hindus, but the Churches have had more success in later centuries among the lower castes and the aboriginals, who see Christianity and Islam as escape routes from the degrading social strictures of the Hindu caste system. But then, the suffering Christ, his disciples and the Old Testament strong men all seem so feeble compared with the Hindu gods, who can leap across oceans and carry mountains on the palm of one hand. When Krishna was a little boy, his mother accused him of stealing sweets. Krishna denied it. 'Open your mouth,' said his mother 'and let me look.' Krishna opened his mouth. There were no sweets inside. Instead, his mother saw the whole world. Now that's a real miracle!

My last day in Goa was spent watching the final of the World Cup between England and Pakistan. I had a few errands to run in Panjim and I paused outside an electrical shop, where a small television was flickering in the window, to see what the score was. The owner dashed out. 'You must be English. Come inside!' I entered the darkened shop to find about fifty shadowy shapes sitting on the floor, their eyes glued to the largest television screen in stock. They brought me a chair and a cup of tea. 'Our hearts are with you,' said one elderly gentleman. Of course, I realised that their hearts were not so much with me as against the Pakistanis, but it was still very agreeable to be with such staunch supporters of my national team. They cheered every English run. Their favourite cricketer was Ian Botham, not only for his swash-buckling style of play, but for a remark he once made, which I've had quoted to me in India more times than I can remember. 'Pakistan,' said Botham, 'is the sort of place where you'd send your mother-in-law.' Despite the wholehearted support of the Indian crowds, Pakistan played brilliantly and deserved their win. We analysed the match over more tea. The fifty chaps in the shop were downcast and it was more like a funeral tea than a match tea. I was bathed in sympathy. Since I began to travel on the Indian subcontinent, I've become a great watcher of cricket. There's nothing quite like it for striking up friendly conversations with Indians, Pakis-tanis and Sri Lankans – even if it's only on the level of 'Tendulkar good.'

By this time, I had had enough of holiday and was eager to be on my bicycle again. But it was already the end of March and the heat was building up. To make a direct run to Rameshwaram across the burning plains and highlands of the centre didn't seem at all sensible. In any case, there were whole tracts of country on that route which had nothing of historical or religious importance. So I decided to make my way to Rameshwaram along the much more interesting coast. But which coast?

My friend Heather was flying out to Bombay to join me for a holiday towards the end of April, and I was booked to return to England myself early in May. That left me with about three weeks for cycling, probably just enough time to reach Rameshwaram, if I hurried, but not enough time to do it justice. So I had the perfect reason for spending another winter in India. I could fly out to Madras in November and cycle all the way down the east coast, poetically named the Coromandel Coast, to Rameshwaram, then go on from there to Sri Lanka. Meanwhile, the west coast, the Malabar, with its necklace of fascinating historical ports, would fill in my remaining three weeks very nicely and take me down to the furthermost point of India, Kanniyakumari, where the waters of the Bay of Bengal and the Arabian Sea meet the Indian Ocean. Kanniyakumari is the confluence second in holiness only to the Kumbh Mela site in Allahabad and it would be an interesting place of pilgrimage in its own right. Also, my arrival there would mean that I had cycled the whole length of India, from Chandigarh in the foothills of the Himalayas down to the southernmost tip.

The only argument against this plan was one of comfort. The sun was getting hotter every day and my skin was suffering, as I was cycling southwards. If I followed the Malabar Coast south-east to Kanniyakumari, I should have the full power of the morning sun directly on my face. So I decided to do the journey the other way round, taking the train to my destination then cycling north.

I booked a sleeper to Kanniyakumari and was intrigued to find that the ticket and the baggage label on my bicycle still bore the old English name of Cape Comorin. When I arrived there, to be welcomed by the stationmaster in a spotless white suit, I couldn't believe that a place in India could be so clean. My hotel bedroom was almost Mediterranean, with its polished tile floor and white cotton bedspread. It was on the top storey, reserved for foreign tourists, and had stunning views of Swami Vivekananda's rock to the west and the sacred confluence of the seas to the south. Mine was the only white face in town, but I was greeted cheerfully when I took a holy dip in the *sangam*, fully clothed like all the modest

Indians, and joined the crowds on the beach to watch the spectacular sunsets and moonrises over the seas.

It was the start of three idyllic weeks. Suchindram, Kovalam, Trivandrum, Quilon, a boat on the Kerala backwaters to Alleppey, Cochin, Calicut, Tellicherry, Mangalore – all names to conjure with, redolent of the spice trade and mercantile wealth. The glory may have faded, but a more cosmopolitan outlook was still evident. The south, though rural, was more advanced than the north, probably because of their more enlightened view of women. I found many women managing hotels and restaurants, where they set a higher standard of cleanliness than I'd found in the male-run hotels of the north. They had even heard of bleach and proper brushes for cleaning lavatories. In Kerala, which has the lowest birth-rate and the highest rate of literacy in the whole of India, at something like 97 per cent for both sexes, women seemed to lead much freer lives. I was always happy to see groups of them in restaurants, having a good gossip together – something I had never seen in the north – and girls at the beach in saris or shalwar kameez with baseball caps perched jauntily on their heads. It is said that the education of women brings benefits to a society far beyond its cost. If that is the case, the south of India is well on its way. After the backwardness of Bihar and the Deccan, it was a really cheering ride.

When I got back to Goa, I took the train to Bombay, where I was just in time to meet Heather off her plane. With two people sharing, even the grandest hotels in India become affordable, at least for a few days. We checked into the Taj Mahal Hotel, where the splendidly turbanned Sikh commissionaires were astonished to be put in charge of a bicycle, when they normally spend their time parking the Mercedes of Bombay's glitterati. They were astonished, but also greatly amused, and asked me to take their photographs, posing in front of the majestic entrance with Condor.

Condor rested in their garage for three weeks, while Heather and I swanned about India in a very different style. We both enjoyed the tour, but I think my pleasure was greater than hers. Until you've crossed Asia on a bicycle, you can never fully appreciate the luxury of clean sheets and a hot bath.

# **10** Reconnaissance

[1996–97]

A FTER MY RIDE TO KISHKINDHA, the Ramayana trail went cold for a while. I was commissioned to write a handbook about the places one might go to escape the English winter. My suggestions had to be based on first-hand knowledge, so I needed to spend weeks in the course of the next year in such arduous places as the Costa del Sol, Tenerife, Tunisia, Mediterranean Turkey and California. It would have been the perfect assignment, had I not had to pay all the fares myself!

When I'd finished all the bus journeys and the uncomfortable long-haul flights, I had to spend the summer researching the chapters of practical advice and writing the book. That involved another sedentary six months, crouching over my typewriter. By the time the book came out, I was longing to get on my bicycle again and ride off to freedom. Madras to Rameshwaram didn't seem far enough. I needed a really long trip, and only the world would do. I'd already cycled from Rome to Lisbon along the Roman roads. Now I picked up the circuit where I'd left off. I flew away in December 1993, to Salvador, the first Portuguese capital of Brazil, and cycled across South America, Australia and Indonesia, then along the Silk Road from China back to Rome. That second bike-ride round the world took me two years. Then I moved house, with all the tramping round estate agents and general upheaval that involves.

So it was late in 1996 before I came back to Rama and Sita. I did some more research in the library of the School of Oriental and African Studies and realised that I still had a lot of work to do in India. Quite apart from Rama's journey south to Rameshwaram and Sri Lanka, all unexplored territory, there were incidents and places I had overlooked on my earlier rides across the north. To do the job thoroughly, I needed to go back and start from the beginning again. I'd missed out Ayodhya altogether and that was one of the most important places on the journey. I'd lost Sita's home and the scene of her abduction in the confusion of Nasik's alleyways; and there were things I needed to check in Kishkindha. As for Madras to Rameshwaram, I didn't know that coast at all and had no idea of the accommodation situation beyond Mamallapuram. Would I need a tent? Would I have to take a mat and sleeping bag for nights in basic pilgrim hostels? Or could I count on reasonable hotels? I do occasionally launch myself off into the unknown, but I'm always happier if I've been able to do a bit of reconnaissance. I had every intention of cycling that leg of the journey, but it would do no harm to take a quick train-ride down the coast first and see if I could spot any hotels from the window. Altogether, I had a tremendous amount of ground to cover and only two months available to cover it in. It was an impossible schedule for a bicycle, so I set out reluctantly on my own, leaving my faithful Condor upended in my study.

I invested in a new suitcase for the journey, one which had tuck-away straps and converted into a rucksack, when required. It would leave my hands free to fight my way on to crowded Indian buses and trains. Strapping it on my back, I set out for Delhi on a dark winter morning towards the end of November. There was a light sprinkling of snow as I walked cheerfully to the Baker Street Airbus stop. I was off to India again, happy to be escaping another English winter – and another Christmas!

From Delhi I took the Lucknow Mail, changed for Faisabad and spent some days in Ayodhya. Then on to Allahabad, Nasik, Hospet, Bangalore and Trivandrum. My friend Heather flew out to Trivandrum to join me in December and we spent Christmas in a very smart ayurvedic health resort called Manaltheeram on the Kerala coast, where we were massaged by women who hung from the rafters on ropes and walked all over us. From there we took the train over the Cardamom Hills to Madurai. Heather flew home and I continued south by train to Rameshwaram, then north up the Coromandel Coast to Madras. Apart from our week in Manaltheeram, it was a high-speed tour, but a very satisfactory one, as I managed to accomplish everything I'd set out to do. The additional information about the commonly accepted Ramayana sites, which I gained on the trip, is included in the relevant chapters.

But the epic has an alternative topography. According to some scholars, the events of *The Ramayana* took place within a much more limited area. Their theory is that when the three exiles left Chitrakuta, they wandered due south through what is now Madhya Pradesh, and Valmiki's Lanka is not the island of Sri Lanka but a location on the shores of a nearby lake. There are as many candidates for this lake as there are Ramayana scholars, but most agree that it was within the territory of the Gonds, the largest tribal group in Madhya Pradesh, and was later stretched into a sea to make Rama's crossing seem more miraculous. 'Lakka' is used in the Gond language to denote a very important place. To fit into this interpretation, Rama's camp for the war with Ravana was situated on a hill just north of Jabalpur. Another popular interpretation takes them down into Andhra Pradesh, and posits that Sita was abducted not from Nasik, near the source of the Godavari river, but from Bhadrachalam, which is only about 180 kilometres inland from the Godavari delta. There is some internal evidence in Valmiki to support these theories. For instance, Rameshwaram is flat and sandy, with no rocks available for building a bridge across the straits to Sri Lanka, whereas Madhya Pradesh is strewn with very suitable boulders; and the sala trees which Valmiki mentions don't grow in Sri Lanka, but are abundant on the Chota Nagpur plateau in the north-east corner of Maharashtra. It is not within the scope of this book to give a critical examination of these theories and try to decide between them. I shall just be totally Indian and believe them all.

I had studied these theories in the SOAS library, but had decided early on that I would follow the commonly accepted route down to Sri Lanka. I thought no more about them until I had an interesting encounter on a train.

I was on my way north from Rameshwaram to Madras, having completed my reconnaissance of the south-east coast. Between Madurai and Chidambaram an Indian, neatly dressed in a Western suit, joined me in my first-class compartment. At first, I was rivetted by his shoes. They were made of mirror-bright black plastic, moulded in one piece, with imitation laces imprinted on the top. I'd seen such shoes often enough in the bazaars, but I never expected to see them on such an elegant person. When I could drag my eyes away from them, I looked up into a warm, friendly face. My companion was the Salvation Army General for Tamil Nadu. He told me that he was a poor farmer's son, who owed everything to the education he had received, free of charge, in a Salvation Army school. In those days, life in the country was desperate. One bad monsoon could ruin a farmer and put not only the farmer himself, but his sons and grandsons, into debt for the rest of their lives. Now things were easier, because there were farm subsidies.

'You see, the Prime Minister, Deve Gowda, and the present Governor of Andhra Pradesh both come from modest farming backgrounds,' he said, 'and they are really trying to help country people, not just seizing power, taking the wealth it brings and forgetting their roots. Even the wages of the poorest rural labourers have risen from ten to thirty rupees a day.'

I had seen Deve Gowda ridiculed in the press as a country bumpkin, who didn't know how to behave on smart official occasions and took all the members of his large extended family with him, for a free ride at State expense, whenever he went to conferences abroad. It was interesting for me to hear a more sympathetic view, expressed by a man who was closer to village India than the cleverclogs of the national dailies.

We then went on to talk about religion and he outlined the work of the four divisions of the Salvation Army in India: Gospel, Education, Social Work and Medical. Tamil Nadu alone had 50,000 full-time 'soldiers'. It was obviously an influential organisation. But what interested me most was that the General had grown up a Hindu in a Hindu village and so was able to explain a great many things which were puzzling me. For instance, who were the swarms of black-clad men, who were touring south India in coaches? I had seen crowds of them in all the temples on my travels in the south and none of the Indians I had asked seemed to have any idea who they were or what they were doing. According to my friend on the train, they were devotees of a twentieth-century god, Ayappa. Vishnu came to earth as a virgin named Mohini and married Shiva. Ayappa was their son, and was obviously very powerful, being an amalgam of the two greatest gods in the Hindu pantheon. His strength appealed particularly to young and middle-aged men. His jungle temple at Sabarimalai in Kerala was open only at certain times of the year, and December/January was the most auspicious time, which was why I had seen such a concentration of pilgrims.

Ayappa seems to me to be an excellent example of the flexibility of Hinduism. It is the world's most ancient formal religion, but it constantly renews itself by absorbing new gods and adapting to new needs. That is the key to its survival. Ayappa was little regarded until the 1980s, when the number of his devotees shot up dramatically. There are now millions of them, and donations to the Sabarimalai temple have risen from 2.4 million rupees in 1970 to an estimated 100 million rupees a year in the 1990s. A pilgrimage to the temple is a very exacting affair. The temple is difficult to reach and those undertaking the pilgrimage must abstain from sex, meat and eggs and must sleep on the bare floor for forty-one days. In an age of overindulgence, this very austerity must add to Ayappa's appeal to his predominantly middle-class followers.

The Salvation Army General viewed it all with a certain amusement. 'People joke about these black-clad Ayappans,' he said. 'Black is such an ill-omened colour. Fancy their leader picking it! At one time, there was no black material at all to be found in the bazaars. So the people who've really benefited from the cult (apart from the temple priests, of course) are the dyers and cloth merchants. They've suddenly had this call for millions and millions of black dhotis. It's made their fortunes!'

When we got round to discussing *The Ramayana*, the General reminded me of its alternative topography. I'd made good time on my general reconnaissance, so I had a few days to spare. I was intending to spend them in Madras, one of my favourite Indian cities, before taking the train back to Bombay to catch my flight home. But as we talked about Rama and Sita, the idea of a quick exploratory trip into unknown Andhra Pradesh became more and more appealing. If I could change my ticket and fly to London direct from Madras, I should have ample time to visit the pilgrim centre of Bhadrachalam, an alternative site for Sita's abduction.

The Lufthansa office was on Anna Salai, the main street of Madras (or Chennai, as the politicians prefer to call it now). I walked along, past the rows of second-hand booksellers, marvelling at the Indian passion for self-improvement. 'Pulling your Own Strings'. 'The Self-Talk Solution'. 'Take Control of Your Life'. 'You Can Negotiate Anything'. 'How to be a Winner'. 'More Ways to Win'. All were written by Americans with names like Herb Cohen and Dr Wayne W. Dyer. There was a market for any book along Anna Salai, even a 1993 Ikea catalogue and a 1990 almanac. As usual, I was a walking moneybag, an incitement to everyone. How could they relieve me of some of my burden of wealth? Perhaps a sari? Socks? A watch? Men's underpants? A plastic helicopter? A rickshaw? A cheaper hotel? A more expensive hotel? Or what about begging? 'One pen for my daughter, madam?' Usually, I can walk straight through it, looking to neither right nor left, though on hot, tired days the hassle in the streets can be one of India's most wearing experiences. I buy fruit in the markets, but for other items I go to regular shops. As for the beggars, I give money only to old women, who are often widows thrown out by their sons-in-law. Men, even beggar-men, are better cared for and usually have someone to feed them.

I couldn't reroute my Lufthansa ticket, but I bought a single to Bombay on one of the cheaper airlines, which are springing up in India as elsewhere. That gave me six days for

Andhra Pradesh, so I went straight to the Central Station to book my train ticket to Vijayawada. I was served by a hugely fat, indolent booking clerk in a purple sari, which left slithery rolls of lard exposed at the waist. 'How many carats?' she asked, pointing imperiously at my Greek lion ring. 'Eighteen.' 'What is weight?' She sat with her pen poised over a pad and her calculator handy, waiting to work out its exact value. She was furious when I didn't know and gave me a ticking off for my casual attitude to my valuables. Meanwhile, the patient queue built up behind me.

The Government Museum in Madras has the world's finest collection of south Indian bronzes. I went there specially to see the large standing figures of Rama, Sita and Lakshmana, but I was intrigued to find a sixteenth-century bronze of Ayappa, here called Aiyanar. He was riding on an elephant and had a cobra, a crescent moon and a skull in his hair. In Hindu iconography, the cobra is a symbol of Vishnu and the crescent moon and skull are symbols of Shiva. There were also reminders of Vishnu in the two stylised lotuses, which Aiyanar's elephant carried on his head. According to the explanatory notice in the museum, Aiyanar was worshipped as the tutelary deity of villages. Ayappa, with his black-clad hordes of urban devotees, has come a long way from such humble beginnings!

In the evening, there was a large Christian wedding reception in the hotel garden, just under my balcony. JASWANTH WEDS ANITA was strung up in lights and there was a dais on the lawn with two thrones for the happy couple. The groom was a solid product manager for Glaxo and the bride, in her red and gold sari with a white veil, was a graduate schoolmistress. When the priest had blessed the cake, a senior colleague of Jaswanth's stood up and gave an enormously lengthy description of Jaswanth's steady career in Glaxo and commended him for shouldering his family responsibilities after the death of his father. As for Anita, she had three younger brothers and was therefore skilled in childminding and housekeeping. There was only the slightest mention in passing of her degree and her teaching career. Fortunately, the *thalis* for 350 were expeditiously served and the Western pop music soon came to an end. It was a wealthy, but very sober affair, which didn't interfere with my early night.

I had to be at the railway station at 4.45. The rickshaw wallah who pedalled me through the empty streets was swathed in pullovers, shawls and scarves. I sat behind him in my shirt sleeves and cotton trousers, enjoying the balmy air of Madras's perfect winter climate. Even the hours before dawn were pleasantly warm. I wondered, as I always do on these occasions, why so many retired people endure the northern winter, when they can live in warmth and comfort in a good hotel in the tropics for less than the cost of their grocery bill at home.

It was an eight-hour journey along the coastal plain to Vijayawada, through rice paddies and tobacco fields fringed with palm trees. When we turned inland, to the head of the mighty Krishna delta, I saw a filthy, seething industrial city surrounded by bare granite hills. Vijayawada was seriously unattractive, and I soon wished I hadn't come. Even the rickshaws, of which there seemed to be far too many to make a living, were dirty and ramshackle.

The best hotels in town rated no higher than category D in my India Handbook. Despite that, they were all full. I failed to get into any of the ones recommended and had to make do with the grandly named Raj Towers, which was hardly a place to raise the spirits. When the lift door opened, a large lizard popped out into the lobby, and there were cockroaches as big and shiny as babies' shoes strolling down the corridors. Old women sweepers crouched down with twig brushes, stirring up the dust from the fitted carpets. In places where there are no vacuum cleaners, carpets are always a disaster. Stained and greasy, they make the perfect breeding ground for vermin. I much prefer a simple concrete floor which can be scrubbed.

The hotel was so dark and depressing that I deposited my luggage in my room and walked round immediately to the best hotel on my list, which I knew was full that night, to see if they could possibly reserve me a room for the next night. They couldn't. But at least they had a travel desk which I could consult. Bhadrachalam looked an awkward place to reach by public transport; and if the Raj Towers was the best hotel I could find in a major city like Vijayawada, I guessed that the accommodation up country would be dire. So I enquired about a car and driver, to get me to Bhadrachalam and back in one day. I could then catch the night train back to Madras and civilisation.

The young man at the desk was delighted. 'I am so happy that you are writing about *The Ramayana*,' he said. 'Lord Rama is our Lord. He broke the bow and married Sita at Bhadrachalam. But you must not go there by car. There are forests and mountains. The roads are lonely. It isn't safe for you to travel alone. You must go on the bus.'

Andhra Pradesh is one of the poorer states of India, with a concentration of tribal peoples in the highlands. It has been fertile ground for the Naxalites, a radical Communist anti-landlord movement which spread rapidly through the northern states from its starting point in Naxalbari, south of Darjeeling. In 1967, the Naxalites' leader, Charu Mazumdar, with the encouragement of China, called for an armed struggle and the encirclement of the cities by the peasantry, as in Mao Zedong's revolution. The current strength of the movement is unknown, as it is opposed to any participation in parliamentary politics and is highly factionalised. But land-grabs in the 1970s threw 3,000 villages and 41,000 square kilometres of land in Andhra Pradesh into turmoil, and there have been sporadic outbreaks of guerrilla activity throughout the 1980s and 1990s, often in alliance with criminal groups. The Naxalites are clearly still a force to be reckoned with among the rural and tribal peoples, and it was they who were causing the nice young man at the reception desk so much concern.

He rang the bus station to find out the times of the early morning buses. 'I rent out cars and I could earn 1,350 rupees if I let you have a car and a driver. But the Lord Rama would not wish me to put you into such danger. The bus at 6 o'clock in the morning is the best one. Take that – and when you get there, go to the police station and ask the police where to stay. Don't listen to the rickshaw wallahs or the men at the bus station. There are bad people in Bhadrachalam.'

So here was yet another version of the story. Bhadrachalam was the scene of Sita's wedding, not her abduction, and the main pilgrim destination was said to be a Rama temple. I was not sure if the site was worth six hours each way on a bus through the Naxalites of Andhra Pradesh, plus a night in a probable dump of a hotel. I decided to sleep on the problem and went back to the Raj Towers for dinner.

Andhra Pradesh is one of only two 'dry' states in India (the other is Gujarat). Prohibition was introduced in 1994, after a most successful campaign by village women, who were angry because their husbands were spending the housekeeping money on arak. They went on cooking strike, ambushed liquor lorries and even set fire to the offending liquor stores. But prohibition has been a mixed blessing. The cheap bootlegged hooch which has replaced arak occasionally kills off whole villages. And though wives may now be receiving more of their husbands' wages, the state has lost considerable revenue from excise duties – a loss it can ill afford. So the future of prohibition is in the balance.

Meanwhile, the Raj Towers happened to be one of the few hotels in Vijayawada with a Permit Room. A notice in the lobby read:

'Information. Permit Room is in the first floor. As per A.P. prohibition rules, only foreigners, NRIS tourists and persons from other states are permitted to avail liquor, beer, wine, etc. in permit room. For further information, contact at Reception or our Permit Room Manager. Management.'

I decided to give it a try. I found the Permit Room and stuck my head round the door.

'What do you want?'

'Dinner.'

'Downstairs restaurant.'

'I want beer too.'

'Restaurant not possible. Beer Permit Room only.'

'Can I get a snack here, if I order a beer?'

'No.'

I peered into the gloom and saw a man who was obviously the manager, surrounded by four waiters. An animated discussion was going on. Suddenly, the manager rushed to the door and showed me inside.

'Yes. Snack OK.'

'Good. Is there a menu?'

'No. Fried rice.'

'That will do nicely. One fried rice, please, and one beer.'

'One glass beer, 230 rupees.'

'It can't be! That's far too much. Forget it. I'll go down to the restaurant.'

'90 rupees then?'

We agreed the price, and the manager produced a two-page application form for a permit. He told me the permit cost 100 rupees, but when it looked as if I might walk out again, he hastily added, 'For you, no charge.' I was their only customer, lost in a sea of tables for four, all elegantly spread with green and white gingham tablecloths, plates, glasses and crisp table napkins. The waiters were friendly young men, who were desperate not to lose me. They crowded round as I filled in the form, commenting on my age, address and profession. The manager was more aloof, stony even, and insisted on taking a photocopy of my passport. It was a great performance for one glass of beer, but when my ice cold Kingfisher and fried rice finally arrived, I was glad I'd made the effort. The waiters were delighted. They came and sat at my table throughout the meal, chattering like magpies. I was the first foreigner three of them had ever met.

I had just returned to my bedroom when there was a loud bang on the door and three policemen burst in. One was in uniform, brandishing a lathi; the other two were plain-clothes officers with heavy walking sticks. I smiled sweetly.

'Good evening, gentlemen. What can I do for you?'

'Liquor. Prohibition.'

'I don't have any liquor.'

The senior officer had a quick look round the room, then smiled and wished me good night. They continued down the corridor, bursting into each of the rooms in turn. It was such a noisy search that anyone with liquor would have had ample time to hide it.

I had satellite television in my room, so I switched on for a peaceful evening's viewing. I was sitting still and quiet in my armchair, when I spotted something flash by out of the corner of my eye. Then something else . . . And something else . . . The room was alive with mice, running around in the dim light of the reading lamp. I stood up and they all fled under my bed. I've learned on my travels to accept the odd little mouse. I can cohabit with one or two. But I had never seen so many as there were in that bedroom and I panicked. I started to pack my bag. If I couldn't get a train to Madras that night, I should be happier spending it on the station, rather than trying to sleep in that bed with all the mice under it. I knew they were harmless, but my imagination went into overdrive. What if they swarmed all over me in the dark? But then I had an idea. I was carrying a container of Deet, the most powerful insect repellent, and I sprayed it liberally up the four legs of the bed and into the carpet round the feet. I reckoned that if Deet was strong enough to kill mosquitos, it would smell extremely unpleasant to mice. It would probably not kill them, but it would be nasty enough to deter them from climbing the legs of my bed.

I slept reasonably well, but I woke at 6 o'clock and decided that I couldn't stand Andhra Pradesh a moment longer. I abandoned the trip to Bhadrachalam and woke up a sleeping bundle of rags in a battered rickshaw to take me to the station. I was too late for the early train to Madras and hours too early for the Coromandel express. But the relief I felt at my escape from the poverty, dirt and mice turned my cup of platform tea into nectar and I sat in quiet content, watching the station come to life. A goat grazing on the tracks bucked indignantly when a man came along to hose down the rails; and I was chased unceremoniously out of the first-class waiting room by an army of women in sky-blue saris, who shoved all the chairs aside, with a tooth-edging scrape of steel on concrete, to ply their little twig brushes. They were followed by another sky-blue regiment with mops. In Vijayawada, they were certainly living up to the station motto:

Indian Railways. India's Pride.
By cleanliness we do abide.

A cameo which stays vividly in my mind from that morning is the sight of a shabby, downtrodden, indigent woman, who was balancing her few possessions in a jute sack on her head. Beside her on the platform were her three beautifully behaved, immaculately dressed children. Her little boy wore a pure white suit, spotless from the crisp collar down to the knife-edge creases in his long trousers. The older girl was wearing a long gold dress with a purple georgette wrap. The younger one floated by in a kind of ballgown, purple organza with a gold wrap. Both sisters had sprays of jasmine woven into their smoothly brushed hair. Their home was undoubtedly some miserable shack, with no running water or electricity. Yet the children were well enough turned out for an audience with the President. Such gallantry in the face of terrible odds never ceases to amaze me. India deserves to prosper in the end.

# **11** The Coromandel Coast

[1997–98]

*Madras – Mamallapuram – Pondicherry – Chidambaram –*
*Kumbakonam – Tanjavore – Ramnad – Rameshwaram*

S UNSHINE, HEAT, HUMIDITY, CROWDS, colour, the gleaming
white smiles of rice eaters, wood smoke, that enchanting
sideways rocking of the Indian head, goats, pony carts,
water buffalo being milked along the highway, diesel fumes,
cacophonous horns and more cars than ever before. I was
back in India, riding in a taxi from the airport to the centre
of Madras.

This was the winter when I planned to complete my
Ramayana ride. I would cycle from Madras to Rameshwaram,
then cross to Sri Lanka, to visit Ravana's kingdom, Sita's
prison and the scene of the final battle between Good and Evil.
My friend Katherine had flown out with me, to share what
promised to be a beautiful cycle-ride down the Coromandel
Coast. I was looking forward to some company for a change,
especially as Katherine has the virtue of cycling at the same
speed as I do. I don't have to puff and pant to keep up with
her, nor do I have to hang around waiting for her to catch up.

When we landed in Madras, it was 10 o'clock in the
morning and the sun was already fierce. Coming from an
English November, we were quite overwhelmed by the heat.
We were also tired at the end of the long flight and didn't feel
we had the strength to fight with the traffic into the city
centre. Unusually for India, the suburban train prohibited
bicycles, so we had no choice but to find an airport taxi and
persuade the driver to rope our two bicycles on to the roof.

Madras has changed since I first knew it in 1988. Now
called Chennai, it has grown both outwards and upwards to

become a major business centre, and has lost its indolent southern air. The main street, Mount Road, has become Anna Salai and there are some totally unmanageable new names like Periyar E V R High Road. (Fortunately, the taxi drivers and rickshaw wallahs still live in the world of Parry's Corner, North Beach Road and Popham's Broadway.) Spencers old-fashioned 'departmental store', where I once bought whole nutmegs and a pair of ill-fitting green knickers, has been pulled down to make way for Spencer Towers, the sort of anonymous shopping mall you can find all over the world. The only Indian touch remaining is the Thought for the Day, which lifts the minds of the shoppers above their groceries with such philosophical gems as: 'There are victories of the soul and spirit. If you lose, you may be the winner.'

But for me, perhaps the worst change of all is the desecration of what used to be one of the most beautiful restaurants in the world. 'The Raintree', in the grounds of the Connemara Hotel, is a garden of fragrant night-blooming flowers, where the tables are laid under mature trees. There used to be a girl who did classical Indian dancing on a makeshift platform, accompanied by her mother on a harmonium. It was a peaceful place under the stars, with exquisite food and service. Now half the trees and shrubs have been chopped down to make an auditorium crammed with tables, and there is a professional stage with stage lighting. The evening I dined there, three solemn young men on pipe, violin and drum played tunelessly and endlessly. Then a dancer came on for a short turn, while one of the young men sang. It was slick, but uninspired. The Madrassi diners had disappeared, to be replaced by holiday Westerners in shorts, plus a few American businessmen, who were talked into ordering Indian wine by the wily head waiter. The Sunday buffet dinner was as delicious as ever, but the price had rocketed. It was a sad disappointment. The place had lost its sylvan charm and I doubt if I shall ever dine there again.

Yet despite these changes for the worse, Madras is still the most relaxed metropolis in India, with plenty of Edwardian character. It was the site of the East India Company's first settlement in 1639 and consequently has some of the finest and oldest English Renaissance architecture in India. Fort St George is a splendid agglomeration of public buildings, including St Mary's Church (1678–80), where Clive of India was married in 1753 and where the tombstones and regimental plaques give an insight into the public lives and personal tragedies of those who died in the service of the Madras Presidency. The secular buildings are still in official use, as the Secretariat and Legislative Assembly of the State of Tamil Nadu.

I once saw the stout, queenly figure of the Chief Minster of Tamil Nadu, Jayalalitha Jayaram, sitting under a tree in Fort St George, listening to the grievances of a queue of suppliants. She is a former film star, who succeeded to the office of chief minister on the death of her lover and one-time co-star, M G Ramachandram (or MGR, as he was known to his devoted fans). During the hysteria which attended his state funeral, Jayalalitha distinguished herself by fighting for pride of place with MGR's wife, Janaki, also a film star; and during her own time as chief minister, she was renowned for her conspicuous consumption – an Imelda Marcos love of shoes, the most lavish wedding ever seen for her stepson, and a cavalcade of 500 cars when she travelled about her state. After years of corruption, political in-fighting and battles with the Central Government in Delhi, she was sentenced to a year's imprisonment in February 2000. India is at last trying to curb corruption in high places with sweeping anti-graft laws, and Jayalalitha had violated these by allowing the construction of a seven-storey hotel in a protected hill resort near Madras. In this, as in everything else, she was in the forefront. She was the highest ranking person ever to be convicted under the newly applied laws. Despite all her misdemeanours, she remains tremendously popular in Tamil Nadu, where she is known as 'Amma (Mother) Jayalalitha'. When her conviction was reported, her supporters rioted in the streets and, like true Indian pyromaniacs, set fire to the buses. A number of people died in the conflagrations and one man was so distraught that he committed suicide.

Fort St George is a quiet, leafy area to wander around on a hot day, but my favourite classical building is St Andrew's

Church, the Scottish Kirk in Egmore. Consecrated in 1821, it looks a bit like St Martin's in the Fields on the outside, steeple and all. But the inside is spectacularly original. It has a circular nave with a dark-blue star-studded dome supported on sixteen Corinthian columns. The pews beneath it are semicircular, in raffia and teak for coolness. The apse faces and balances the entrance porch across the marble floor. It stands in what would once have been beautiful grounds, before they were put to more practical uses. Now they provide outdoor classroms under the trees for small children, a clinic, outbuildings occupied by the poor and a Destitute Feeding Centre. The church is obviously still at the heart of a thriving community.

Yet though there are so many Christian churches in Madras, including the Catholic Basilica of Saint Thomas (said to be built over the tomb of Doubting Thomas, who first brought Christianity to India), Tamil Nadu is the most Hindu of all the Indian States. It has an impressive list of major temples and is almost exclusively vegetarian in diet. Tamil is the oldest surviving language in India and the state voted out the Congress Party, when its leaders, all from the north, tried to introduce that hybrid upstart, Hindi, as the official language. The Tamils are Dravidians and proud of it. They inhabited India long before the Aryan invaders came and swept them south, and they are fiercely jealous of what they consider to be their unadulterated cultural heritage. They are probably the dark-skinned Rakshasas in *The Ramayana*.

Katherine and I had both visited Madras before, so we had 'done' all the sights in the guide books. We checked into the Atlantic Hotel and had contrasting experiences, which were an early reminder of the Indian love affair with bureaucracy. I needed to confirm my Indian Airlines flight from Trivandrum to Colombo. The Indian Airlines office was a vast marble hall full of employees, only five of whom seemed to be working. There were three passenger queues, each requiring a numbered token for a separate operation. There was one queue to book a flight, another to pay the cashier, and a third queue to hand over the cashier's receipt and get the ticket in return. Fortunately, the only queue I needed was the booking queue, as I already held a ticket, so my wait in the office was little more than three-quarters of an hour. Meanwhile Katherine, who had no ticket at all and was starting from scratch, went to Thomas Cook in Monteith Road to book a flight from Trivandrum to Bombay. She booked, paid by credit card and was issued with her ticket, all in the space of six minutes!

We had one bit of essential sightseeing to do. I had read of a gigantic statue of Hanuman, newly constructed in a temple on the outskirts of Madras, near St Thomas Mount, and I was naturally keen to see it. But tracking it down was not easy. The hotel reception had never heard of it, nor had the staff in the Government Museum. I went to the Tourist Office and drew a similar blank with the first two men I asked. But a third arrived, just as I was about to leave in despair, and directed me to the Prasanam Anjaneya Temple at Nanganallur. As Anjana was the name of Hanuman's mother, a temple with Anjaneya in its title seemed a distinct possibility, worth the considerable effort it would require to get there.

We wanted to arrive in time for the evening *darshan*, so we joined the commuters on a crowded suburban train from Egmore Station. By the time we reached Palavantham, the rain was coming down in sheets. We took an autorickshaw and for the next two miles rattled along a rough track, jolting over potholes and raising tidal waves from the puddles. It was dark and we began to wonder why on earth we were subjecting ourselves to so much damp discomfort. But then we saw the magnificent Hanuman. He towered nine metres high, carved out of one huge slab of black marble. He was not the warrior Hanuman, brandishing his mace, but the devoted servant of Rama, standing humbly with his hands together in the attitude of prayer. He wore a crown and an emerald-green lurex skirt, which glittered in the lamplight. Behind him was a steel staircase, which the priests climbed to light the oil lamps on either side of his head, arms and stomach. There were crowds of worshippers. They flocked there, according to the priests, because he was an extremely powerful Hanuman, who always granted requests. We were not allowed to take photographs, so I bought a small one in a frame which now sits in my study. Close up, he seems to have whiskers and looks more like a rather fierce cat than a monkey.

The torrential rain, which had drowned us in Palavantham, continued to hammer on our windows all night. Tamil Nadu has a strange monsoon. In other parts of India, the really heavy rains fall between June and August, starting in the south of the subcontinent and working their way northwards. But Tamil Nadu is relatively dry in the summer. It catches what is known as 'the retreating monsoon' between October and December. November is the peak month for rain, but as the daytime temperature rarely falls below 30°C, we were not really worried about getting wet. We waited for a break in the clouds and were able to set out at 8 o'clock in the morning.

On our ride down the Coromandel Coast, we planned to keep as near as possible to the seashore. So our route out of Madras should have involved a short ride to North Beach Road followed by a comfortable cruise along the promenade, past the aquarium on Marine Beach and St Thomas Basilica. But once across Anna Salai, we found that our road to the beach was axle-deep in flood water and we had to weave our way through the crowds of Saturday morning shoppers to find an alternative route to the sea. Then we had to make another detour, this time from the flooded promenade, through a district of thatched fishermen's shacks, where an amazing number of new-born black kids were tethered. But when we eventually reached the coastal highway, we found it clear of water and perfectly surfaced. Cycling became a delight. The honking horns of the outskirts soon gave way to peaceful casuarina groves on our right and sand dunes on our left. Bird-life was abundant, particularly on the salt flats where herons fished and vigilant kingfishers perched on telegraph poles. There were coffee stalls in the villages and coconut-sellers, who slashed off the tops of the nuts with machetes and handed them over with a straw stuck in the hole. When the coconut milk was drained, they chopped the shell in two to offer us the surprisingly soft, moist flesh. At only one or two rupees, these fresh coconuts were ideal food and drink for cyclists. When the heavens opened, which they did from time to time, we sheltered under a tree together with the locals. In one village, a girl in a hurry upended a giant saucepan to shelter under as she rushed along the street.

It was our first day out on our bicycles and neither of us had done any training, so I was uncertain how far we should be able to ride. I thought we might have to spend the night at one of the garish seaside resorts, such as Paradise Beach, just south of Madras, or lay out a large sum of money for the Taj Group's complex, Fisherman's Cove, at Covelong. But the road was flat and between downpours there was a slight drizzle, which kept the air agreeably cool. We crossed Madras and covered the 60 kilometres to Mamallapuram quite easily by mid-afternoon. There we were marooned. The rain came down in torrents for the next three days, submerging the roads and hiding the potholes. Cycling would be dangerous as well as wet.

But there are many worse places to be marooned than Mamallapuram (sometimes called Mahabalipuram), once the seaport of the Pallava Kings of Kanchipuram. We checked into a beautiful new hotel, very inexpensive for its standard of comfort, where our room had a balcony overlooking the central garden. When it was raining too hard to go out, Katherine embroidered and I read Horace on the balcony, or we both did crossword puzzles. In the brief lulls between downpours, we made sightseeing sorties to view the magnificent Pallava sculptures, and shopped for breakfast buns in the Western-style bakeries. Mamallapuram has a thriving tourist trade, so it caters well for those who like the occasional change from curry. It was an indolent life, which we really enjoyed after the tiring flight from London and the bustle of Madras.

It was my fourth visit to Mamallapuram, but I was still overwhelmed by the beauty of its monuments. They were all produced in the space of two centuries (seventh to the ninth AD), during the greatest flowering of the Pallava dynasty. There are friezes carved out of the granite cliffs, while the beach is littered with shrines and giant animals sculpted from granite outcrops. There is also the Shore Temple, which is thought to be the first temple in the south of India constructed of stone blocks, rather than carved as a cave from the living rock.

The most spectacular sculpture covers an immense cliff-face, about 8 metres high by 25 metres wide, and tells the story of the descent of the River Ganges to earth. To achieve this, the ascetic Bhagiratha fasted and performed austerities for a thousand years. When the gods finally granted the boon, the human race was terrified that the power of the Goddess Ganga's waters, crashing down on to the earth, would destroy it. So the great god Shiva undertook to receive the impact of the downpour on his own head, where it would lose its force by meandering for centuries through the maze of his long, matted locks until it flowed, tamed and gentle, down to the ground. The relief depicts the moment when the waters of the Ganges descend from Shiva's hair, watched adoringly by the gods, mankind and some beautifully carved elephants and monkeys. The King and Queen of the Nagas, semi-divine cobras with human torsos, swim up into the current, which was made more realistic on special occasions by the release of a flow of water from a cistern above the relief. Bhagiratha, who made it all possible, is shown torturing his body by standing for years on one leg with his arms in the air, mocked by a small cat, who has adopted exactly the same pose. It is one of the amusing details which adds to the charm of the relief. Another carving nearby shows an idyllic pastoral scene. Krishna, who like Rama is an incarnation of Vishnu, is lifting Mount Goverdan on his little finger to shelter a group of herdsmen from the rain god Indra's fury. The cows and their calves, in particular, are sculpted with loving delicacy. It is so fortunate for us that these beautiful carvings were executed on granite. They have hardly worn at all in fourteen centuries and appear as fresh today as they did on the evening when the last sculptor laid down his chisel.

On the beach, the most significant sculptures are a row of four large, ornate shrines, carved out of one gigantic granite outcrop, while a fifth shrine is carved from a separate boulder nearby. Like the temples of ancient Greece, they are stone replicas of earlier wooden structures. But the beach favourites are the granite elephant, lion and recumbent bull, all much larger than life. Indians pose for their photographs in front of them, while swarms of little children try to clamber all over them.

If you like romantic ruins, the famous Shore Temple is their epitome. Eroded by centuries of salt and wind, it stands with its foundations in the sea, its main shrine to Shiva catching the first light of the rising sun over the Bay of Bengal. Its orientation is thought to have enabled fishermen out in their boats to pay homage to the god. To the west lies a ruined courtyard, its surrounding walls topped with dozens of identical sculptures of Shiva's Nandi. This bull, which is Shiva's vehicle, is always represented in recumbent form in the environs of a Shiva temple, pointing like a faithful gun dog in the direction of the main shrine. A second sanctum in the Shore Temple is dedicated to Vishnu Anantasayana, 'he who sleeps on the serpent Ananta'. This contributes to the mystery of the place, as it is most unusual to have shrines to these two major gods in one and the same temple.

Tamil Nadu is the land of temples. There are thousands of them, many so important that they appear in every guide book and every tome on Indian art and architecture. When so many experts have written about them in so much detail, there seems to be no point at all in trying to cover them exhaustively myself. So unless they relate directly to *The Ramayana*, I shall simply comment on the works of art or temple ceremonies which particularly take my fancy. I have written at length about Mamallapuram, because it was perhaps the most magical of all the temple sites I saw, as well as being the most significant in the evolution of southern temple architecture.

Our fourth day dawned with clearish skies, so we set out along sandy streets with huge puddles to rejoin the excellent new coastal highway. We cycled all day through wetlands and rice paddies, thronged with heron, egrets and flashing blue kingfishers. For part of our journey, we had the Kaliveli Tank on our right, an important staging post for migratory water-fowl. I am not usually interested in birds; in fact, I have a phobia of little fluttery creatures. But the Indian varieties, being larger and more colourful, are splendid to watch. There were pelicans drifting by like comic mailbags and marsh birds stalking arrogantly to seaward on their long stilts of legs. Inland, minah birds and hoopoes scavenged for crushed beetles on the tarmac and were so tame that they let us cycle within centimetres of their beaks without flying away. They were such bright, engaging birds that they could have settled on my handlebars, or even on my hands, and I wouldn't have minded at all.

By late morning, the sun had broken through and it was almost unbearably hot. We sheltered for two hours over three bottles of Pepsi each and a bunch of bananas, to the great fascination of the people of Marakkanam, who came in their dozens to stare. There was a lodge of sorts in the village, but it was too basic to be used, except *in extremis*. So we struggled on to Pondicherry, stopping at intervals to rest and cool down in the shade. It was over 100 kilometres, which was a bit too far for comfort on our second day's cycling, but we were glad we'd made the effort when we sat down to dinner that evening in Le Café. It was perched on a rocky outcrop, with the waves crashing beneath, and though the fare was south Indian not French, as we had hoped, it was still a vastly pleasanter and more sophisticated place than anything we could have found in Marakkanam.

Pondicherry, as everyone knows, was a French enclave until it was handed over to India in 1954. It is very French in its layout and architecture. Some streets have French names, the town hall is still called the Hotel de Ville, there is an imposing seventeenth-century Jesuit Cathedral, Notre Dame de la Conception, and the policemen still wear képis and short French cloaks in the rain. It must have been a charming seaside town under the French, but the first time I passed through, in 1992, it was virtually indistinguishable in its maintenance (or lack of it!) from any other place in India. Since then, there have been improvements. The Alliance Française, together with the wealthy Aurobindo ashram (which owns too much property in the town, according to the locals), have been restoring the streets between the seafront and the canal. There are now some really smart houses in that area, whose flowery gardens spill clouds of bougainvillea over their whitewashed walls into the garbage-free streets.

Some of these well-maintained buildings form the Sri Aurobindo Ashram, one of the most popular ashrams in India with Westerners. It was founded in 1926 by Sri Aurobindo Ghosh, a Bengali whose opposition to British rule forced him to leave Calcutta. He had a system of 'integral yoga', which attempted to merge traditional Indian yogic philosophy with modern science. His disciple and successor, a Frenchwoman named Mirra Alfassa (popularly known as 'The Mother'), founded the city of Auroville, just outside Pondicherry, and named it after her master. It was to be a city where everyone lived together in harmony, irrespective of race, nationality and creed. The President of India himself attended its opening in 1968, and delegates from 121 countries poured a bag of their native soil into an urn symbolising the unity of mankind.

We stayed in a hotel on the seafront owned by the ashram, where portraits of the now deceased Mother watched over us in our bedroom, and in all the other rooms of the gracious, crumbling villa. She was such a dominant figure that we had to go and see her town. We booked on a coach tour, rather than cycling there under threatening skies, and were impressed with Auroville's 'yoga of work'. Hand-built furniture, ceramics, sculpture, hand-woven garments, hand-woven paper, all the products of its factories, were of superb quality, and had I not been on a bicycle with two limiting panniers, I might have bought up the whole visitors' shop. In the heart of Auroville stands the Matrimantir, an extraordinary globe, 30 metres in diameter, standing on a base in the shape of a lotus bud. Upward-sweeping ramps represent lotus leaves and the guide told us that the entire globe will eventually be covered with brass flowers ('gold, the colour of beauty'). Inside is a marble meditation chamber, illuminated solely by the largest man-made crystal in the world, presented by Zeiss, which refracts the light from a tracking mirror on the roof.

The shop and the Matrimandir are the two impressive features of Auroville. Otherwise, it seemed to us to be a sad place. Designed on the grand scale by a French architect,

Roger Anger, with 70 settlements spread over a 20 kilometre area, it has so far attracted only about a thousand permanent citizens, almost all from Europe, though its numbers are swelled by resident visitors. The town centre, apart from the Matrimandir, is still unbuilt; and the districts, through which our coach wove its way, were still quiet woodland. With names such as Certitude, Peace, Discipline, Fraternity, each had its designated specialism (alternative technology, computer science, sport, handicrafts, experimental agriculture, etc.). But they stood virtually empty, a forlorn reminder that high social ideals have little attraction in our materialistic world.

The rain held off for our tour, but it came down in torrents again in the evening. Accustomed as we were to cold English rain, it took us a few days to realise that we could stay out for hours in the tropical stuff and not come to any harm. In fact, we began to appreciate the rain for the luxuriance it brought with it. In our hotel garden, the red hibiscus was just beginning to bloom and there were bright red, yellow and orange cannas, purple bougainvillea and some rich creamy yellow flowers with glistening dark-green leaves. In the streets, women in transparent ankle-length macs over their brilliant saris were carrying great armfuls of lotus blossoms. The whole of Pondicherry was ablaze with colour.

When we checked out of our seaside hotel, we had to wade along the promenade up to our knees in water, but we knew that the highway would be raised on an embankment and in good condition for cycling, so we persevered until we reached it. That day, we were rather like the Israelites crossing the Red Sea, with water everywhere except on us. There was sea to our left, puddles on the road from the previous night's storms, black thunder clouds to both north and south, but miraculously we cycled all the way to Chidambaram without feeling a single spot of rain. Even when the road surface deteriorated to sandy, flooded potholes about 25 kilometres before we got there, the passing motorists were courteous and no one drowned us in a bright red tidal wave. The soil was so red along the coast that the puddles looked more like blood than rainwater under the dark sky. The rice paddies were a brilliant emerald green and there were coconut groves as far as the eye could see, but it was a poor area, despite its fertility. We passed old women with bundles of firewood on their heads, who were too destitute to afford a blouse under their saris, and old men dressed only in loincloths, staggering along on the bow legs of childhood rickets.

We cycled into Chidambaram along West Car Street, and it seemed as if the rural poverty we had just seen had spilled over into the town. It was a shabby little place, more like a backwoods village than one of the most important pilgrim destinations in the whole of India. Goats and cows wandered round the streets of beaten earth, scavenging for garbage, and the only secular building of any size was the imposing cinema. Popular Indian films are spectacular escapes from reality and the offerings of Chidambaram's palace of dreams drew the usual long queues throughout the day. In the bustling streets of the centre, there were old wooden houses with thatched roofs and pillared verandahs. They jostled with the market stalls for proximity to the temple walls, like the higgledy-piggledy buildings in the shadow of mediaeval English cathedrals. But the lowliness of its surroundings only served to glorify the temple, whose ornate towers were visible from every quarter. The temple was the geographical centre of the town and the centre of its life. It was the great temple of Shiva Nataraja – Shiva, the Lord of the Cosmic Dance.

On my own pilgrimage, I was following the path of Rama, an avatar, or incarnation, of the god Vishnu. But the god most closely associated with the south of India is Shiva. So I think the time has come when I should try to make sense of the multitude of Hindu gods and map out their relationship to one another.

೧೩ ೮ೌ

## The One or the Thirty-three Million

*Hinduism is the world's oldest living religion. While other faiths trace their development over centuries, the Indians work in* millennia. They have an overwhelming number of religious texts, from the Sanskrit Rig Veda, which evolved round about the twelfth century BC as a group of 1,028 sacrificial hymns, through the Brahmanas, the Upanishads and the two great epics (The Mahabharata and The Ramayana) to the Puranas (c. AD 1000–1500). Dating these works is extremely difficult, because many were passed down orally for centuries before they became written texts and, in any case, their dates are irrelevant because, as Professor Wendy O'Flaherty points out in her introduction to Hindu Myths, 'myths do not have dates'. They are revised, reworked, adapted and modernised by each succeeding generation. But whatever their date, and whatever gods they are attached to, myths express the basic concerns of humanity – creation and destruction, birth and death, god and man, good and evil. They attempt to answer the fundamental questions: 'Who are we? Who made our world? Why are we here? What are our duties? What will happen to us when we die?'

According to the Upanishads, there are 30,306 Hindu gods, though their popular number is often given as thirty-three million. These gods play out answers to life's fundamental questions in their myths, but the piling of layer upon layer over the centuries has produced the kind of multi-faceted answers which are not found in other faiths. Christianity and Islam, for example, which rely on one book of divine revelation, have only one answer to every question, which tends to make their followers more dogmatic than the devotees of Hindu gods.

The main reason for Hinduism's continuing success is that it enables the individual to approach God within the limits of his competence. If he is an illiterate villager, he may worship a tree or a snake, making offerings to ward off disaster and ensure a good harvest. At this level, the distinction between religion and magic is somewhat blurred. At the other end of the scale, there is the philosopher, who grapples with universal truths. All are Hindus and their relationship with their god, on whatever level, is equally meritorious. There is a priestly caste, the brahmins, who perform the temple rituals, and are often paid to approach a god on behalf of a lower caste individual, who feels himself to be unqualified. But the brahmins do not lead the prayers in a temple. The temple ritual simply focuses the mind of the worshipper. His prayers to his god are his own personal affair.

*Another important reason for the success of Hinduism is its all-encompassing nature. This has enabled it to absorb other gods and philosophical systems, when they have become particularly interesting, or threatening. For example, when its offshoot, Buddhism, was making converts and drawing Indians away from orthodox, brahminical Hinduism, the Buddha was simply made an avatar of Vishnu, and that kept the Buddhist converts within the Hindu fold. If Christianity were ever perceived as a threat, I'm sure the same thing would happen to Jesus. Hindus never proselytise. To be a Hindu, you have to be born into the faith. But they don't like losing members to other religions.*

*Despite the fighting which breaks out from time to time between Hindus and Muslims, the Hindus are remarkably tolerant. It's not unusual to see pictures of Jesus and the Ka'aba at Mecca hanging up in shops and railway stations alongside images of the Hindu gods. When the daughter of an Indian friend converted to Christianity, I asked her if she was upset about it. 'Of course I wasn't,' she replied. 'I just got statuettes of Jesus and the Virgin Mary and put them in the puja room, along with all the other gods.' And she was speaking with genuine acceptance of another's beliefs, not out of indifference to her own religion; Indi is a practising Hindu and a devotee of Durga. As Ananda Coomaraswamy once wrote, 'There are many paths that lead to the summit of one and the same mountain.'*

*The myth of creation brings order to chaos, and I shall now try to bring order to the multitude of Hindu gods by arranging them in ranks, though I am aware that any stratification is bound to oversimplify the mass of complex inter-relationships within what has been termed 'a pantheistic monism'.*

*Imagine a pyramid. At its peak is the One, the Almighty, the Absolute. On the level below, stand the three great gods of the Hindu trinity: Brahma, Vishnu and Shiva, popularly known as the Creator, the Preserver and the Destroyer. These three have wives, families and, in the case of Vishnu, a range of avatars and helpers, all of whom may be worshipped separately from the god himself. Below these three come a group of still important survivors from the original gods of the Aryan invaders, who were Indo-European and had a similar pantheon to the Greeks and Scandinavians, each of their gods being related to one of the* natural elements or to a specific task or emotion. Then, at the broad base of the pyramid, there are all the thousands of minor gods – the gods of the villages, fields, trees and animals, the gods of diseases, the planets and the days of the week, to list but a few. All the Hindu gods, whatever their rank in the hierarchy, have merged, divided, and gained or lost power over the centuries, so that it is difficult to be categorical about their nature and their powers. Finally, permeating all these layers from top to bottom is the Great Goddess, the Earth Mother, who was worshipped in India long before the patriarchal Aryans arrived and is still a vital force.

### The Top of the Pyramid

At the heart of Hinduism is a profound philosophical agnosticism. I shall not attempt to define the indefinable in a few crisp sentences. Four quotations from religious texts will give the general idea and show the difficulty of elucidation:

'Whence has this creation arisen? Perhaps it formed itself, or perhaps it did not. The One who looks down on it, in the highest heaven, only that One knows – or perhaps it does not know.' (Rig Veda)

'The breath of life is Brahman. The messenger of Brahman is the mind.'

'Space it is which brings out name and form. That within which they are is Brahman, the immortal, the Self.'

'Which is the one god? It is the breath of life, Brahman, the beyond.' (Upanishads)

Unlike Jehovah in Genesis, the One God of the Hindus, or Brahman, is both the material out of which everything is created and the efficient cause of creation. Brahman is a state of being, Being itself, and at the same time, the source of multiplicity. It is a neuter noun, which is unknowable, 'which exists beyond questioning'. It is sometimes called simply 'that' or 'who?' It was there before the gods.

The ordering of creation is a particularly Vedic concept. Brahman measures things, organises them, spreads them out, balances opposites and props the elements apart to form the natural world. But there is also an obsession with ordering language, with defining things in words, because to define is to create. The earliest summary of grammar and syntax was compiled by a Sanskrit grammarian, Panini, who lived in India around 500 BC. Brahman created in accordance with the Vedas, so did the Vedas exist before Brahman? There are even instances in the scriptures where the Vedas are called Brahman. And then there is the primal word 'Om', or more correctly, the trisyllable 'Aum' (a-u-m standing for the three most ancient Vedas). This sacred word encompasses the universe and is beyond time and Brahman. It is the essence of everything sacred, used at the beginning and end of prayer, at the beginning of meditation and during the performance of yoga, when the mind is absorbed into Brahman.

'What was and is and is yet to be, all that is Aum;
And whatever else the three times transcend, that too is Aum.'
(Upanishads)

The beginning of the Gospel according to St John is reminiscent of this: 'In the beginning was the Word, and the Word was with God, and the Word was God.'

Hindu religion at this level is all very metaphysical, a far cry from anything which the Indian man in the street could ever begin to contemplate. But it helps to explain how the Indians came to invent that vital concept in mathematics, the zero, and why they excel in the further reaches of contemporary physics and astronomy. The Indian mind has an ingrained predisposition towards speculation and abstract debate.

### The Hindu Trinity

Brahman is so powerful, so dazzling, so all-embracing, that the concept cannot possibly be grasped by a limited human being. It has to be broken down into different aspects and personalised, if we are to have any chance of coping with it. So the unfathomable Brahman has been divided into three major gods.

Brahma, the Creator, is clearly a personification of Brahman, but it is a later name. If the Creator appears as a mythological personage in the Vedas, he is usually called Prajapati or Hiranyagarbha. He originally had five bearded faces, one for each direction (or each of the four Vedas) and one on the top of his head. But Shiva consumed the fifth face in the fire of his third eye, because Brahma had spoken disrespectfully. Brahma has four hands, each of which carries an object selected from: a book (representing the Vedas), a rosary, a sceptre, a bow, a spoon, a lotus or a water jug. These objects are symbolic. For instance, the rosary which he is counting represents time; and the water pot alludes to a myth that the whole universe evolved out of water. If his image is coloured, it is usually pink or red. His wife is Saraswati, the goddess of learning, music and the arts. She is credited with the invention of writing and is worshipped when children first begin to learn their alphabet. All the important Hindu gods have creatures as their vehicles. Brahma and Saraswati both have the swan, the symbol of knowledge, and are often shown riding a swan or seated in a chariot drawn by swans. Many gods stand on a lotus flower, as it indicates divinity in a general sense, but Brahma and Saraswati may also sit in the centre of a lotus. The lotus flower is rooted in mud and grows up through water into sunlight, so that it also symbolises enlightenment. When associated specifically with Brahma, it is a symbol of the origin of the universe.

Religious iconography is a fascinating study and some knowledge of it adds greatly to the interest of temple-touring. The Hindu gods, like Christian saints, can always be recognised by their symbols. As the religion developed and new gods evolved, some of the older ones merged. This created a problem for the artist, as he had to symbolise all their combined attributes. The only way out of that difficulty was to give the amalgamated gods extra hands – usually four, but sometimes eight – in which they could carry all the required objects and make the required gestures. For as well as the symbols, there is a gamut of mudras, stylised gestures, which indicate character or disposition. For instance, if the fingers are together and pointing down to the ground, it means that the god is of a charitable nature, and if they are pointing upwards, palm towards the viewer, the god is protective.

Brahma is closely associated with time, which is why he carries its symbol, the rosary, in one of his hands. In Hindu cosmology, the basic cycle, through which the universe passes, is the Kalpa or Day of Brahma. Each of his days is equivalent to 4,320 million years and each night is the same length. After 360 of these days and nights, or one year of Brahma's life, the world is consumed by fire, but the gods, sages and elements remain to begin the next cycle. Brahma's life is expected to last for 100 of his years, at the end of which time, everything, including Brahma himself, will be resolved into its original elements.

Over the centuries, Brahma has diminished in importance, pushed into the background by the other two members of the triad, who have gained in power and assumed Brahma's creative function. Images of Brahma are still made, but they occupy a subsidiary place in the scheme of temple decoration. They rarely appear in the main shrine, and there are now only two temples in the whole of India which are dedicated specifically to him, one in Rajasthan and the other in Orissa. In some of the creation myths, Brahma committed incest with his daughter to produce mankind, and it has been claimed that this distasteful idea may be the chief reason for his decline in popularity.

Vishnu, the Preserver, is a prime example of the way in which the status of a god has changed through the ages. In the Rig Veda, he was not in the major league, but was a minor god, one of the manifestations of solar power. By the time he appeared in the Epics and Puranas, he had become the greatest god, assuming all three powers of creation, protection and destruction. As he rose in eminence, he absorbed a number of minor gods, popular folk deities and heroes, who became his avatars. There are twenty-four of these, ten of them forming the most important sub-group: the Fish, the Tortoise, the Boar, the Man-Lion, the Dwarf, Parashurama, Rama, Krishna, Buddha and Kalkin. The first nine have already appeared on earth to destroy evil, while Kalkin is yet to come. We are living at present in the Kali Yuga, the age of darkness, when righteousness and the rule of law are being eroded. At the end of this age, Kalkin will ride out on a white horse, brandishing a fiery sword and shining like the sun, to save mankind and establish a golden age of truth and goodness.

Vishnu is instantly recognisable. His skin is blue, the colour of the heavens and also the colour which symbolises determination and strength of character. His face is beardless, his expression benign, and he is always dressed in yellow, the colour of knowledge, happiness and tranquillity. His two upper hands carry his most important symbols – the wheel or discus and the conch shell. The wheel represents the Universal Mind and Vishnu's limitless power to create and destroy the revolving worlds. The conch shell, which is a multiple spiral arising from one point and spreading in ever-widening circles, is a symbol of the creation of the universe, especially as its connection with the sea alludes to the myth that creation evolved from water. In addition to these key symbols, Vishnu may carry a lotus flower or a mace, representing his authority, or he may hold up one of his hands in the reassurance mudra. His sign, which he wears in the middle of his forehead, consists of two vertical lines, often with the round dot of the Supreme Being between them. Sometimes the lines are joined at the base, to make a kind of shield shape, but they are always vertical, as they link Vishnu with water, whose property it is to descend. Indian devotees of Vishnu (Vaishnavas) demonstrate their allegiance by wearing this sign. Vishnu's vehicle is Garuda, who is half man, half eagle. Lakshmi or Shri is his wife, but she is such an important goddess in her own right that I shall deal with her separately later.

In one of his most common portrayals, Vishnu as Narayan, he is shown reclining on the immense coils of the serpent king, Sheshanaga , who protects him under a canopy formed by some of his thousand cobra heads. Sheshanaga (sometimes called Ananta, the Infinite) is the residue left over from the disintegration of the universe at the end of one of its cycles. The serpent floats on the cosmic waters, rocking Vishnu to sleep. While Vishnu sleeps dreamlessly, there is an interval in the cycle of creation. But when he begins to dream, a lotus blooms from his navel. In the centre of the lotus blossom sits Brahma, who carries out the actual work of creation under Vishnu's command. This is a very cunning appropriation by Vishnu of Brahma's creative role. In addition to his great cosmic sleeps, Vishnu and many other gods have an annual nap from June/July to October/November. This four-month period is considered unlucky, with the result that weddings and other important ceremonies are deferred until the gods reawaken.

Another form in which Vishnu is worshipped is simply as a pair of footprints, perhaps alluding to the three daily steps of his Vedic predecessor, the Sun God – rising, noon and setting. Or *perhaps they represent the steps taken by one of his avatars, Vamana the dwarf, who wrested control of the earth and heavens from an over-powerful ruler by a trick involving giant steps.*

*The various avatars of Vishnu give clues to their origin. Some carry the discus and conch shell, the lotus or the mace; some have a hand raised in the reassurance mudra. Rama and Krishna are both blue-skinned, like their great Original, and Rama carries the marks of the discus and conch shell on his palms, like stigmata. All the incarnations have Vishnu's vertical sign on their foreheads.*

*In the Vishnu group of deities, one has assumed surprising importance over recent years. He started life simply as an assistant to one of the avatars, but more prayers are now directed towards him than towards many of the great gods. He is, of course, Hanuman, the monkey general who helped Rama – and the god who originally sparked off my interest in* The Ramayana, *when I saw a poor man praying to him one morning in Ujjain. In the original Valmiki epic, Hanuman is a less significant character than Sugriva, the King of the Monkeys, but in the Uttara Kanda, the seventh and last book of* The Ramayana, *which is considered to be a later addition, Hanuman is given greater prominence, with hundreds of lines devoted to his miraculous childhood, his overwhelming physical strength and his erudition. Since then, his power and popularity have steadily increased.*

*Hanuman is usually represented as a powerful man with a monkey's face and a particularly long, flamboyant monkey's tail. Occasionally, he has five or ten heads, representing avatars of Vishnu. He carries a mace and most frequently a mountain on the palm of his hand. This refers to an incident in* The Ramayana, *when he flew to the Himalayas and brought back medicinal herbs to cure the wounded. When he is worshipped as the God of Grammar, he appears in priestly robes, studying a huge tome. He is red, the most auspicious colour, and the colour of prowess. Vishnu's sign is on his forehead and he is sometimes accompanied by Vishnu's vehicle, Garuda.*

*Hanuman was Rama's devoted friend, who diligently, even miraculously, performed all the tasks which Rama assigned to him. He fought valiantly on Rama's side against Ravana and the* forces of evil, so that his worshippers see him as the god who helps them in time of trouble, their mighty champion against misfortune. He has his own shrine in most of the temples dedicated to Vishnu and his avatars, and there are many small Hanuman shrines in the streets, where passers-by stop to worship. Even in temples to gods outside the Vishnu group, his image is sought out on friezes and pillars, where it is daubed with red paint and becomes an unofficial shrine. Hanuman has always been worshipped fervently in the villages, but he is now said to include the urban middle classes in his following, perhaps because they have more problems than most people in today's society.

Shiva, the Destroyer, *the third member of the trinity, is as primitive and complex as Vishnu is urbane and straightforward. He may well trace his origins back to pre-Aryan times, as an interesting seal of a god with many of Shiva's characteristics has been found at Mohenjodaro in the Indus Valley. It is a product of the Harappan civilisation, roughly dated c. 2300–1750 BC. The seal shows an ithyphallic god, seated in the lotus position, with huge horns on his head. He is surrounded by adoring animals, all exquisitely carved. The name of Shiva is unknown in the Vedas, but the yogic god of the Indus Valley may have merged with the Aryan god Rudra, the terrible, howling god of the storm. As Shiva means 'auspicious', he may have started life as a euphemistic epithet applied to Rudra to placate him. In some of the Vedic hymns, Rudra, who has both benign and malign aspects, is declared to be the only god, the Creator and Preserver as well as the Destroyer. Shiva is mentioned by name in the Epics, where he is subordinate to Vishnu. But, because things are never simple, Vishnu and the other gods sometimes pay homage to Shiva. There are many instances in* The Ramayana *of Rama worshipping him.*

*Shiva is Vishnu's rival. To his devotees (Saivas), he is Mahadeva, the Supreme Being. He represents destruction and the malevolent forces of life, but because rebirth follows death in the cycle of the universe, he also has the power to regenerate and procreate. In his temples, he is usually worshipped in the form of the phallic linga. His third aspect is that of Mahayogi, the naked ascetic, the god of meditation. By the power of his austerities,* miracles may be worked, spiritual knowledge acquired and union with Brahman eventually attained.

A god with such diverse powers obviously appears in many different forms, each one representing a particular aspect. He is fair-skinned, but he has a blue throat because he drank poison at the time of the churning of the primal ocean by the gods. He has a third eye in the middle of his forehead, whose glance is so fiery that he keeps it closed, except at the destruction of the universe. He sits in the lotus position, dressed in a tiger-skin, with snakes coiled round his neck and arms (reminiscent of the god of the animals on the Harappan seal). In his four hands he may hold a trident, an axe, an antelope, a bow, a club with a skull on the end, a cord to bind offenders, or a drum in the shape of an hourglass. He often wears a garland of skulls and is smeared with ash, as the god of cremation grounds and ghosts. His wild hair is decorated with the crescent moon, perhaps the horns which adorn the Harappan deity, and a small mermaid figure representing the goddess Ganga, whose waters he tamed. (The Vaishnavas also stake their claim to Ganga with a myth that she sprang from Vishnu's feet). Sometimes Shiva is simply an emaciated, two-armed, meditating ascetic, with none of the usual symbols in his hands. And in the temple at Suchindram, near Cape Comorin, his shrine is empty, except for a mirror, which symbolises Shiva in his unmanifest aspect. The priest who sees his own reflection in that mirror attains union with the Absolute.

Shiva's vehicle is Nandi, the bull. His sign consists of two or more horizontal lines, with or without the dot which claims his preeminence as the Supreme Being, and with or without a representation of his third eye bisecting the lines. Even though his terrifying images are softened by the 'fear not' mudra, it is hardly surprising that his followers prefer to worship him in the more abstract and positive form of his phallic symbol.

In Chidambaram, Shiva is worshipped as Nataraja, The Lord of the Cosmic Dance, one of his more attractive representations. In it, he is performing the wild Tandava, with one foot high in the air and the other foot crushing the dwarf of ignorance. He is surrounded by a ring of flames. His hair, which shelters Ganga, appears in art in a whole range of positions, from flat at the start of the dance to vertical at its climax. In one of his upper hands *he holds the fire which destroys the universe, while in the other he carries the hourglass drum, whose beat is the pulse of life – or perhaps the drum is the source of sound, the mystic word which is Brahman. His lower right hand is in the protection mudra, while his lower left points to his stationary foot. This gesture not only shows the conquest of ignorance, but attests that his feet are the only refuge for the soul. The elevated foot stands for release from illusion. The presence of Ganga in his hair has been cited as an example of the mutual taming of two opposites: Shiva mitigates the potentially destructive power of Ganga's waters, while Ganga cools Shiva's head, thus preventing the fiery god from destroying the world with his flames. Such a complicated figure as the dancing Shiva is obviously capable of many interpretations. The above is just one of them.*

*Shiva has two children. The elephant-headed Ganesha may be India's most popular god, whose image appears in almost every home. Gentle and affectionate, he has endearing weaknesses like his greed for sweets. He is the god of wisdom and prudence, so that his image is placed over the doors of banks and libraries. As the remover of obstacles, he is worshipped at the start of any undertaking, particularly at the beginning of a journey. His vehicle is the rat, the elephant's perfect working partner: a rat can creep through small holes and deal with obstacles which Ganesha's huge bulk and strength cannot remove. There are hundreds of charming stories about this much-loved god, but it is unfortunately not within the scope of this book to narrate them. Shiva's other son is Kartikeya or Skanda, the God of War, whose vehicle is the peacock. He is a popular god in the south of India, where he is worshipped under the name of Murugan. Shiva's wife is so powerful that she will be dealt with later under the heading of the Great Goddess.*

### The Aryan Gods

*When the Aryans swept into the north of India, they brought with them a pantheon similar to that of the Greeks. As Sanskrit has the same root as Greek and Latin, some of their gods even had names which are instantly recognisable to us. For instance, 'ignis' is the Latin word for fire and Agni is the Vedic Fire God. In the Vedas, three of these gods are preeminent.*

*The King of the Gods was* Indra *who, like Zeus and Jupiter, was the god of the firmament, rain and the thunderbolt. He predominates in the Rig Veda, and more hymns are addressed to him in the Vedas generally than to any other god, except Agni. He is still referred to as the chief god in* The Ramayana, *though much of his power has already been taken over by Vishnu, and by the time of the Puranas, he has definitely fallen out of the first rank. He remains the chief of the less important gods.*

*Indra carries the thunderbolt and he may also have a bow and arrows, a conch shell (linking him to Vishnu), a hook or a net, depending on whether he is shown with two arms or four. He has a thousand eyes all over his body and his vehicle is the white king of the elephants, Airavat, who has four tusks and a few extra trunks.*

*The Vedic god who occupied an important place in an agricultural society and is still worshipped today is* Surya, *the God of the Sun. He is the god to whom water is offered and the famous Gayatri Mantra chanted every morning at his rising. This prayer, from the Rig Veda, is so sacred that many people will not write it down. As a non-Hindu, I have no such inhibitions, though I find it difficult to decide between the various interpretations. It seems to translate as something like, 'Earth, sky, heaven. We meditate on the excellent light of the divine sun. May he illuminate our minds.'*

*Although he has lost some of his power to Vishnu, Surya still has a few temples dedicated to him, notably the splendid Sun Temple at Konarak in Orissa. He is sometimes shown with a lotus in each of his two hands; sometimes he is four-handed, displaying Vishnu's wheel, conch, lotus and protective mudra. His chariot is drawn across the heavens by seven horses, or one horse with seven heads, each symbolising one of the seven colours of the rainbow. His charioteer is the god of the dawn, Aruna (cf. Latin Aurora).*

*The third great Vedic power is* Agni, *the god of fire. As the god of the sacrifice, a most important element in Vedic worship, he is the priest of the gods and the god of priests, serving as the link between gods and men. Even today, fire plays a vital part in the most significant rituals. At weddings, for instance, the bride and groom throw offerings into a ceremonial fire and the marriage is solemnised when they make seven circuits of the flames together.*

At the end of life, it is Agni who accepts the body as an offering on the funeral pyre.

Agni is a red, pot-bellied god with three legs and two to seven hands, in which he carries the implements used in fire ceremonies. He has one or two heads, and flames issue from his mouth or mouths to lick up the butter which the priest offers to the sacrificial fire. Seven streams of glory radiate from his body. His vehicle is a ram.

Other significant Vedic deities are Vayu, the Wind God, who is the father of Hanuman; Kama, or Kamadeva, the God of Love; Yama, the God of Death; Varuna, the God of the Oceans; Chandra, the Moon God, whose other chief name is Soma, under which name he is the god of soma or amrita (nectar), the substance from which the gods derive their strength; and Vishwakarma, the divine architect of the universe and god of craftsmen.

### The Rest

At the base of the pyramid stand the other thirty thousand or thirty million deities. Some scholars claim that the cult of the river is the oldest indigenous cult, and the most sacred of the rivers is the Ganges, or the goddess Ganga. It is an act of worship to walk down one bank of a river from its source to its mouth and back up the other bank. In addition to the sacred rivers, there are sacred mountains and sacred forests. In fact, the whole of India is sacred and is worshipped under the name of a modern goddess, Bharata Mata.

Among living things, the cow is particularly sacred, as the symbol of Mother Earth, and snakes are commonly worshipped by country people. Tree gods are found on Harappan seals, and yakshas, the goddesses who live in trees, are still propitiated with offerings of food, shreds of cloth tied to the branches and red-daubed stones placed at their roots. Some trees, like the tulsi, the Indian basil, which is sacred to Vishnu, are worshipped daily, while others are worshipped only at certain festivals. The sun, moon and stars are worshipped, as are the days of the week. For the Hindu, everything in the universe is sacred.

Because the Absolute and the three major gods of the Hindu trinity are so awe-inspiring, most Hindus have a personal god, *an* ishwara devi, *who is more approachable. For example, Krishna and Rama, who are both human avatars, with some of a human being's frivolity and weaknesses, are more accessible than Vishnu himself. Hanuman and Ganesha, about both of whom many amusing stories are woven, are even easier to approach, as are the more benign consorts of the gods.*

*The Way of Devotion,* bhakti, *is the worshipper's direct approach to God through the* ishwara devi *of his own choice. It is open to all, irrespective of caste or sex, without the need to use brahmins as intermediaries. When it came into prominence in the Middle Ages, it was in fact opposed by the priests, as it disregarded traditional Vedic rituals. For Vaishnavas,* bhakti *usually focuses on Krishna or Rama; for Shaivas on Siva's* shakti, *one of his female forms. It is a mass movement, celebrated with enthusiastic chanting and dancing. The worshipper is lost in adoration and is embraced by God's love.*

*Personal gods, though they may be as minor as the tree outside a peasant's back door, are all pathways to Brahman. The Bhagavad Gita, the section of* The Mahabharata *which is revered as one of the Hindu's most sacred works, is the earliest expression of* bhakti. *Krishna says, 'Those who worship other gods worship only me.' In the Gita, Krishna is on earth and is acting as Arjuna's charioteer in a battle. At a certain point, he reveals himself to the mortal Arjuna as the Universal Being, transcendent, limitless, million-armed, glittering, with the sun and moon in his eyes. Arjuna is powerless against such brilliance and begs Krishna to hide his glory again in human form, which Krishna obligingly does. Krishna is approachable by man, but he is none the less Brahman.*

### Devi, or Mahadevi, The Great Goddess
*All the Hindu deities have so far been male, except for Brahman the Absolute. But just as the One God is neither male nor female, so the three great gods of the Hindu trinity, being personalisations of Brahman, belong to both sexes and to neither. Their 'wives' are not simply their consorts; they are their* shakti, *or divine force. In his Ardhanari manifestation, Shiva even appears as half man, half woman, divided vertically down the middle. There is a particularly beautiful example of this form, sculpted anywhere between* AD 450 *and* AD 750, *in the main cave on Elephanta*

*Island, near Bombay. The female half is gentle and sensual, with a mirror in her hand, but she merges so successfully into her opposite, tautly masculine half that, at first glance, the figure seems completely normal. Ardhanari is a mystic concept, miraculously worked in stone.*

*Like other ancient peoples, the early inhabitants of the Indus Valley worshipped a powerful Earth Mother, who was responsible for fertility. She is represented on Harappan seals. With the arrival of the patriarchal Aryans, who were nomadic warriors rather than settled agricultural people, the fertility goddess fell out of favour, or was suppressed in the official Vedic religion. But she continued to be the dominant force in the countryside, where she was worshipped in many forms.*

*Modern scholarship suggests that she became accepted into contemporary mainstream worship in two phases. First, the male gods were given consorts. Then, in the Middle Ages, under the growing influence of Tantric and Shaktic movements (yogic practices which take erotic and forbidden routes to divine ecstasy), these once token consorts became powerful manifestations of the gods' powers.*

*Vishnu's consort, Lakshmi or Sri, is the personification of abstract nouns meaning 'good fortune' and 'prosperity'. A golden goddess, she arose from the primal waters seated on a lotus and usually holds lotus blossoms in her two upper hands. Gold coins rain down from one of her lower hands, while the other is in the boon-granting mudra. Vishnu is the cosmic ruler and Lakshmi is his power to bestow wealth, order and fertility. When Vishnu took the mortal form of Rama, Lakshmi came to earth as Sita. For his Krishna incarnation, she was Radha. Her festival is Diwali, the Festival of Lights in October/November, when lamps are lit all over the house, inside and out, in the belief that Lakshmi will not enter a dark place. Diwali is the start of the financial year, when businessmen open new accounts and offer special prayers to the goddess of wealth. Until recent times, there were no temples to Lakshmi in her own right, but it is perhaps a sign of our more materialistic age that modern temples are now being built to this popular goddess. The hectic red and yellow Lakshmi Narayan temple in Delhi, built by the wealthy Birla family in 1938, is an example.*

*Just as Shiva is a more complex god than Vishnu, so his shakti is extremely complicated. He has a whole catalogue of consorts. As the beautiful Parvati, 'the mountaineer', Uma, 'light', or Gauri, 'the brilliant one', his shakti is his benign, creative force. As Kali, 'the black one', Durga, 'the inaccessible', and Bairavhi, 'the terrible', to name but a few, the consort is his wild, destructive power. Kali is perhaps the most notorious of these manifestations. She is the black-skinned, naked haunter of cremation grounds, dripping blood and holding a severed head and a cleaver. Her girdle is made of severed arms and she wears a necklace of skulls. Animals are sacrificed in her temples, and there was a terrible incident a few years ago when a man decapitated his small son to propitiate her, recalling older, darker tantric rites. Her devotees, who call her Mother Kali, claim that she is fierce in order to destroy evil.*

*Durga, 'the inaccessible one', seems to have emerged as a goddess around the fourth century AD and was attached to Shiva as one of his more powerful consorts. Over the last century or so, she has become more accessible and is now the most important female deity of the Hindus, particularly among strong-minded middle-class women. She is worshipped today in her own right. If she is shakti, she is the shakti of the Absolute, not simply of Shiva. Durga is a handsome yellow-coloured goddess with eight arms. In her eight hands she carries symbols selected from: a trident, a sword, a shield, a bow, an arrow, a snake, a bell, a drum, a cup, a wheel, a conch shell and a water pot (to form a composite of all the gods in the trinity). She rides on a tiger and is often shown slaying Mahihasura, the buffalo demon. She has nine popular forms, called Nava-Durgas, which are worshipped during the first nine days of Dussehra, or Durga Puja, in September/October. Dussehra celebrates the slaying of the buffalo demon, the triumph of good over evil. On the tenth day of Dussehra, Rama's victory is commemorated, with the burning of Ravana's effigy.*

*With the modern prominence of Durga, the Earth Mother has at last begun to resume the status denied her by the high-caste masculine Aryans. She has taken a couple of millennia to do it, but Mahadevi has finally pulled herself out of rural obscurity and taken her seat at the Hindu top table. As Hinduism deals so much in symbols, I like to think that Durga's elevation is a sign of increasing maturity and self-respect among India's women. I hope it means that they are now standing on the threshold of something approaching true equality.*

Friday is the big night in Chidambaram's temple. It's the night when the most elaborate rituals take place at the shrine of Shiva Nataraja. I walked through the shuttered streets of the outskirts, drawn by the temple illuminations, reflecting how comfortable and unafraid I always felt in India's darkness. London seems much more threatening at night. The great courtyard of the temple was busy, but there was a casual air about the place. Families were picnicking, children were playing tag, cows were strolling around amiably, while old men sat gossiping in groups under the colonnades. I nearly tripped over a sleeping dog. For the Indians, religion is such an integral part of their lives that they don't have to dress up or put on solemn faces to sit in the temples. They are completely at home there.

As I approached the shrine, I saw the gleaming white robes of the officiating brahmins flitting through the lamplight. Hundreds of them form a hereditary priesthood, the *dikshitars*, who care for the temple on a rota. Some were little boys, looking very important as they did the fetching and carrying. But as God is both male and female, only the married men whose wives are still living may perform the most sacred rites. The *dikshitars* are highly reverenced in Chidambaram and are recognisable in the streets, even without their robes, as they wear their hair long and tied in a bun to one side of the nape – a style which causes problems for the older, balder ones!

The evening ceremony in the main shrine began at 6 o'clock. The great silver doors were opened, but Shiva himself remained hidden behind a curtain. The duty priests first anointed Nandi, Shiva's bull, with a mixture of milk, coconut milk and water, cracking the coconuts on an iron spike. The mixture ran down from the statue into a runnel and I was amazed to see devotees pushing and shoving to lap up the dirty liquid as it drained down from the shrine. By now, I was hemmed in by a mob of expectant worshippers. A battery of oil lamps was lit, some of them brass candelabras as big as Christmas trees. The *dikshitars* kept opening and shutting the silver doors, which were also picked out with lights. All these lamps radiated heat and the air grew hot and tense with excitement. Apart from myself, there were only two Westerners, a young Italian couple. The girl was fascinated, but the boy kept asking, 'Che si passa? Niente!' (What's happening? Nothing!) He was bored, fidgety and petulant, but he wouldn't go away. He just stayed there and spoilt the ceremony for her. I was glad I was on my own.

After some frantic sweeping up with twig brushes, the curtain was finally swept aside to the clanging of bells and clashing of cymbals. Shiva Nataraja was revealed. The crowd pressed forward, raising their hands above their heads in prayer and slapping their cheeks. When the *dikshitars* lifted the great candelabras and described circles with them in front of the idol, the worshippers gasped and went into a frenzy of silent fervour. Shiva was smothered in so many garlands and jewels, that only his faint, inward smile was visible, and his eyes which give and receive *darshan*. His elegant dancing form, surrounded by its ring of fire, was completely obscured. When the noise and excitement died down a little, a soft tenor voice rose into the night air. I looked towards the corner of the sanctum and saw a modest, bespectacled man, rather like a clerk in his neat navy trousers and white shirt, with a briefcase in his hand. He was not a brahmin, so he was not allowed into the shrine. I learned later that he was an *oduvar*, 'one who sings', a member of an ancient line of temple chanters. His songs of devotion to Shiva, in Tamil not the brahmin Sanskrit, have been passed down from father to son for centuries, since the days before the foundation of the present Chola temple.

Shiva was revealed to us, as he is revealed twice every day to his worshippers. But what was not revealed, and is never revealed to the profane, is the 'Chidambaram secret'. Behind the statue of Shiva Nataraja is a curtain decorated with gold bilva leaves. It conceals the source of the temple's sacred power – an empty space. It is the very spot on which Shiva performed his Tandava, his cosmic dance of creation and dissolution. It is therefore the centre of the universe. And it is a reminder to Hindus that God is nowhere and everywhere.

At the end of the two-hour ritual, I walked out of the great east gate into the night, past the brightly lit temple stalls full of trinkets and plastic toys, through the courtyard of a Vishnu temple where pop music seemed to be playing, then over the canal by the thatched huts of the poor to the Hotel Tamil Nadu.

Dinner there was a gloomy affair. The dining room was a hall the size of a football field, with linoleum flooring, fluorescent lights (half of which were off) and brown formica-topped tables. Apart from Katherine and myself, the only other customers in this vast, echoing expanse were a party of nineteen senior schoolgirls with their teacher. Being used to girls of this age, we expected giggling, squealing and ani-mated chat, but they sat in absolute silence. Their teacher seemed to be asleep, until the food appeared, when she opened her eyes to tuck into it. Not a word was uttered over dinner, and they all trooped out as silently as they had eaten. We polished off our indifferent *thali*, washing it down with a couple of bottles of Kingfisher. Like the rest of the hotel, the dining room was overmanned with lethargic staff, typical of Indian state-owned hotels. They talked among themselves and seemed to resent any attempt to catch their eye. Our room was serviced, if we demanded it, by an old man who kept offering to bring us beer at all sorts of inappropriate hours. There was a potentially pleasant garden, with cattle-grids to keep out vagrant cows. But goats could jump over the wall and often did. One day, I watched in fascination from the rooftop verandah, as a black and white kid stripped every single green shoot from a carefully pruned and watered bush, while the gardener rested idly in the shade of a tree. It was presumably the job of his caste to garden, not to chase off marauding animals, even if they were destroying all the plants which he himself had so lovingly tended. Much as I love India, there are times when I despair of it!

As there was nothing else to do in Chidambaram, we dodged the rain to make some daylight visits to the temple. I always prefer to go round interesting sites quietly on my own with my guidebook, at least the first time, but in many countries that's an impossible luxury. Guides and pseudo-guides are a menace and it's often better to pay one mosquito, rather than to spend all day beating off clouds of them. Since Michael Wood made a television programme there, the mosquitos get very excited when they see Westerners. They all claim to have been in the programme and to be able to introduce you to the *dikshitars* featured in it. Even at a banana stall far from the temple, there was the same cry: 'Come with me, madam. You meet Rajah. I know Rajah. Friend of Michael Wood. I know where he lives. Very learned scholar, madam. On BBC television.'

My chosen guide was a short, slight young man with a baby in his arms, followed at a respectful distance by his wife and two other children. He was trying to earn some extra money in the temple, because the thatched roof of his house had been destroyed in the monsoon and he needed to get it reroofed. The five of them were living temporarily with friends, but the cottage was so small and cramped that the young man brought his family to the temple in the daytime, to get them all out from under their friends' feet. At least it was dry in the temple halls. He was not an official guide, but he knew the temple well and loved it, so he was able to tell us all sorts of traditional tales and point out many small things that we would never have noticed ourselves. For instance, he showed us a unique group of sculptures on one of the *gopuras*, the towering temple gates. They were statues of Ganesha, the elephant god, as a bridegroom with his bride, who was a beautiful girl, not an elephant, surrounded by their wedding guests. Now Ganesha is always celibate. In fact, he is the god of bachelors. So these sculptures are the only known representation of Ganesha's wedding in the whole of India. Of course, I have no way of checking this little nugget of information, so I hope my guide got it right. But even if he didn't, it's a charming idea about a delightful scene.

As Shiva is worshipped in the temple as Lord of the Dance, there are two sets of carvings of 108 classical dance positions. On the inside of the south *gopura*, Shiva's wife, Parvati, is shown dancing them all. Our guide related the story of a competition, to which Parvati challenged her husband. They were both fantastic dancers and for days and nights on end they executed such dazzling steps that there was nothing to choose between them. Then Shiva made such a bravura leap that one of his earrings went flying. Without pausing in the dance, he picked it up from the ground and clipped it on to his ear again with his toes. To perform this feat, he had to lift his leg right up until it was vertical. Modesty prevented Parvati, as a lady, from performing such an indecorous action, so Shiva was declared the winner of the competition. Another version claims that the carvings show Kali, who was competing with Shiva for the right to occupy the present temple site. She was defeated and now has her own temple nearby. As always in Hindu mythology, layer is piled upon layer, and version contradicts version. But does it matter?

By the time we had finished with Mamallapuram and Chidambaram, we were feeling 'templed out' and ready for some uncultural, unreligious cycling. There were eighteen temples and a monastery in our next town, Kumbakonam, but we didn't visit a single one of them! Unusually for me, I got diarrhoea and stayed in bed most of the first day, while Katherine arranged with the hotel manager to have our extremely muddy bicycles cleaned. I did make a token attempt to visit the Ramasvami temple, which was said to have Ramayana frescoes, but I got lost in the maze of the town centre; and when it started to bucket down with rain, I gratefully gave up the search. We did, however, hire a car the next afternoon for a drive into the country to see the magnificent Chola temples at Darasuram and Gangakon-dacholapuram. Chola art (tenth and eleventh centuries), with its tall, elegant, sinuous figures and long, narrow faces with pointed noses, is my favourite of all the Indian schools, and I was not disappointed. The Chola carvings, which covered every pillar and every niche, were exquisite. But both temples were dedicated to Shiva, who is not the god of *The Ramayana*, so I shall not describe them in detail. We were driven to the temples by a taxi wallah called Murugan, after Shiva's son, and the priests who took us round were quick to point out sculptures showing Vishnu paying homage to Shiva. The rivalry between the two deities is deeply felt in Tamil Nadu. I was very pleased with myself that afternoon, because I finally managed to memorise the name of the celebratory temple built by the Chola King Rajendra I – Gangakondacholapuram. Working backwards, it means 'the city (puram) of the Chola who conquered (conda) the Ganga', and refers to Rajendra's victories in the Ganges Valley and Bengal. Now the wealth of its sculpture is all that remains of its former glory. It stands alone and empty in the middle of fields, inhabited by goats and cats.

The manager of our Kumbakonam hotel was a chemistry graduate from Madras, who had worked in Saudi Arabia until he had saved enough money to build a house back in India. He was a nice, sad-faced man, who was very protective towards us. When we headed for the hotel bar, a gloomy place full of men, he was obviously uneasy and insisted on accompanying us. Over the Kingfishers and peanuts, he told us about his cousin, who was a doctor in general practice in England.

'My cousin is always ticking me off for lack of ambition. I haven't been to England yet to see him. I could never afford the fare. But he sometimes comes over here and he can't understand how I can go on living in India. He says it's a filthy place – and perhaps it is, by Western standards. But I'm all right. I earn 5,000 rupees a month (about £77 at the time) and I get my meals in the restaurant. In any case, I don't know what sort of a job I'd be able to find in England. I think I'm better off here, in "filthy" Kumbakonam.'

His kitchen boy had made a good job of cleaning and polishing our bikes, but they looked as bad as ever at the end of our muddy 38-kilometre ride to Thanjavur, or Tanjore, as the British used to call the capital of the Chola kings. We found clean rooms looking out over a lush garden, where the trees were thronged with argumentative minah birds. There was a real treat of a restaurant in the city's most expensive hotel and, miracle of miracles, a proper supermarket, our first since Madras! We went mad over the dried apricots, Nescafé and toilet rolls. Travel in India really makes you appreciate life's little luxuries, the everyday purchases which we take for granted at home.

We spent a happy morning wandering through the alleys and shady courtyards of Thanjavur Palace, a rambling, run-down complex within the city fort. The art gallery there was crammed with magnificent Chola bronzes, made using the *cire perdu* (lost wax) technique, of which the Cholas were masters. There was a notice at the entrance, welcoming visitors. The style was so wonderfully flowery that I copied down every word and comma. Here it is:

Welcome to the Art Gallery

These icons, which have, behind them, historical values, spiritual lore and cultural mores of this part of Indian heritage, are meaningfully mute with wordless expressiveness. They influence, however, the viewing personages like you to come out with instinctive processions of emotive articulations in their own way style. You are welcome to record your feelings.

May we have the benefit of your munificence for promoting our selfless commitment to preserve these icons?

E. Venkata Chalam, I.A.S.
Chairman, Art Gallery Society.

We had to visit Thanjavur temple, as it's reckoned to be the finest expression of Chola architecture and is a World Heritage monument. King Rajaraja's magnificent structure is all the more appealing to Western taste because its buildings have not been tricked out with gaudy paintwork. Its grey granite towers rise majestically into the sky, exquisite in their carving, but austere. The fourteen-storey *vimana*, the spire over the holy of holies, is topped with an 80-ton dome of solid granite and is the tallest temple spire in India – not a difficult feat to achieve in the south where, for some reason, the gate-towers usually dominate. Nandi the bull did less well though. Legend relates that his statue had magic powers, and kept growing and growing. When it swelled to such a size that it threatened to overwhelm the temple, a nail was driven into its back and that put a stop to its outrageous growth. As a result, the Thanjavur temple Nandi is only the second largest in India. There were beautiful statues in polished black basalt; and to make sure that we realised it was a Shiva temple, no fewer than 250 Shiva lingas encircled the main courtyard. But what struck me most were the Chola frescoes. They were discovered only recently under layers of white-wash, so they had retained their freshness and their quirky humour. I particularly liked the duck in jewels and a sari, saying her prayers.

The next day we cycled into the Chettinad, said to be full of deserted palaces, though we didn't see any. The merchant princes who had once made the region prosperous had mostly left and set up business elsewhere, though there were still a few tobacco plants and diamond-cutting workshops. We had seen very few tourists in the great temple cities, as it was the rainy season. Now, in the sparsely populated Chettinad, we were right off the tourist trail and saw absolutely none. It was scrubby, eroded country, with little cultivation. Only the goats prospered. They were beautiful creatures, with pale beige coats and deep chocolate markings.

The roads were peaceful. There were few cars, and those there were travelled quietly, as there were no lumbering ox-carts to incense the motorists and make them lean on their horns. There were granite-cutting workshops and we saw whole families, from grandma down to toddlers, sitting by the roadside shelling peanuts, or roasting them on charcoal braziers. And sometimes we cycled over sheets of peanuts in their shells, spread out on the asphalt to dry. The people fixed us with silent, curious stares, but didn't respond to our greetings. A pair of young men on a motorbike rode beside me for a good five kilometres, staring silently. Then they overtook me and drove ahead, swivelling their heads round to keep me in their sights as long as possible. Perhaps they had never seen a white face before, except on television. The only people who reacted noisily were gangs of school-boys, who often chased us. They mocked us, shouting, 'Naughty boys!' I said, 'silly boys', and they added that phrase to their repertoire. 'Silly boys, silly boys!' they screamed with delight. There was no way of escaping them. Our bikes were much better than theirs, and much better maintained, but they were fully laden and we were burdened with years. Even when we accelerated to 25 kilometres an hour, they somehow managed to keep up, with a terrible clanking of unoiled chains. We were only free of them when we cleared the villages. Then they would drop off one by one, turning up some wayside path to go home. They were harmless boys, with their little piles of dog-eared school books tied to their rear carriers. They obviously had English lessons and were terribly excited to find two real live English women cycling down their road. But 'What is your name? What is your country? Naughty boys!' becomes very tedious as conversational exchange.

Pudukottai, Karaikkundi, Devakottai Road, Ramanathapuram. It was marshy country, carefully irrigated, but the streams had swollen and the village tanks turned to lakes in the persistent rain. On one 60-kilometre stretch, we crossed 96 canal bridges. There were sections where the culverts simply couldn't cope and the water rushed over the highway. We cycled up to our chains in swirling floods, our pedalling feet dipping under the water alternately. Where the floods had destroyed the asphalt, it was all we could do to keep our balance and keep going. Had we put a foot to the ground to save ourselves, we should have been standing up to that knee in brown water and silt. The egrets and herons were happy, but the peacocks sat disconsolate in the shelter of the banyan trees, ruffling their wet feathers. It was so warm that we didn't bother to put on our waterproofs.

This was the region where I feared that we might find nowhere presentable to stay, but we were pleasantly surprised. There were gleaming new hotels in every little town, built by men who had made a fortune in Indian terms by working in the Gulf States and Saudi Arabia. As the hotels were new, everything still worked. We arrived dripping, but we could plug in our kettles for coffee and enjoy a really hot shower – the small luxuries which make a day's cycling in the monsoon seem worth the discomfort. Deluge followed deluge. We reached Ramanathapuram (known to the locals as

Ramnad) between downpours and saw a small tank fringed with palm trees from our window. Within minutes it was totally obscured, hidden behind the next curtain of rain. It was so wet that even the little frogs were sheltering in the hotel vestibule!

It was difficult to imagine, at the height of the monsoon, that the Chettinad was arid, drought-stricken country for most of the year. The people there rely on an ancient and highly sophisticated system of tanks to store the annual rainfall. In Ramnad, speculators had filled up many of the old tanks to provide more profitable building land in the centre of the town. Unfortunately, the rainwater still drained into what used to be tanks, so that the shops and houses along the main street were awash. We got used to shopping in bare feet, as the locals did, with our trousers rolled up to our knees. We waded along with the shoppers, cows and goats. Cycles and rickshaws wove in and out around us, and the cacophony of horns was even angrier than usual, as motors stalled in the flood waters and caused traffic jams. We thought we might be marooned in Ramnad till the end of the rains, but the traffic policeman assured us that the floods were very local, just in the town centre. The highway was clear. So we waited for a lull in the morning torrents, then ventured forth on our last lap to the holy island of Rameshwaram.

The policeman was right. As soon as we cleared the town, we were on dry, well surfaced highway. We were heading east now, into the sun and a strong wind which blew even more forcibly against us once we were out of the shelter of houses and palm groves. The road ran along a sandy spit, which narrowed as we neared Matapan. A large fleet of fishing boats lay at anchor to the south, and we could smell the Mandapam fish-processing plant long before we saw it. Then we began the steady pull up to the crown of the splendid new Indira Gandhi Bridge, which joins the mainland spit to the island. Over two kilometres long, it runs beside the older railway bridge, where men dangled on ropes removing barnacles from the piers. Busloads of pilgrims sped past us in both directions, many of them black-clad Ayappans. Those who were leaving Rameshwaram had already taken their ritual bathe in the sea and been doused at the temple wells, so they had hung their wet clothes out of the bus windows to dry. They all gave us cheery waves. The afternoon heated up and we realised that the island was much bigger than it looked on the map. It was a toilsome ride, through scrubby thorn bushes which offered little shade, but we had our reward as evening fell. The road climbed to the top of the island's highest hill and we saw the town of Rameshwaram spread out before us, its mighty temple towers silhouetted against the darkening sky and the sea. After two weeks on the road, we had reached our destination. We freewheeled down to the seashore, checked into the beachside Hotel Tamil Nadu and prepared for our next meeting with Rama, Hanuman and their army of monkeys and bears.

## ∞ ∞

### Across the Bridge to Lanka

*At first, Rama was downhearted when he heard Hanuman's description of Ravana's kingdom. Although that mighty monkey had been able to destroy Ravana's citadel, the Kingdom of Lanka still seemed impregnable. Defended by millions of demons, it perched high on rocky pinnacles rising sheer from the sea. There was no anchorage for ships and the waters were infested with sharks and crocodiles. But King Sugriva took Rama to task for despairing like an ordinary man. His army of monkeys and bears was so valiant, and he himself so full of confidence, that Rama had only to get them across the sea and they would crush Ravana and his Rakshasas with the greatest of ease.*

*The planets were in the most favourable conjunction and Rama's right eyelid was twitching, which was always a good omen, so the army set out from Kishkindha that very day. Rama rode on Hanuman's shoulders and Lakshmana on Prince Angada's. They marched towards the sea in high spirits, the monkeys leaping and turning somersaults in their excitement. Under Rama's command, they skirted the cities and highways, marching through flowering forests where they could feast on fruit and honey. There were so many monkeys and bears that* when they reached the ocean and camped beside it, they were 'resplendent as a second ocean, whose waves were yellow as honey'. But they looked at the turbulent waves and their hearts sank.

At this juncture, Rama had a piece of good fortune. Ravana had a younger brother, Vibhisana, a wise and virtuous demon. It was he who had persuaded Ravana to spare the life of the captured Hanuman. Now, he tried to convince Ravana that he had acted unjustly in abducting Sita and should return her to Rama without delay, thus avoiding a war which was bound to end in defeat. But Ravana was surrounded by toadies and boastful generals, who assured him that Rama and his monkey army would stand no chance at all in battle against the might of the Rakshasas. Long arguments ensued, but Ravana was proud and unrepentant, so Vibhisana stormed out of the royal presence and flew away from Lanka.

When he and his four attendants appeared in the sky above Rama's camp, fully armed and covered in celestial jewels, the monkeys were terrified. They were convinced that he had come to kill them, or at the very least to spy on the disposition of their troops. Only Hanuman advised Rama to give him an audience. Vibhisana was delighted to be summoned. He flew down and fell at Rama's feet, begging for protection against his vengeful brother and promising to help in the destruction of Ravana's kingdom. He spoke with such wisdom and sincerity that Rama embraced him and anointed him King of Lanka.

Vibhisana advised Rama to seek the assistance of Varuna, the God of the Oceans; only with his help could the monkey army cross over to Lanka. Rama prayed to Varuna, asking him to clear a passage through the waves for his army. He sat on the seashore for three days and nights, waiting for Varuna to appear. When his patience ran out, he threatened to dry up the ocean with one of his divine arrows, but Lakshmana, for once less impetuous than his brother, dissuaded him. Then Varuna rose from his waves. Emerald in hue and decked with pearls, he appeared in a circle of clouds and winds, attended by the Rivers Ganges and Indus. The God of the Oceans explained that he could not give up his nature, even for Rama. But though he could not solidify his waters, he was prepared to allow a bridge to be built over them. He promised to calm his waves and quell his sharks and crocodiles.

Rama summoned Nala, the son of Vishwakarma, the Divine Architect of the Universe. He was a gifted monkey, created in heaven with the other animal leaders to assist Rama. With the architectural skills he had inherited from his father, he set to work designing a remarkable bridge, ten leagues in width and over a hundred leagues long. All the monkeys and bears were eager to help. They rushed into the forest in their hundreds of thousands, tearing up trees by the roots and rolling gigantic boulders down to the shore. They piled them into the waters and, little by little, the splendid causeway crept out into the ocean. In five days it was finished, and it was such a miraculous sight that even the gods in heaven gazed down on it in wonder.

Then the mighty army began its crossing. Rama climbed on to Hanuman's shoulders and Lakshmana on to Prince Angada's. King Sugriva and King Vibhisana marched beside them, but the monkeys were too excited to keep to their ranks. Some dived into the water, some sprang into the sky , flying through space like birds, while the hordes who scampered across the bridge made a noise like thunder, drowning the roar of the sea. When they were all safely across Nala's bridge, Rama found them a sheltered camping ground, abounding in fruit and fresh water. And the gods came down secretly from heaven and anointed Rama with sea water, promising him victory and eternal dominion over earth, sky and water.

### How the Chipmunk got his Stripes
This charming story does not appear in Valmiki, but it is told in one of the official guides to Rameshwaram.

While the monkeys and bears were piling up logs and boulders to build Nala's bridge, Rama sat on the beach watching a chipmunk. The little creature was helping in the construction work. First he dived into the sea to get his fur wet, then he rolled in the sand, ran up on to the bridge and shook himself. The sand fell from his fur into the cracks between the boulders and cemented them together. Rama was touched by his devotion, so he picked him up and stroked him. Where his three fingers travelled down the chipmunk's spine, three dark stripes appeared, which all chipmunks carry to this day as a sign of Rama's blessing.

# 12 Rameshwaram to Sri Lanka

*Rameshwaram – Ramnad – Manumadurai – Madurai – Trivandrum*

F ROM THE MAP OF SOUTH INDIA, it looks as if it might be possible to walk across from the mainland to Sri Lanka. First, the Indira Gandhi Bridge crosses the Pamban Channel to Pamban Island with its great pilgrimage temple at Rameshwaram. From Rameshwaram town, another 22 kilometres of ever narrowing sandy spit leads to Dhanushkodi at the island's eastern tip. From there, a chain of reefs dots the shallows across to Talaimannar on the western tip of Sri Lanka's Mannar Island. Now called Adam's Bridge, these rocky outcrops are said to be the remains of Nala's bridge in *The Ramayana*, even though their span of some 30 kilometres falls far short of the miraculous 100 leagues (480 kilometres) bridged by the monkeys and bears. A regular ferry used to operate between Rameshwaram and Talaimannar, but it has been out of service now for many years, since the beginning of the bitter civil war between the Tamils and the ruling Sinhalese in Sri Lanka. The Jaffna Peninsula is one of the Tamil Tigers' strongholds.

There were many Ramayana sites to be visited in Rameshwaram, but the tall *gopuras* of the Ramanathaswami Temple dominated the little seaside town and drew us there with the crowds of morning visitors. The temple is one of the most important pilgrim destinations in the whole of India. Although not strictly at the southernmost tip of the subcontinent, it is counted as one of the four temples at the cardinal points, which should be visited at some time in their lives by all good Hindus. (The other three are Haridwar in the north,

Dwarka in the west and Puri in the east.) Then, according to popular tradition, Rameshwaram is the place where Rama set up three Shiva lingas, one built of sand by Sita and two brought by Hanuman from Mount Kailash, Shiva's Himalayan abode. Rama needed to worship Shiva at the end of the war against the Rakshasas to expiate his guilt, because he had killed Ravana in battle and Ravana was a brahmin. So Rameshwaram is associated with both Rama and Shiva, and consequently draws both Vaishnavas and Shaivas on pilgrimage.

Architecturally, the Ramanathaswami Temple is famous for its magnificent *mandapas*, the lofty perimeter corridors which are so long that they melt into the distant gloom. Each of the hundreds of elaborately sculpted granite pillars is identical, its scrollwork and lotus motifs crowned with a capital in the shape of a prancing horse's head. Unlike the rounded columns of classical Greece, those in India are rectangular, with sharp angles and deeply recessed sections. They present a strange, jagged perspective, so that entering a corridor is like walking into a vastly elongated dodecahedron. It seems to be a fairground trick with mirrors, hallucinatory, except for the temple elephant, who is a very real object, munching her sugar cane in the shadows.

The first shrine inside the east gate is dedicated to a bright vermilion Hanuman. Unusually, as he is not one of Shiva's group of gods, he stands behind a linga. When he flew to Mount Kailash to bring Rama two Shiva lingas, he took rather a long time over it. The most favourable conjunction of the stars for the worship of Shiva was in danger of passing, so Rama had to go ahead and atone for his brahminicide at a sand linga made by Sita. Hanuman was desperately disappointed. To console him, Rama gave him one of the Mount Kailash lingas and decreed that all devotees should worship it first. They still do to this day.

Visiting the Ramanathaswami Temple is real family fun. There are 22 sacred wells within the complex and worshippers pay two rupees each to be doused with holy water from all 22 of them. A merry time is had by all. Groups of pilgrims first take a ritual, purificatory bathe in the sea, then they enter the temple and process from one well to the next with dripping hair, saris and dhotis. They laugh and splash one another, and the temple floors are awash. English cathedrals were never so jolly.

The first time I visited the temple, I was welcomed inside and invited to join a group of black-clad Ayappan pilgrims doing the round of the wells. I got a thorough soaking, as did they, and we all took funny photos of one another. When I went there with Katherine, a more punctilious guard was on duty, who barred our entry because we were not Hindus. He would allow us no further inside than the perimeter *mandapas*. But there is usually a way round these difficulties. A boy came along whistling and swinging a bucket. He was one of the well attendants who draw the water for the dousings. He offered to take us round the wells for 50 rupees each – rather more than the Hindus' 2 rupees, but it was worth it. He put red tilak marks on our foreheads and marched us brazenly past the duty brahmins. Then he teamed us up with a family to begin the circuit. Grandparents, parents and toddlers were all keen on a total drowning, but the bucket-boy told us that a splash on the head was equally beneficial, so we just got our hair wet. We noticed that some extremely elegant Indians were also avoiding the dousing. They simply held out their hands at each well and received a spoonful of holy water, which they dropped on to their heads. By the end of the morning, there were laughing, dripping pilgrims everywhere. They completed their round of the wells, then went into the sanctum to make offerings to the Shiva linga. We managed to avoid that. Having paid 50 rupees for our tour of the wells, we were in no mood to pay the even greater sum which would no doubt be required of non-Hindus for *puja*. Instead, we went to the bazaar and bought two bottlebrushes to clean the mud off our bicycle chains and stocked up on breakfast buns and snacks.

We hired a lethargic young guide named Cannon to take us round the other Ramayana sites. He was Cannon by name, but far from a cannon by nature! He told us that it was impossible to get to Dhanushkodi on our bicycles. A tornado in 1964 had washed away the road and torn down the villages on the peninsula, leaving nothing but sand dunes and a few gaping ruins. To reach the eastern tip, where the monkeys had started building their bridge, we must take a motorcycle-rickshaw to the last remaining fishing village, then hire a jeep to cross the sands.

We rode through the flooded outskirts of Rameshwaram, then along a straight asphalt road which used to be a railway line. The fishing village was a poverty-stricken hole, with low thatched hovels, an unappetising tea-hut and a cart selling coconuts. We hung around there for over an hour, while Cannon drank tea and chatted in the hut. There was no sign of a jeep to take us to the point and Cannon made no effort to enquire about one. We ourselves were helpless, because none of the fisherfolk could understand us. When the sky blackened with storm clouds, we insisted on leaving. We had seen that a bus serviced the village and we thought we could do better on our own, without Cannon, on a sunnier day.

On the way back into Rameshwaram, we stopped at a small temple along a causeway, built on the very spot where Vibhisana, Ravana's younger brother, had joined forces with Rama. It was now raining in torrents and the streets were virtually impassable. A lorry had stalled in a deep pool and six men were struggling to push a cart round it. It was piled to a staggering height with dining chairs, insecurely roped, so that every lurch through the mud threatened to send them all toppling. When we finally got through the traffic jam and the raging cacophony of horns, we took our rickshaw up to a small temple on the highest point of the island. Here Rama had stood and looked out across the waters to Sri Lanka. The holy of holies contained nothing but a pair of footprints, simply garlanded, with a smiling brahmin in charge, who actually looked pleased with the 20 rupees we gave him for *puja*. Usually, they scowl and look offended, in the hope of shaming foreigners into even larger donations.

We had hoped to make another attempt at Dhanushkodi without Cannon, but he looked so crestfallen when we dismissed him at our hotel entrance that we took pity on him and hired him again for the next day. It dawned sunny, but we still insisted on going to the fishing village under proper cover inside the bus. One windy, rainy afternoon in an open-sided rickshaw was quite enough. We'd been chilled to the bone and knew from our shivers that we were on the verge of nasty colds.

On the way to the fishing village, we had a most interesting encounter. The bus stopped at a primitive wayside shack and out stepped four immaculate people, looking as well groomed as film stars. How do they manage it when they live in such basic conditions? The young couple were extremely elegant, he in an orange Lacoste polo shirt and beige trousers with knife-edge creases and she in a beautiful lilac sari. They came from Sri Lanka and both spoke competent English. They introduced the young man's Sri Lankan mother and Indian father, whom they were visiting for a few days. What interested me most was that they had come over from Sri Lanka in a fishing boat. Since the ferry service had been suspended, that was evidently the way the locals went back and forth. I brightened up immediately I heard this.

'How can I get a place in one of those boats?' I asked. 'I'm planning to visit Sri Lanka and I've been told that the only way I can get across there from south India is by flying from Trivandrum to Colombo. But that obviously isn't the case.'

I already had my flight ticket, but I would have been quite happy to sacrifice the fare if I could actually cross over beside Adam's Bridge and land in Sri Lanka with Rama. The young man was discouraging.

'That crossing's all right for us,' he said, 'because we know all the local people. But it wouldn't do for you. It's too dangerous. You see, there's gun-running for the Tamil Tigers between Rameshwaram and Jaffna. We have to cross secretly at night, because the Indian Navy patrols the strait and if we're caught, we're arrested and sometimes jailed, whether we're carrying guns or not. A few people have even been shot on sight. You could cause a diplomatic incident!'

I thought it over. I was sorely tempted to persevere and try to bribe my way to an illegal crossing, but I decided in the end that discretion was the greater part of valour. Having been arrested the previous year by the Chinese police, I had no wish to repeat that kind of experience in India. I would take the sensible course.

The bus rumbled into the fishing village, where we struck lucky. We were just drinking a coconut milk at the cart by the terminus, when a four-wheel-drive truck arrived, full of cheerful pilgrims from Karnataka, who were on their way to perform *puja* in the sea at Dhanushkodi. They hauled the two of us up into their truck and we sped off down the remaining strip of asphalt, leaving Cannon behind; he preferred to linger over his tea and cigarettes in the hut. Once the road finished, we careered wildly over the dunes, swerving in and out of the ruined buildings to avoid quicksands. The faster we went, the less likely we were to get stuck. We were hurled from one side of the truck to the other, but amazingly no one was hurled out, thanks to the ropes we could all hang on to.

When Rama worshipped Shiva at the sand linga built by Sita, the great god himself appeared with his consort in the sky overhead. He pardoned Rama for killing the brahmin Ravana, and pronounced that anyone who bathed at Dhanushkodi would be freed from all their sins. So when we reached the end of the peninsula, everyone jumped out of the truck and rushed into the sea with shouts of joy. The pilgrims had their own brahmin travelling with them. He began his Sanskrit chants and we all crouched down in the shallows to pour the holy seawater over our heads. Despite the presence of the priest, there was much laughing and splashing. Hinduism can be such a jolly religion. The pilgrims' journey may be arduous, but once they reach their destination, little is demanded of them. Brahmins have to go through the rituals, but for the other castes it's sufficient to have arrived. Many pray fervently, but just as many don't. They enjoy being together in a sacred place and receiving *darshan*, if there's an idol to bestow it. It's a pleasant outing with a holy purpose, and if it frees the pilgrim from sin, that's a real bonus.

We paddled throughout the ceremony, then careered back to the village, suitably shriven. We celebrated our sinlessness with a lunch of freshly caught fish. I've no idea what they were, but they were served up straight from the frying pan on to a banana leaf and were absolutely delicious.

There was one Ramayana site left, the Villundi Tirtham, halfway along the spit between Rameshwaram and

Mandapam. When Rama brought Sita back from Sri Lanka to the mainland, she was thirsty after her journey. So Rama struck the seabed with his staff and a freshwater well sprang up in the middle of the waves. Whether the well has divine origins or not, it is certainly an amazing phenomenon. We walked along a rickety pier, far out over the sea, and came to a well, where the water was indeed fresh. Just as we were testing it, the heavens opened and we got another soaking.

That evening our colds matured. In other circumstances, we would have stayed where we were and nursed them. But our hotel, Rameshwaram's best, was depressing in the extreme. It stood in a superb situation on the seashore and we had a balcony overlooking the sea. Under other management, it could have been a delight. But it was the usual lackadaisical state-run affair. Our bedroom walls were filthy, the fan came down through a gaping hole in the ceiling and the air-conditioning apparatus had been fitted into the wall with grey cement which had been left unpainted. We had a television and a choice of four chairs and a stool to sit on, but the lighting was too dim for reading. If we went out into the relative brightness of our balcony, there were so many flies that we had to cocoon ourselves in our mosquito nets. Another day there was out of the question, so we struggled back the next morning to our smart new hotel in Ramnad.

The town turned out to be totally devoid of paper handkerchiefs, tissues or toilet rolls. When our own supplies from England had run out, we were reduced to packs of 'Fancy Table Napkins', which were non-absorbent and very hard on the nose. But we ate extremely well. Every evening, pavement stalls sprang up opposite the hotel. A man cooked delicious onion omelettes on a sheet of tin over an old tar barrel, while a woman and her daughter crouched on the muddy pavement cooking samosas, bhajis and chick-pea patties over a paraffin stove. Their beautiful clean saris dragged in the dirt, but their gold bangles glittered cheerfully in the firelight and they did an excellent trade. The food may have been cooked in the street, but it was sold straight from the sizzling fat, so it was perfectly safe to eat. One of us shopped for the food, while the other went to the nearest

English Wines Store for bottles of Kingfisher. The other customers always stood politely aside when the memsahibs arrived and insisted that we go to the front of the queue; and the cooks, who looked a bit worried the first time we bought their food, beamed with delight when we went back for more. We feasted every night in our hotel room. The omelettes cost us all of two rupees each and the samosas, bhajis and patties one rupee. Our beer was the expensive item, at 45 rupees a bottle. Government policy deliberately taxes factory-produced alcohol beyond the means of working men, with the result that they turn to dubious bootleg liquor, sometimes with fatal consequences.

Our colds eventually disappeared, as colds do, and we were eager to be off on our bicycles again. We still had a long way to go. When Rama crossed over to Sri Lanka, he took the direct route across the Palk Strait from Rameshwaram to the Jaffna Peninsula, a journey of about 30 kilometres. We were not so lucky. We had to travel right across the south of the subcontinent, from the Bay of Bengal to Trivandrum on the Arabian Sea, a journey of some 450 kilometres. From there, I had a flight booked to Colombo, to begin my tour of Ravana's kingdom, while Katherine planned to return home.

On the first day of our convalescence, we took it easy. We cruised in fine weather along an idyllic country road, where the grass verges were a brilliant green after the rain and huge trees offered their shade. We passed contented livestock and children bathing in village tanks, while the women washed their brilliant saris and spread them out over bushes to dry. From time to time, the smooth asphalt would break up into a sea of mud, water and stones, where pigs, dogs, cows and crows were scavenging on refuse tips. We had entered a small town. Ten minutes later, we had fought our way through the crowds and the suffocating diesel fumes, and were back in rural tranquillity. We covered only the 37 kilometres to Paramakudi and checked into the Krishna Lodge overlooking the bus station. Buses revved up their engines and gears screeched through the afternoon and night, but it was the best we could do.

There was one important Ramayana site between there and Madurai – the Perumal Temple of Hanuman in

Manumadurai. It was small but important, as it had a most unusual idol of Hanuman in a royal crown. We spent a long time, and drank many cups of tea and coffee over enquiries at roadside stalls, before we eventually tracked down the temple in the maze of Manumadurai's narrow streets. It turned out to be a modest rectangular platform with pillars and a roof, leading to a black stone shrine. When we arrived, a purple silk curtain with gold lettering was drawn across the sanctum and a handbell was ringing behind it. Then the curtain was drawn aside and the saffron-clad priest emerged carrying holy vessels. At first, I saw only Rama, Sita and Lakshmana but, as my eyes became accustomed to the darkness inside, I realised that there was a huge black Hanuman towering over them. The glint of gold, which was obviously his crown, was almost invisible in the gloom. A woman came out of a nearby house and we took *darshan* together, but I fled before the priest could offer me the tilak on my forehead in exchange for yet another large donation.

We bought bananas for our lunch and ate them under the trees beside the Vagai river. We had perfect cycling until we reached the outskirts of the great pilgrim city of Madurai, which is also a major industrial centre of well over a million people. This time, we were not contending with rain and mud, but heat, dust and frantic drivers. It was an exhausting end to a long day's ride, but we knew that comfort awaited. We checked into the excellent Park Plaza Hotel, where both our room and the rooftop restaurant offered magnificent views of the floodlit Sri Minakshi Temple, and we had good hot water, bedside lamps, armchairs and a daily complimentary basket of fruit. We celebrated at dinner time with a whole tandoori chicken between us, as well as an egg biryani – more protein in one meal than we'd managed to find in four weeks of travel across vegetarian Tamil Nadu. After all those nights in depressing state-run hotels and bus station lodges, we were back in Western tourist land, and it was paradise.

Madurai can boast eight millennia of history. A leading centre of Tamil culture, its merchants traded internationally and were well known to the Greeks. The present city owes its shape to the Nayakas (sixteenth to eighteenth centuries), who laid out its streets in the form of a lotus flower with the temple of Sri Minakshi at its heart. It is they who were responsible too for the outrageously baroque temple gateways. These hectically coloured *gopuras* are packed from top to bottom with statues of gods, demons, animals and monsters, to form a gigantic compendium of Hindu mythology. To Western eyes, they are quite overwhelmingly tasteless, more suited to the portals of Disneyland than to a serious place of worship. After seeing the restrained grey granite of the Chola Kings in the temples of Thanjavur and Gangakondacholapuram, I couldn't really take to these monstrous multi-coloured extravaganzas. But the Indians could. They flocked into the temple at an estimated rate of 10,000 a day, seething round the shrines to watch the nightly ceremony of the idol of Shiva being transported to Minakshi's bedroom and the morning ceremony of his transport back to his own sanctum. The temple is a shrine, museum and market, all rolled into one. And it's a great place for tailors. They pursue tourists to the gates, offering to measure them up for a suit and have it ready by the end of their temple tour. They even advertise within the temple: Kali A Grade Tailors has a large hoarding of the black goddess, tongue protruding, hatchet in one hand, decapitated head in another, to promote their expertise!

We were now in mid-December and we had lost a number of days' cycling through monsoon floods and bad colds. With only two days left before Katherine's flight to London, and three before mine to Sri Lanka, we had to take the night train over the Cardamom Hills to Thiruvananthapuram (the city of the divine snake Ananta, on whose coils Vishnu reclines in the main temple) – or Trivandrum, to give it its more manageable name.

I know Trivandrum well. The capital of Kerala State, it's as easy-going as the Keralans themselves, and very unpretentious. There are no great highways or grand buildings – just winding lanes, where pleasant whitewashed houses are half-submerged in exuberant tropical plants. I wanted to give Katherine some idea of the region, so we took a one-day tour to Kovalam Beach, to the old palace of the Rajas of

Travancore at Padmanabhapuram and the meeting place of the three oceans at Kanniyakumari. It was Diwali, the festival of lights, when dozens of small oil lamps are lit both inside and outside every home and business in honour of Lakshmi and also, by popular tradition, to guide Rama and Sita back home to Ayodhya after the defeat of Ravana. We were lucky to be travelling by bus that evening. Every little village from Kanniyakumari to Trivandrum was a sparkling fairyland, where Lakshmi's oil lamps mingled ecumenically with Christmas decorations. The combination of the two was delightful, and heartening in its ready acceptance of both faiths. There are many Christians in south India and they mingle easily with the Hindu majority. Each community joins in the other's festivals and consequently enjoys twice as many holidays as the purists.

I was not taking my bicycle to Sri Lanka. My friend Heather, who has often gone cycling with me in the past, was joining me in Colombo for Christmas, but without her bicycle; and my Sinhalese friend, Rani, who lives in Kandy and is quite definitely a non-cyclist, had offered to take me to all the Sri Lankan Ramayana sites. Poor Condor would obviously be a hindrance there, so I had to find a temporary home for him in Trivandrum. To my surprise, the hotel was unwilling to take responsibility, even though there were watchmen on duty both day and night. I was at a loss until I thought of the railway station, where there was a huge cycle park. I found that it operated only on a daily basis, but the guard referred me to the longer-term park for cars and motorcycles behind a barbed wire fence. I enquired there, without success. It was a park for cars and motorbikes only. 'Cykels' were not allowed. I went away despondent. Then I had another idea. I went back and offered to pay the motorcycle rate.

'If the manager checks,' I said cunningly, 'my cykel will appear in your books as a motorcykel, so he won't know.'

The boy on duty was amazed. 'But it will cost you one rupee a day. *And* you will have to pay a deposit!'

'How much is the deposit?'

'Two rupees, paid in advance.'

I went and fetched Condor from the hotel and an extremely satisfactory place was found for him, hidden away under cover in the depths of a shed and locked up with my own cycle-lock and Katherine's for good measure. I paid my princely deposit of two rupees, got a numbered receipt for my 'motorcykel' and went off, highly satisfied with my afternoon's work, to catch up on the English newspapers in the British Library.

The hotel did agree to take charge of my cycling gear, though it took them so long to produce my room bill, find change, calculate the storage charge, find change for that, and issue the two receipts, that I began to fear for my flight. But my motorcycle-rickshaw rushed me to Trivandrum's tiny airport just in time for me to complete the stringent security checks and I boarded the Indian Airlines plane for the 50-minute flight to Colombo.

# 13 Christmas in Colombo

WHEN I LANDED at Bandaranaike International Airport, I couldn't believe that I was in the same subcontinent. The terminal processes millions of tourists, unlike sleepy Trivandrum, and is well organised to deal with them. I was struck by its cleanliness and good order, which put every airport in India to shame. There was even an efficient accommodation bureau, where I chose a hotel, negotiated a discount and booked a car to get me there, all in the space of fifteen minutes.

Heather and I were booked into the Mount Lavinia Hotel for the Christmas period, starting on 19 December, but I arrived in Colombo on the 15th and she was due to fly in two days later. So I had to find an interim hotel which was not too far from the airport. Downtown Colombo was 30 kilometres away and, according to my guidebooks, was a noisy, grubby place with few tourist attractions. It was dangerous too, as it was a target for the Tamil Tigers. It seemed a better and altogether safer idea to stay in Negumbo, a well-known seaside resort to the north of Colombo, only 8 kilometres from the airport.

Here the disappointment began. I had expected so much of Sri Lanka. Friends had given me enthusiastic accounts of their holidays on the island, and my own first impressions at the airport had been excellent. My hotel was clean and well appointed. I had a comfortable, air conditioned room with its own little slice of verandah, from which I could see the cannas round the manicured lawn, and the swimming pool beside the beach. It was not the Ritz, but I was not paying Ritz prices and I thought it was value for money. So far, so good. But when I went down to the smart restaurant for my dinner, I found that the fare was nothing but bland 'international cuisine', cooked specially for the Christmas package trade. That first night, after five weeks of unmitigated curry, I was quite happy to tuck into insipid boeuf stroganoff with garlic spaghetti. But the ghastly breakfast of stewed coffee, artificial pineapple juice (in the tropics!), tosbutterjam and a soggy omelette sent me out into the town to investigate the alternatives.

Modern Negumbo is a string of hotels facing the narrow, rather scruffy beach. Behind them all runs Lewis Place, with its pancake houses, Chinese and German restaurants and shops selling snorkels and postcards. By the time Heather arrived, I had discovered a breakfast café which made wonderful pancakes, but had failed in my search for a really good restaurant for dinner. Negumbo had abandoned Sinhalese food for foreign fare, which it cooked badly. I was to find the same sad state of affairs almost everywhere in Sri Lanka.

I walked into Negumbo Town to do some shopping, as I could see that Lewis Place would provide nothing useful. I bought bananas and tangerines in the oper-air market, finding them poorer in quality, yet more expensive, than those I was used to in south India. But there was a supermarket of sorts and it was there that I found my greatest treasure – a round box of processed cheese portions! At home, I wouldn't touch Kraft Velveeta, but the wealth of cheeses we enjoy in England is one of the things I miss most on my travels. A picnic lunch of Velveeta with freshly baked rolls was an enormous treat.

Away from the beach resort, I was surprised to find that Negumbo was a typical subcontinental dump, where animals scavenged in the refuse. I had somehow expected better. There was a network of Dutch canals, a Dutch fort and some fine Dutch gabled houses, relics of the days when the town was the centre of the Dutch cinammon trade. But the canals were foetid, as canals everywhere tend to be, and the grand buildings were ill-maintained. As I was exploring them, the sky grew black and the heavens opened. In Trivandrum, on the west side of India, the monsoon had already passed and the weather was dry and sunny again. But Sri Lanka lies off the eastern coast, so I was back in the retreating monsoon, which had soaked Katherine and me almost every day from Madras. I had to take refuge in a rickshaw, and by the time I reached my hotel, Lewis Place was ankle-deep in water and it was paddling time again.

In Negumbo, I had my first taste of Sri Lankan begging, which is quite different from begging in India and Pakistan. There, beggars are ragged. They pursue you with out-stretched hands and cries of 'Ma, ma'. Begging is a profession, like any other, and beggars are instantly recognisable. People like guides and rickshaw wallahs, who perform a service for you, often come out with tales of woe in an effort to extort a bigger tip than you were thinking of giving, but that is 'baksheesh', which is quite distinct from alms. All the other people who engage you in conversation, people who are not in rags and are not performing personal services, do so because they are interested to talk to you, not because they are after your money. In India and Pakistan, you know exactly where you are and can talk to strangers with confidence. Sri Lanka was different. There were no beggars to be seen in the streets. Begging was a covert operation. Wherever I went, I was hounded and hassled by well-dressed people, who spoke good English and had proper jobs.

'My father is dead. We are a big family. My daughter is clever in school.' That was the nightwatchman at the hotel, who came creeping up to me as I lay out by the swimming pool after dinner, looking at the stars.

'I am collecting money for the rehabilitation unit at the hospital. The minimum donation is 100 rupees.' That was a smartly dressed young man, who pursued me in Lewis Place. He could give no proof of his charitable credentials and I was too suspicious to give him any money at all, let alone 100 rupees. He was one of many who accosted me in the street, walked along beside me uninvited and involved me in very tedious conversation ('What is your country, madam? How many children? What is your husband's profession?'), which

I was too polite to ignore, then told me they were teachers of the deaf, auxiliaries in hospitals, social workers or poor fishermen, and asked me for large sums of money. Every chance conversation with a Sri Lankan seemed to end in importunity, and I soon reached the stage where I suspected everyone of begging and avoided contact with the local people. This was a great shame, as travel is nothing but staring at buildings from a goldfish bowl if there is no human connection.

Heather arrived, as expected, and after two days together in Negumbo, we transferred by car to Mount Lavinia across the tense centre of Colombo. The Tamil Tigers had planted a bomb the previous year in the busiest part of the city, killing eighty people and injuring over a thousand. We were there over Christmas, 1997, when the people of Sri Lanka were preparing to celebrate fifty years of independence. Prince Charles was coming in February to participate in the ceremonies. It was the ideal time for the Tamil Tigers to assert their own claim to independence from the Sinhalese. They were threatening a bombing campaign both before and during the Prince's visit, when the world's media would give them maximum publicity. So public buildings were sandbagged that Christmas and the military presence in the city was strong. There were even khaki guards in trenches outside government offices. But Mount Lavinia was far enough south of the capital to be at peace. We checked into our beautiful beachside room in the Mount Lavinia Hotel, once the official residence of the British Governor of Ceylon, and prepared to enjoy nine days of luxury.

We booked cars to visit the famous ruins on the island, such as the ancient capital, Anuradhapura, with its sacred bo tree, more than 2000 years old. It was grown from a cutting taken from the very bo tree in Bihar's Bodhgaya, under which the Buddha achieved enlightenment, and was brought to Sri Lanka by Princess Sangamitta, a daughter of the Indian Buddhist Emperor Ashoka. At the same time, her brother, Prince Mahinda, introduced Buddhist teachings. That was in the third century BC, and the Sinhalese majority on the island has been Buddhist ever since. The bo tree in Anuradhapura has become a major pilgrim destination for Buddhists from all over the world, because the original bo tree in Bodhgaya died and had to be replaced. So the Anuradhapura bo tree is the only remaining living connection with the Buddha himself.

It is tempting for a history addict like myself to describe all the fascinating sites we visited. But Rama is a Hindu prince and this book is an account of his travels and an exploration of his place in Hindu life. The fortresses of Buddhist kings and the ruins of Buddhist monasteries, however imposing, are outside its scope.

There is just one point to make about Buddhism. It arose in northeast India, in the foothills of the Himalayas, where Gautama Siddartha was born in 563 BC. By the time of his death, eighty years later, he had thousands of followers and had established a rational offshoot of Hinduism, which was destined to become one of the world's most influential philosophical systems. Rama too was born in northeast India and *The Ramayana* is known, from internal evidence, to be a northeast Indian epic. According to some scholars, there is an ancient Buddhist legend of a pious Prince Rama, who embodied the Buddhist ideal of equanimity. Are the two Prince Ramas one and the same person? Both geography and chronology seem to point in that direction, as well as the virtuous character of Valmiki's Rama. Their inter-relationship becomes even more tangled when an attempt is made by the brahmins to reabsorb the Buddha into the Hindu mainstream by declaring him to be, like Rama, an incarnation of Vishnu. The argument spirals round in ever-decreasing circles to the point of Vishnu's conch.

Between excursions, Heather and I sat on our balcony and read, sometimes going for a walk along the hotel's private beach, where we couldn't be pestered. We once bathed in the sea, but the waves were so high and the undertow so fierce that I was sent flying, then dragged under for a few terrifying moments. The culprit wave forced so much sand into my middle ear along with the sea water, that I was partially deaf for weeks and had to have medical attention when I got home.

Apart from its lovely rooms, the Mount Lavinia Hotel was another disappointment. The staff were poorly trained and had no idea how to behave towards guests. Porters pushed ahead of us through doors, then let them slam in our faces; receptionists forgot messages; and the head waiter in their very expensive restaurant simply pointed to a table and was most put out when we insisted that he escort us there and seat us in the accepted manner. Add to that the indifferent quality of the food and we soon began to dine out, at a small restaurant called The Anglers, just round the corner from the hotel, where we got real Sri Lankan food, served by a pleasant young man whose wife and mother were in charge of the kitchen.

Although Sri Lanka profited from tourism, there seemed to be a surly resentment of Westerners, unlike anything I had met before in former Southeast Asian colonies. Under a succession of aggressive and economically inept political leaders, the people had been disappointed in their aspirations and had become discontented. Their problems were exacerbated in the 1950s, when Solomon Bandaranaike enacted the Sinhala Only law, which banned the use of English and Tamil in government offices, schools and universities. It was an own goal. English had been the national language, binding together Sinhalese, Tamils and Christians of Dutch, Portuguese and British descent. Many well-educated, professional Sri Lankans had only 'kitchen Sinhala' and were forced to emigrate to find work. So, while the law provided better job prospects for some Sinhala-speakers, it drained the country of English-speaking talent it could ill afford to lose. It also impoverished many Tamils, who had spoken Tamil at home and English at work. Now they were quite unable to find employment. Their protests led to violence and the rivalry between Sinhalese and Tamils, which had been contained under colonial rule, escalated into demands for a separate Tamil state and the emergence of the Liberation Tigers of Tamil Eelam (LTTE), or the Tamil Tigers for short.

My friend Rani was one of Bandaranaike's victims. As an English-speaking Burgher (the name given to all Christians of European descent, whether they are Dutch or not), she was suddenly without a job. She was a music teacher and it was impossible for her to teach Western classical music in

Sinhala. She was not fluent in the language and, in any case, Sinhala lacked the necessary vocabulary. So she was obliged to come to England to find work. I met her in an English boarding school, where she was giving piano lessons and teaching music theory, saving every penny she earned, so that she could eventually retire back to Kandy with sufficient funds for comfort.

Another case, which is even sadder, is the case of two medical specialists. After Heather left me, I had another interim period before I went to Kandy to stay with Rani. The Mount Lavinia Hotel was affordable for a week or so, when Heather and I were sharing expenses. But on my own, the cost of the room would have been way outside my travel budget, so I had to move. I found a pleasant enough beach hotel, which was run by a friendly couple as their semi-retirement project. They were English-speakers and they told me that their daughter had trained as a doctor at a London teaching hospital. She went on to become a specialist in neurology, married a cardiac specialist, and both now had appointments in the States, at a magnificent hospital in Dallas.

'Will they come home one day?' I asked. 'Sri Lanka could do with more doctors, and two such highly qualified specialists could do tremendously valuable work here.'

Her mother shook her head sadly. 'They'll never come back. We just have to accept that and try to save enough money for the airfares. That's partly why we run this hotel – so that we can earn enough to go out to Dallas and see them and the grandchildren from time to time. You see, if they came back, their British and American qualifications would not be accepted. They would have to take their medical degrees all over again, and they would have to write the exams in Sinhala, which they hardly know at all. Then, if and when they qualified, they would have to accept government postings, which could be anywhere on the island. They could even be sent to two different places, with no regard at all for the children. We need their skills here. I realise that. But can you blame them for not coming back?'

In the face of such severe anti-English legislation, the British High Commissioner was doing his best. He made a very clever speech over Christmas, in which he produced all the usual arguments for the use of English: that it was now the international language, the language of science and technology, the language of some of the world's finest literature, etc. But he staked a much more subtle claim for it too, well suited to the political climate of Sri Lanka. He told his audience that they should not think of English simply as the language of their old colonial masters. It could be regarded as the language of revolution. English was the language in which Senanayake, Gandhi, Nehru, Jinnah, Nyerere and Makarios had all negotiated their independence from Britain. And now it was their language of freedom, the language which made it possible for them to play their part, as free peoples, in the work of the United Nations.

The older Sri Lankans all spoke English with varying degrees of competence, but I felt sorry for the young people, who were being deprived by their politicians of the necessary key to progress. The hairdresser in the Mount Lavinia Hotel spoke enough English to get by. 'My parents speak good English,' she explained. 'I speak little bit. I learn from tourists. I know shampoo, blow dry, all those things, things for my work. My children – no English at all. Very bad. They don't learn in school.'

What I found most shocking was the cynicism of the politicians. There was one rule for them and another for the rest. They made sure that their own children grew up speaking English, and went to England or America for their university education. One of the Bandaranaikes was at Girton College, Cambridge, with me, shortly after her father introduced the Sinhala Only law.

The people I met lacked the arrogance of their political leaders. In fact, they undervalued themselves and their culture to a depressing extent. In Colombo, many women had cast off their saris and wore dreadful turquoise and sugar-pink Western clothes, all short skirts, flounces, puffed sleeves and glittery buttons. So many restaurants served foreign food that it was difficult to find anything Sri Lankan to eat. In the city centre, notices outside clubs and bars read VIP ROOM. FOREIGNERS ONLY. And, worst of all, when I took a rickshaw from the Mount Lavinia to my modest beach hotel, the shocked rickshaw wallah said:

'You not go stay there, madam.'

'Why not?'

'Our people. Not foreign.'

'But I like your people. You're very nice. I like to stay in hotels with you, to get to know you.'

He looked at me in disbelief. Little did he know how glad I was to be escaping the loud-mouthed Westerners on Christmas packages, who were eating and drinking themselves sick in the Mount Lavinia Hotel. My quiet, civilised Sri Lankan hosts in their small beach hotel were much more to my liking.

Sri Lankas have a real self-image problem. They copy everything Western, yet they seem jealous of Westerners and scorn the language in which they had a head start. So many of them are resentful. I couldn't help contrasting their attitude with that on the mainland. In India and Pakistan, the sari, dhoti and shalwar kameez are the traditional dress, and that's what most people wear. Their normal food is curry, and that's what they serve, whether foreigners happen to like it or not. They demonstrate a healthy national pride. And they are so confident in the worth of their own culture, that they are quite happy to use the language of another when it suits them. They have had the wit to retain English as the lingua franca.

Heather had left on 29 December, so I celebrated New Year's Eve alone. I went up to The Anglers, where the nice young man was delighted to learn that I was staying in the Ranvali Beach Resort. It belonged to his aunt and uncle! He ran me back there after my delicious freshly caught sole, as he didn't like the idea of my walking down to the beach on my own. New Year's Eve happened to coincide that year with the start of Ramadan. The sliver of new moon which signalled the start of the fast rose over the sea, together with an evening star of exceptional radiance. I sat out on my balcony, enjoying the brilliant stars until midnight, when the sky over the Mount Lavinia Hotel exploded in a rain of rockets and catherine wheels. I toasted the New Year in Bagpiper Indian whisky, congratulating myself on my free grandstand seat.

I had shopping to do before I left for Kandy and I decided to try the local train into Colombo. It was a beautiful ride, as the track ran all the way along the beach. To my amazement, the fare was only 7 rupees return, compared with the 700 rupees each way which Heather and I had paid for a motorcycle rickshaw, and the extravagant 1800 rupees one rainy day when we needed a proper taxi!

Rani is a connoisseur of food and wine, but Sri Lanka has no wines of its own and imported wines are far too expensive for everyday drinking. My hosts told me that there was just one shop in Colombo which stocked vintage French wines, so I tracked it down and bought a bottle of Pouilly Fumé and one of Brouilly to take as my house-guest presents. Then I divided up my luggage, two-thirds to leave in the Ranvali and one-third to take in my rucksack to Kandy. I now had most of my belongings scattered in three different places – Trivandrum Railway Station, my Trivandrum hotel and Mount Lavinia – so I walked to the station with a very light step. After my Christmas break, I was back on the Ramayana trail. I was off to meet Ravana in his mountain fortress above Kandy.

## ☙ ❧

### Preparations for War

*A flurry of reports was reaching Ravana about the vast army of monkeys and bears which was preparing to advance on his stronghold. He decided to sow dissension. Summoning one of his most skilful negotiators, a demon called Shuka, he sent him off to negotiate secretly with King Sugriva. Shuka flew to Rama's camp and, hovering in the air above Sugriva's head, addressed him in the most flattering terms.*

*'O Lord of the Monkeys,' he said. 'I bring you greetings from your brother, King Ravana. You have nothing to fear from him, so why don't you go back to Kishkindha with all your troops and live in peace there? What concern is it of yours if that great monarch has taken the wife of a crafty prince? When even the gods are powerless against the might of King Ravana, the Scourge*

*of the World, what chance do a band of monkeys and bears have? If you stay, you will certainly be massacred. You would be well advised to accept my royal master's protection and go home in safety to your wives and children.'*

*The monkeys were furious when they overheard Shuka's speech and leapt into the air to punch him and tear out his wings. But Rama heard the commotion and restrained them: it was unlawful to kill an ambassador.*

*Sugriva spurned Shuka's approach with great dignity. 'Ravana is not my brother or my friend, and I shall annihilate him, along with all his family and all his people. My army will reduce his Kingdom of Lanka to ashes. Even if he makes himself invisible, enters hell or takes refuge on Mount Kailash, Rama will find him and put an end to his wickedness.'*

*Shuka returned with tattered wings to report his failure to Ravana. He gave him a detailed account of the strength and disposition of Rama's troops, and Ravana grew afraid. Turning over a number of schemes in his mind, he devised a plan to thwart Rama's attack. If he could only persuade Sita to submit to him, Rama would no longer be interested in rescuing her and would go away. He would make a final attempt on her virtue by turning to sorcery.*

*Summoning the magician Vidyujiva, he ordered him to conjure up a phantom of Rama's head and a golden bow exactly like Rama's. Then he went with Vidyujiva to what used to be the ashoka orchard, before Hanuman uprooted it. He found Sita lying under the one remaining tree, still pining for Rama. Vidyujiva laid the false head on the grass before her. It was covered in blood and dust, but the face and hair, and even the jewel on the brow, were recognisable as Rama's. Ravana brandished Rama's phantom bow and told Sita that his troops had entered the monkeys' camp under cover of night and killed Rama as he slept, along with Hanuman and Sugriva. Lakshmana had fled with all the monkeys and bears, and Vibhisana had been taken prisoner. The invasion was over. Sita was now a widow and there was nothing to prevent her from becoming Ravana's wife.*

*Sita was overcome with grief and begged Ravana to kill her immediately, so that she could be reunited with Rama in death. While she was pleading with him, a messenger arrived to* summon Ravana to a meeting with his counsellors. He left the orchard and an amazing thing happened. The head of Rama disappeared. Vibhisana's wife was one of the demonesses deputed to guard Sita. She explained that the head was just a magic trick; that Rama was alive and well, and was even now finalising his plans for the attack. As she spoke, they heard the distant roll of drums and the earth began to shake with the tramp of marching feet. Sita dried her tears and her spirits rose as those of the demons plummeted.

When he was within striking distance of Ravana's citadel, Rama led his generals up the green slopes of Mount Suvela. From its summit, they commanded an excellent view of Lanka and the disposition of Ravana's troops. They saw a land of woods and groves, shady avenues and orchards, where bees swarmed and birds, intoxicated with love, sang among the fragrant fruits and flowers. In the centre of this earthly paradise rose Mount Trikuta, sparkling like gold, a mountain so high that it was beyond the reach of birds. 'It could not be scaled, even in thought.' On its peak, Vishwakarma, the divine Architect of the Universe, had built Ravana's opulent city of Lanka. Its parks and palaces were surrounded by ramparts of gold and silver, defended by a second wall of dark-skinned demons.

Then Ravana himself appeared above one of the gates, wrapped in a cloak the colour of hare's blood, embroidered with gold, 'like a cloud dyed with the tints of sunset'. Seeing him, Sugriva was seized with sudden fury. In one mighty leap, he bounded across from the summit of Mount Suvela, snatched Ravana's diadem and threw it to the ground. Ravana attacked him and those two powerful kings fought hand to hand, 'like two wild cats fighting over a piece of meat'. Both displayed great valour and cunning. But Ravana became frustrated at failing to overcome his opponent and tried to cast magic spells. When Sugriva realised what was happening, he leapt up into the sky triumphant, leaving Ravana exhausted at the gate.

Sugriva's daring had cheered the army, but the omens were terrible. Harsh winds blew, the moon shone red, the sun and the planets strayed from their courses, rain fell mixed with blood and the mountains shook with fear. 'I foresee a terrible calamity, boding universal destruction and death to monkeys, bears and demons,' cried Rama in despair. He decided to make one last effort to avert disaster. Reflecting that a king should always try conciliation before he went into battle, he sent Prince Angada on a final diplomatic mission, offering clemency to Ravana if he would return Sita and beg Rama's forgiveness. Angada faithfully conveyed the message. The proud King of the Rakshasas was furious. 'Seize him and put him to death!' he cried. But Angada, 'who in his splendour resembled a blazing torch', overpowered the guards and hurled them down from the palace roof before leaping to safety. His final offer rejected, Rama had no choice but to declare war.

# **14** Lanka at Last!

W HEN I REACHED Colombo Fort Station, the first vision to greet my eyes was that of a tall youth, etiolated like a stick of celery, with pink hair, a green T-shirt, white sandals and a pair of green, yellow, pink and mauve striped trousers. The first-class observation car, which I was to ride up to Kandy, was full of noisy young French people. When Sri Lankans asked them the inevitable, 'Coming from?' or 'What is your country?' they shouted in chorus 'Fromage!' I was back among my fellow Europeans. The station announcer spoke in the cultured BBC English of Lord Reith's day, like Alvar Liddell reading the wartime news. There were seats in my carriage labelled RESERVED FOR CLERGY. And I was approached by my first overt beggar in Sri Lanka. With piteous groans, he thrust his hand at me through the carriage window. I had a pocketful of small change – not a fortune, but a reasonable number of rupees. He took the money, counted it, then threw it into my lap in disgust. I picked it up carefully and put it back in my pocket. Rupees are rupees. That arrogant station beggar was the last straw. I didn't like Colombo and hoped that life would be more agreeable elsewhere on the island.

The train ride up to Kandy was a delight. We soon left the suburbs of Colombo behind us and began to climb up through wooded hills. Unlike the busy main road to Kandy, which you have to travel if you are visiting any of the inland historical sites, the railway line was a peaceful serpent, twisting and turning through gaps in the rocks, hemmed in by shady trees.

When I first got into my carriage, I despaired at the noise. I was sure that I was going to have my journey ruined by some loud pink-haired lad, but I was lucky. The reserved seat next to me was taken by a quiet young woman, a biologist working for the Department of Agriculture, who had a PhD from the University of Sussex. She turned out to be a Hindu with a profound knowledge of the Epics. She pointed out some lesser-known Ramayana sites on my map of Sri Lanka and talked of the epic's influence in countries further east, even those which are not Hindu. For instance, I'd forgotten, until she reminded me, that the most common name of the Kings of Thailand is King Rama. We chatted amicably between spells of reading and passed a very pleasant journey together.

A glance at the map will show how easy it is to identify Sri Lanka with Valmiki's Kingdom of Lanka. The tear-shaped island has flat coastal regions, while the centre south is mountainous. The little train climbed 450 metres to reach Kandy. Ravana's fortress was situated much higher than that, in the mountains overlooking Nuwara Eliya, a favourite British hill station in the days of the Raj. The island's highest peak pierces the clouds at 2,524 metres. It is now called by the difficult name of Mount Pidurutalagala, but it is presumably Mount Trikuta, the mountain 'so high that it could not be scaled even in thought', where Vishwakarma built Ravana's citadel. Valmiki gives a rapturous description of the natural beauties of the central highlands and their teeming wildlife. Even today, despite the depredations of loggers and speculative builders, the hills are wild and lovely enough to lift the spirit.

The population of the island also fits well with Valmiki's cast of characters. There is still a sprinkling of tribal people, the Veddahs, living in the forests. These are thought by many to be the dark-skinned aboriginal inhabitants, Ravana's Rakshasas. The Sinhalese, who are probably northern Aryans in origin, seem to have made their way down to the island by the sixth or fifth century BC and gradually gained supremacy there. Rama's invasion may be the legendary echo of some punitive attack which occurred in the distant past. This ruling

Sinhalese majority is the group which converted to Buddhism. The Hindu Tamils arrived on the scene too late to feature in *The Ramayana*. Though the first settlers seem to have filtered across from Tamil Nadu some 1,000 years ago, the history of the subcontinent is long and, in Sri Lankan terms, they are recent arrivals. They crossed the Palk Strait and settled in the northern part of the island, on the Jaffna Peninsula, where they predominate, and along the north-east coast. There is also a group of Tamils living in the central highlands, but these are nineteenth century arrivals, low-caste Tamils who were brought over by the British as indentured labourers to pick tea. Most of them stayed on after the British left and Tamil women still pick all the tea on the estates, but they are a distinct group from the Tamils in the north and are not, on the whole, involved in the struggle for Eelam, the independent Tamil state.

Kandy, in the very heart of the island, is Sri Lanka's cultural and spiritual centre, and the Kandyans are justly proud of their heritage. While the coastal ports and the plains behind them fell successively to Portuguese, Dutch and British rulers, the Kingdom of Kandy alone remained impregnable in its mountain fastness. It was only when the British made the island a Crown Colony and started to take its administration seriously that control of Kandy was finally wrested from its last king in 1815.

Rani met me at Kandy Railway Station, dressed as always, whether in England or at home, in a most beautiful sari. After Colombo, I was astonished at the cleanliness and general good order of Kandy. The whole city gleamed in the afternoon sun, as the public buildings had been given a fresh coat of whitewash in honour of Prince Charles and the forthcoming Independence celebrations. Even the balustrade encircling Kandy's huge central lake had been given the treatment, each little section lovingly whitened. The lake, one of the last works of the last King of Kandy, Sri Wickrama Rajasinha, looked so natural in its bowl of green hills that it hardly seemed man-made. When the King had it excavated, he left an island in the middle to house his harem – which the British put to less romantic use as their arms depot! Overlooking the lake on its northern edge stands Sri Lanka's most sacred Buddhist shrine, the Temple of the Tooth. It is a World Heritage site. Like all relics, the tooth of the Buddha may or may not be the real thing, but the golden casket within the impressive building is the focus of Sinhalese faith and the cherished object which draws Buddhist pilgrims from all over the world.

It was good to be in a friend's home after so many weeks of hotels. Rani had built a two-storey house near the Peradeniya Botanic Gardens on the proceeds of her music teaching in England. The upper floor was a flat for her sister, while Rani herself, with her two dogs, had the ground floor and garden. She had a part-time gardener and two Tamil maids, who came in on a daily basis. The two maids were poor thin little women, with no-good husbands and too many children. One of them was pregnant yet again. They had both converted to Christianity, probably because the Church ran some decent welfare services. Rani complained about all three of her staff and her friends too discussed 'the servant problem' with passion. I couldn't help smiling to myself. Little did they know what a luxury it would be for me in my London flat to have just one servant every day, let alone three!

We ate Sri Lankan food, basically rice and very hot curry – curries get hotter the further south you go. We took our main meal in the middle of the day, when the duty maid could help prepare it and eat a decent meal herself. Rani guessed it was her one meal of the day, everything at home going to the husband and the brood of children. In the evenings, we often went into downtown Kandy. It was sometimes difficult to find a rickshaw. Many of the rickshaw wallahs were Muslim and it was Ramadan, so they all rushed home at sunset to eat. But Rani was persistent and we always got into Kandy eventually. There we would snack on 'hoppers', the pancakes which are a local speciality, served either with a side dish of curry or with honey, yoghurt and bananas. One evening we drove for dinner up to The Chalet, a hotel high in the hills overlooking the lake. And one evening Rani cooked her speciality, caneton a l'orange, which we ate with a bottle of Brouilly.

To help us enjoy the feast, she invited her friend, the poet Jean Arasanayagam, round to dinner. Ducks are considered unclean birds and you have to be a Burgher or a foreigner to eat them. I realised only after meeting her what a well-known writer she was and what a strange life she had led. A Christian Burgher of Dutch descent, Jean had married a Tamil, whose high-caste Hindu family had found it difficult to accept her. Despite that, she had suffered with them during the anti-Tamil riots of 1983. In that year, the Tamil Tigers ambushed an army patrol near Jaffna and the Sinhalese went on the rampage, burning, looting and killing in revenge attacks. Within days they had slaughtered thousands of Tamils, and tens of thousands more had been forced to flee the island. Jean and her family had escaped to Tamil Nadu, where they had spent two years in a refugee camp. So Jean was an outsider twice over, victimised by the Sinhalese for being Tamil, and disdained by her husband's Tamil family for *not* being Tamil. I wish I had had all that background knowledge when I met her. I gained it from the book of poems she gave me, *Shooting the Floricans*, which I read only after I left Sri Lanka. She was a cheerful, philosophic woman and it would have been so interesting to talk to her about her experiences, instead of simply making dinner-party chat. Our meeting was another of life's missed opportunities.

My main reason for visiting Sri Lanka was to explore the area around Nuwara Eliya, which was supposed to be Ravana's Kingdom of Lanka, but while I was in Kandy, I also wanted to visit the historical sites which Heather and I had missed. To fit everything in, I needed to hire a car and driver. Rani did the bargaining for me and of course succeeded in getting a much better deal than Heather and I had been able to negotiate for our trips from the Mount Lavinia Hotel. The long-distance hire cars in Sri Lanka are nearly all pocket-sized Japanese minibuses, which run on cheaper diesel fuel and have a lower tax-rating than saloon cars. So we had lots of spare seats and were able to invite Rani's friends to join us for days out.

The day we visited the fortress of Sigiriya was memorable because we took Amara Aluwihare, with us. Amara is a descendant of the Kandyan royal house, and through her I got a fascinating insight into traditional Sri Lankan life. She took us to call on various relations in their beautiful 'walauwe', spacious country homes with pillared halls and verandahs surrounding a central garden. One of these Kandyan aristo-crats, Amara's Aunt Ena, whose father had been knighted as chief of police under the British, emerged into her garden to greet us. A handsome, upright woman of 75, sporting rather than leaning on an ebony cane, she was dressed in an astonishing pea-green pinstripe trouser suit and four types of headgear: a navy and white scarf, a red baseball cap and a calico sunbonnet, all topped with an enormously wide-brimmed cartwheel of a hat in beige straw! The village where she lived was called Aluwihare and we had breakfast there in the Aluwihare Kitchens, a restaurant devised by Aunt Ena as part of a village employment project. She was also involved in the production and marketing of batik and traditional wood carvings. Fifty years previously, she had played the Spirit of Lanka in the Independence Day pageant. With Amara's family, I was a million miles away from the politicians of Colombo. They were no longer wealthy. Their houses were a bit on the shabby side, but they were people of grace, with a social conscience.

We went to Nuwara Eliya on our own, because that trip was serious Ramayana business. The road there from Kandy was flat for a good half of its 80 kilometres, then it climbed 1,500 metres in a succession of steep zig-zags. The hills were covered in tea bushes, compact through endless picking of the fresh, new leaves. They glistened a brilliant green in the morning sun, slighter darker in tone than the emerald green of rice paddies, but a vivid colour all the same, rendered even more lively by the bright saris of the Tamil women leaf pickers. We stopped at one of the estates for morning tea and bought a few boxes at production prices.

Nuwara Eliya was a strange place, a kind of Bognor Regis stranded up at 1,890 metres in the middle of Sri Lanka. There were cross-timbered mock Tudor houses, hotels with names like Collingwood, The Grosvenor and The Ascot Guest House, a country club, an eighteen-hole golf course, a racecourse and a park with a boating lake. Once the favourite hill resort of the British, Nuwara Eliya is now *the* fashionable place for Sri Lankan socialites to be seen, especially around the Sinhalese New Year in April.

We drove some ten kilometres out of the town to the Sita Eliya Temple. It stood beside a mountain stream, where Sita is said to have bathed every morning. Some of the boulders beside the stream had large round indentations, the foot-prints of Ravana's elephant. Mount Pidurutalagala, Valmiki's Mount Trikuta and the site of Ravana's citadel, towered above the valley, its peak lost in the clouds. Sita was held captive in an ashoka grove on top of that mountain and, according to our driver, the local people believe that there is a tunnel running right through, from the summit of the mountain to the stream below, which Sita used every morning to walk from her prison to her bathing place.

The temple itself was a ramshackle affair, a small concrete structure painted sky blue with a patched green corrugated iron roof. On the entrance gable was a painting of Sita, dressed in grey, her hair dishevelled, sitting disconsolately beside the stream. The painting was framed on each side by a small representation of Hanuman. He had laid his mace on the ground and was kneeling down, gazing reverently at Sita. There was quite an elaborate grey granite dome over the sanctum. It thrust its statues of Vishnu, Hanuman and sundry guardian giants and dwarves out through the corrugated iron, to give a measure of artistry to an otherwise primitive structure. The interior was even more basic. The three idols in the holy of holies were nothing but three irregular lumps of black stone, garlanded with marigolds. The biggest, pre-sumably Rama, was dressed in royal blue and gold. An effort had been made to give him a face, with the all-important staring eyes and Vishnu's vertical marks on his forehead. The central figure was Sita in a grey sari, with a silver umbrella over her head. She too had a face of sorts, with eyes and the *bindi*, the red spot of the married woman, on her brow. The third and smallest figure had no face, just three red blobs in a vertical row. It was robed in blue and looked like nothing so much as a black banana with buttons. I'm not sure if this unfortunate object was supposed to be Lakshmana or Hanuman. There was a glossy portrait on the wall behind the banana of a smiling boy with long black ringlets, standing beside a peacock. He could only be Murugan, Shiva's son. I was surprised to find a member of Shiva's family occupying such an important place in a temple dedicated to the consort of one of Vishnu's avatars, until I reflected that the local Hindus would all be Tamils, and Murugan was one of their best-loved gods.

Our driver turned out to be a mine of local knowledge. He drove us past a terraced hillside where the red soil had strange black striations. These were scorch marks, he informed us confidently, caused by Hanuman's burning tail, when he was setting fire to Ravana's Lanka. The Hakgala Gardens, near Sita's temple, were also connected with Hanuman. Hakgala means 'jaw rock', and he told us that the gardens were given that name because they stood on a hill which had dropped from Hanuman's jaw, a fragment of the Himalayan mountain he was carrying to Rama.

Touring with Rani was restful, as I was not plagued by the souvenir sellers, touts and crypto-beggars who usually swarm round tourists. 'Say nothing,' said Rani. 'Let me do the talking.' She came out with a torrent of Sinhalese and they all disappeared like magic.

'What did you say?'

'I told them we were both Burghers and lived here. And they went away.'

Depending on the racial mix, Burghers can be anything from dark brown, through every shade of coffee, to pale and blond, so one fair-skinned, brown-haired Burgher came as no surprise to anyone.

In fact, my whole interlude with Rani was restful and I was quite sad when the time came to leave Kandy. I returned to Mount Lavinia, just missing the son of the hotel, who had left for Kandy that very morning. He was an officer in the Sri Lankan Air Force and was to be responsible, together with Scotland Yard, for Prince Charles's safety at the Independence celebrations. I stayed long enough to amalgamate my luggage and have a last dinner at The Anglers before flying back to Trivandrum.

Twelve days later, at 6.10 a.m. on 25 January 1998, a massive truck crashed through the entrance gate of the Temple of the Tooth. It was a suicide bomb attack by the Tamil Tigers in advance of Prince Charles's visit. The structure of the Temple itself was little damaged and the Shrine of the Tooth was unharmed, but 8 people were killed and a further 25 injured. All were innocent Buddhist worshippers, visiting the Temple to make early morning offerings. Prince Charles was not deterred by the attack, and the celebrations to mark fifty years of independence took place as arranged.

CR 80

### War and Peace

*Rama drew up his forces beneath Ravana's battlements. But before he gave the signal to attack, he had to take a strategic decision. As the monkeys and bears were all sons of the gods, they could change their forms at will. So would it be more advantageous for them to go into battle as men or animals? He discussed the matter with his generals and they decided that it would be safer for them to stay as monkeys and bears, for then there would be no confusion on the battlefield.*

*The trumpets sounded. The monkeys stormed up Mount Trikuta and began hurling boulders and uprooted trees at the walls of the citadel. Then the Rakshasas, armed with magic weapons, riding in golden chariots drawn by a thousand horses or mounted on elephants, stormed out of the gates in their hundreds of thousands, 'like the winds that blow at the dissolution of the worlds'. A terrible battle ensued. The monkeys fell upon the chariots, smashing them with boulders or their bare fists, and the bears tore at the demons with their teeth and claws. The demons retaliated with swords, spears, hooks and harpoons. The battle raged far into the night, until the earth was soaked with blood.*

*Prince Angada took on Indrajit, Ravana's son. He shattered his gold-encrusted chariot and slew his horses and driver. Then he struck Indrajit on the head with a tree. Indrajit, enraged at the attack, made himself invisible, flew into the air and rained down* arrows on Rama and Lakshmana. They were magic arrows, which turned into serpents as they flew. They transfixed the two heroes, then bound them in their coils. Losing blood from a thousand lacerations, 'bristling with arrows like porcupines', Rama and Lakshmana fainted away. Indrajit was sure that he had killed them and flew to Ravana to report his victory. Meanwhile, King Sugriva, Hanuman and Vibhisana were in despair.

Suddenly, a great wind arose, whipping up the waves and causing the mountains to tremble. In a storm of thunder and lightning, Garuda appeared. At the sight of this giant eagle, the serpents which were binding Rama and Lakshmana fled in terror. Then Garuda stroked the two princes with his wings and their wounds healed. They sprang up from the ground, their valour and wisdom enhanced.

'Who are you,' cried Rama, 'you with your golden crown, your perfume and your celestial ornaments?'

'I am your dear friend, your very breath, Garuda. But do not enquire indiscreetly into the cause of my friendship. You will understand everything when you have conquered Lanka and rescued Sita.'

With those words, Garuda embraced Rama, then disappeared into the heavens with the speed of wind.

One after another, the mightiest of the demons rode into battle, only to be defeated by Rama, Lakshmana and their valiant monkey army. Ravana's eyes turned red with rage and, convinced of his invulnerability, he resolved to enter the conflict himself, to destroy his enemy 'as a forest is consumed by fire'.

Rama was astonished when he saw him drive up in his gleaming chariot, surrounded by horrible spectres, his twenty arms bearing fiery weapons and his ten heads glittering with diadems and precious earrings.

'O, what glory, what majesty is Ravana's!' he cried. 'Who can rival the brilliance of the King of the Rakshasas?'

The monkeys attacked him with little success and Lakshmana was carried off the field wounded. Then Rama climbed on Hanuman's shoulders and challenged Ravana to single combat. It was all too easy for him. With his mighty weapons, he smashed Ravana's chariot, broke his bow and inflicted a deep wound.

When Ravana collapsed, Rama chose a flaming arrow shaped like a crescent moon and shattered the demon's diadems. Having humiliated him in front of his army, he sent him back to Lanka, to rest and regroup his forces.

Ravana had premonitions of doom. Brahma had granted him protection from gods and demons but, in his pride, Ravana had not asked for protection against men and animals. He saw now that the human prince Rama and his monkey forces were destined to be his downfall. But he would not go down without a fight. He sent for his brother, the giant Kumbhakarna.

Kumbhakarna was so voracious and so bloodthirsty that he devoured thousands of creatures the moment he was born. Had he not been subdued, the whole world would have become a desert within days. So Brahma ruled that Kumbhakarna should sleep for six months and wake up for just one day, during which time he could appease his terrible hunger and thirst, before going to sleep again for the next six months.

When Ravana summoned him, Kumbhakarna was in the middle of one of his sleeps. The demons sent to wake him up took the precaution of piling mountains of antelope, buffalo and bear meat beside his bed, along with two thousand pitchers of wine, fat and blood, so that he would have something other than them to devour as soon as he opened his eyes. When he woke up and heard of Ravana's troubles, he mounted the battlements and hurled himself down into the fray. The monkeys and bears saw him towering over them, 'quenching the sun with his brilliance, a monster as tall as the peak of a mountain, with eyes like chariot wheels and a gaping mouth like the entrance to hell'. They fled in terror, but Prince Angada rallied them and they found the courage to attack. They rushed at the giant with trees and boulders, but he swung his mace and scattered them on the ground, seizing handfuls of them to cram into his cavernous mouth.

Rama, as usual, waited in the background until the monkey leaders had all challenged the demon and been repulsed. It was only when Kumbhakarna dismissed Lakshmana, disdaining to fight with him, that Rama decided to enter the battle himself. He used his divine weapons to sever Kumbhakarna's arms and legs, finally decapitating him with an arrow belonging to Indra, the King of the Gods. Kumbhakarna's mountainous head crashed down, destroying highways and palaces in its fall, and his giant body toppled into the sea, where the sharks were crushed as it plunged to the depths. The jubilant monkeys, 'whose faces were like opening lotuses', cheered and shouted, and the gods in heaven rejoiced. Only Ravana wept at his brother's unexpected death. He fell down in a swoon and it was left to his eldest son Indrajit to carry on the campaign.

By this time, all Indrajit's brothers had been killed along with the bravest of Ravana's generals. But Indrajit rallied his demon troops and they poured out of the city gates mounted on tigers, scorpions, cats, serpents, jackals as large as hills, crows and peacocks. Indrajit himself shone like the firmament at midday, lighting up the whole of Lanka with his magnificence. The monkeys were no match for this army and soon the earth was covered with their corpses. Indrajit was carrying Brahma's bow. He now made himself invisible and showered Rama and Lakshmana with unerring darts. They fell to the ground unconscious and once again Indrajit rushed back to his father to boast of victory.

Hanuman and Vibhisana did a tour of the battlefield, where their valiant army lay dead and wounded. They found Jambavan, the King of the Bears, riddled with arrows and gasping for breath.

'Is Hanuman still alive?' he whispered.

'Why do you ask about Hanuman and not about the two princes or King Sugriva?' asked Vibhisana.

'Because if Hanuman lives, we still have a chance of survival.'

Hanuman approached the wise old bear with reverence. As the son of the Wind God, he could cover enormous distances at the speed of light. So Jambavan told him to fly immediately to the Himalayas. There, between the unscaleable peaks of Mount Kailasha and Mount Rishabha, he would find a golden mountain, glowing with medicinal herbs. There were four in particular which he must gather and bring back to Jambavan.

In no time at all, Hanuman flew to the Himalayas and identified the mountain by its gleam. But the magic herbs knew that he was looking for them and hid themselves away. In his impatience, Hanuman broke off the whole mountain, trees, elephants and all, and leapt into the sky 'to the great terror of the worlds'. The mountain illuminated him with its radiance as he flew, so that he looked like Vishnu himself, armed with his discus of a thousand fiery rays. As soon as Rama, Lakshmana and Jambavan smelt the herbs, they sprang up, their wounds healed, and the monkey army rose from the dead, like sleepers waking. Jubilant, Hanuman flew back to the Himalayas and put the mountain back in its place.

Indrajit again led his demons into battle. To discourage his enemy, he resorted to magic. He created a likeness of Sita and carried it in his chariot, weeping and crying out for Rama. Then, before the eyes of Hanuman and the other monkeys, he chopped the likeness in two. The monkeys fled in despair, and Rama fainted with grief when he heard of Sita's death. But Vibhisana convinced him that Ravana was too enamoured of Sita to let her come to any harm. It must be a trick.

Indrajit seemed invincible, until Lakshmana determined to kill him. He went into the attack, riding on Hanuman's shoulders, supported by Vibhisana, King Sugriva and all the monkey army. A terrible battle ensued. The two warriors seemed evenly matched, but Lakshmana was armed with the bow and arrows of Indra, the King of the Gods. At the end of their duel, he drew this bow with such force that Indrajit, who had once defeated Indra himself, was decapitated by one of Indra's arrows. His head rolled on the ground like a golden ball and he fell on the battlefield, his weapons and armour smashed. The monkeys let out wild cries of delight and the gods and nymphs, rejoicing in heaven, showered Lakshmana with flowers.

It was time now for the final confrontation, the decisive battle between Ravana himself and Rama. Both were armed with magic weapons bestowed on them by the gods and both were wonderfully skilful in the arts of war. When Ravana hurled a spear or shot an arrow at Rama, Rama took aim and shattered the weapon in its flight. Ravana was equally accurate in destroying Rama's weapons. And both were warriors of such formidable strength, that even those weapons which found their mark, fell useless to the ground. Vibhisana joined in the fight, attacking Ravana's horses. But he was no match for Ravana, and Lakshmana had to rush in to protect him. Then disaster struck. Ravana aimed a magic spear at Lakshmana, which flamed as it flew and clanged with eight extremely loud bells. To Rama's despair, it pierced his brother Lakshmana through the heart. All seemed lost, until Sushena, the monkey physician, sent Hanuman to the Himalayas again for the magic herbs. In a flash, Hanuman was back, carrying the whole mountain. Sushena plucked the herbs, crushed them and passed them under Lakshmana's nostrils. He leapt up, fully cured.

The battle raged for seven days and nights, watched anxiously by the gods in heaven. Indra decided that the contest was unfair, as Rama had to fight on foot, while Ravana had a chariot with splendid horses and a driver. So he summoned his own charioteer, Matali, and ordered him to drive to the service of Rama. Rama also received help from his old friend, the Sage Agastya, who had now joined the immortal gods. Agastya came down from the skies and advised Rama to repeat the potent Hymn to the Sun three times, after which he would be invincible.

Riding in Indra's chariot and protected now by Surya, the Sun God, Rama drove on to the battlefield for the final duel. Though the two contestants still seemed evenly matched, dreadful omens began to assail Ravana. Blood fell from the skies on to his chariot, his horses wept tears and flames together, contrary winds blew clouds of dust into his eyes and, though it was daytime, the whole of Lanka was shrouded in darkness. But still he fought on, showering Rama with hundreds of thousands of deadly weapons, all of which Rama shattered in their flight. Then Rama selected an arrow like a poisonous serpent and cut off one of Ravana's ten heads. It rolled to the ground with its sparkling diadem and earrings, but another identical head immediately sprouted from his shoulders. Rama took aim a hundred times, and a hundred times succeeded in shooting off one of Ravana's heads, only to find that a hundred more sprang up to take their place. His weapons had never failed him before and he began to lose confidence.

At this juncture, Matali showed his true worth. He took Rama to task. 'Why are you carrying on like an ordinary man, unaware of your own powers?' he asked. 'Why don't you use Brahma's weapon?'

Prompted by Matali, Rama took up the flaming arrow which was hissing like a viper. Created by Brahma as a gift for Indra, *this gigantic weapon had passed to the Sage Agastya, who had given it to Rama. Its wings were the wind, its point the fire of the sun, and space was its haft. Composed of the essence of all the elements and swirling with smoke, it resembled the fire of time. Rama charged it with its sacred mantra and fixed it to his bow. The whole of creation was seized with terror and the earth trembled. Drawing back his bowstring, Rama released that lightning arrow with such force that it pierced Ravana right through and buried itself in the ground behind him. The King of the Rakshasas crashed down dead from his chariot and Brahma's arrow, its duty done, returned quietly to Rama's quiver. Lakshmana and the generals rushed up to congratulate Rama, and the monkeys and bears shouted in triumph. The heavens were filled with music and a shower of blossoms fell on to Rama's chariot.*

*But there was mourning among the Rakshashas. Ravana's beautiful queen, Mandodari, flung herself weeping on to his lifeless body, and his other consorts crowded round, lamenting like ospreys and wilting 'like creepers that have been torn down in the forest'. Even Vibhisana wept, for Ravana was, after all, his brother. Though he had sinned, he was courageous in war, loving to his family and a generous, dutiful ruler. Rama consoled him:*

*'We should not mourn for those who, firm in their duty as warriors, fall on the field of battle. No one is always victorious in war. Death has ended our enmity. Ravana is as dear to me now as he is to you. So perform the funeral rites that will lead his soul to heaven.'*

*Ravana was placed on a golden bier, covered in antelope skins and, while the brahmins recited the Vedas and the widows wept, Vibhisana set his torch to the fragrant sandalwood pyre. It was a magnificent state funeral, at the end of which Vibhisana was anointed King of the Rakshasas by Lakshmana and ascended the throne of Lanka.*

*When Rama had carried out all his official duties, he was free to turn his attention to Sita. He summoned Hanuman and sent him as his messenger, to give her the joyful news.*

Valmiki's account of this war is enormously long. It occupies almost the whole of Book Six of The Ramayana and contains many set-piece battle scenes, which are repetitive in the extreme.

It is an epic tale of clashes between giants, where every weapon, every suit of armour, every blow dealt and parried is described in loving detail, along with every boastful threat, every omen and every lamentation. It is the traditional stuff of the storyteller, passed down from generation to generation and ideal for long dark nights around the fire. Read as a book, it is less appealing. The above is an extremely condensed account.

In terms of Hindu iconography, two of the most important episodes are the flights to the Himalayas by Hanuman, to search for the medicinal herbs. They explain why Hanuman is so often represented flying through the air with a mountain on the palm of his hand, rather like a waiter rushing along with a tray. Throughout India and Sri Lanka, there are many hills which are revered because they are said to be fragments of that magical golden mountain. Some of them, like Maruda Malai (Medicine Mountain), between Kanniyakumari and Nagercoil, do in fact grow many curative herbs, while the surrounding hills have only the normal regional vegetation.

## The Alternative Ravana

Ravana and his Rakshasas have been demonised in The Ramayana. The more terrible Ravana can be made, the more valiant and virtuous Rama will appear by contrast. Most authorities agree that India was once inhabited by dark-skinned Dravidians, and that Rama represents the fairer-skinned Aryans from the north, whose influence drove the Dravidians to the south of the subcontinent, chiefly into Tamil Nadu. But whether the Rakshasas of Lanka were the most southerly of the Dravidians or were aboriginal tribesmen, Veddahs from the highland forests of Sri Lanka, is open to scholarly dispute. What is certain is that they fought a losing battle against northern pre-eminence.

In recent years, south Indian and Sri Lankan activists have promoted the view of Ravana as a tragic hero, the brave defender of southern, Dravidian culture against the brahminical culture of the north. His ten heads are interpreted, not as horrendous attributes of a ghastly demon, but as symbols of ten aspects of his kingly character.

Ravana's actions are strongly defended. His supporters point out that the theft of an enemy's wives, daughters or cattle was a common tactic in contemporary warfare. Ravana abducted Sita, *not because he was overwhelmed with lust, but because she would be a useful bargaining counter. This is corroborated by the fact that he always treated her courteously and never tried to overcome her resistance with force. His abduction of Rama's wife was also an appropriate punishment for the horrific, and quite unwarranted, injuries inflicted by Lakshmana upon Ravana's sister, Surpanakha.*

*Ravana was so learned in the scriptures and had performed such remarkable religious austerities that Brahma himself had been impressed and had granted him invincibility in battles with gods and demons. He was a loving husband, father and brother, 'full of gaiety in pastimes and enjoyments' and an accomplished musician. A wise ruler, he always consulted his ministers and allowed them freedom of speech, even when they criticised his actions. Valmiki himself had to concede that Ravana was a mighty warrior, who fought valiantly against divine odds and deserved a magnificent funeral. According to the alternative version, Rama was the aggressor, Vibhisana a traitor, ambitious for the throne of Lanka, and Hanuman was nothing but a tricky, vicious monkey, who set fire to Ravana's capital out of spite.*

## ෪ ෩

### Reunited

*Hanuman hurried to the ashoka grove and delighted Sita with his account of Rama's victory over Ravana. Then King Vibhisana arrived to escort her in a curtained palanquin. She dressed her hair, and decked herself in her finest sari and most precious jewels. As she approached Rama, the monkeys, bears and demons crowded round, trying to catch a glimpse of this beautiful woman who had been the cause of such a terrible conflict. So Rama asked her to leave her palanquin and come to him on foot, in full view of the troops of both armies.*

*Sita, full of admiration for her handsome, valiant husband, gazed lovingly into his eyes. But his words came as a great shock to her. Averting his face, he informed her that he had not waged war for her sake, but to avenge the insult to him personally and to his noble family. Her abduction by Ravana had stained his* reputation. Now that he and his friends had killed Ravana and achieved a glorious victory over the Rakshasas, his honour was satisfied.

Continuing coldly, Rama informed Sita that she was free to leave. 'I can have nothing more to do with you,' he said. 'What man of honour would be such a slave to passion as to permit himself to take back a woman who has lived in the house of another? Looking on your ravishing and celestial beauty, Ravana could never have respected your person during the time he held you in his palace. So how can I reclaim you, I who boast of belonging to an illustrious house? I no longer have any attachment to you.'

Sita wept bitterly at these harsh words, proclaiming her innocence and accusing Rama of jumping to conclusions like a common, worthless man. Then she turned to Lakshmana.

'Raise a funeral pyre for me,' she said. 'That is the only remedy for my grief. Rama's unjust reproaches have destroyed me. I cannot go on living.'

Rama nodded his assent and Lakshmana built up the fire. Then Sita reverently circumambulated her husband, offered a prayer to Agni, the Fire God, and stepped fearlessly into the flames. A cry of anguish arose from the monkeys, bears and demons, and Rama's eyes filled with tears.

Suddenly, there was a great commotion in the heavens, as all the gods arrived in their golden chariots.

'O Creator of the Universe,' cried Indra. 'How can you be unaware that you are Chief of the Gods?'

'I have always considered myself to be a man, Rama, the son of King Dasaratha. Who am I then?'

Brahma replied, 'You are the great and effulgent God Narayana, the fortunate Lord armed with the discus. You are the imperishable Brahman, Existence Itself, transcending the three divisions of time. You are aum, the Greatest of the Great. You are Vishnu and Sita is Lakshmi. It was to rid the world of the demon Ravana that you entered a human body.'

Agni then rose from the flaming pyre, with Sita alive in his arms. 'Here is your wife,' he said. 'There is no sin in her. Neither by word, feeling nor glance has Sita shown herself to be unworthy of your noble qualities. Surrounded by hideous demon women, though tempted and threatened, she never so much as looked at

*Ravana, but was totally absorbed in thoughts of you. It is my command that she should suffer no reproach.'*

*Rama was overjoyed. He explained to Agni that Sita had lived in Ravana's inner apartments for a long time, so that he had felt obliged to put her innocence to the test. Otherwise, people would have said that he was overcome with lust. He himself had known all along that Sita was a virtuous wife, as inaccessible to Ravana as a flame. 'But now her purity is evident to the Three Worlds, and I could no more renounce her than a hero could renounce his honour.'*

*Shiva then pointed to King Dasaratha, who had 'crossed the sea of relativity' and joined the immortal gods. Blazing with glory, that great monarch stepped down from his celestial chariot and embraced his sons, telling them that he now understood everything – how the banishment of Rama, which had grieved him so sorely, was part of the divine plan to rid the world of Ravana. At Rama's request, he unsaid the curse which, in his lifetime, in his human ignorance, he had laid on Queen Kaikeyi and her son Bharata. He now saw that they too had only been working out their destiny. Then he approached Sita reverently, with joined palms. 'My daughter,' he begged, 'Do not take it ill that Rama renounced you. He acted in your own interest, to demonstrate your innocence.'*

*Finally, Indra spoke for all the gods when he said how delighted they were with Rama's exploits. They wished to reward him with whatever would please him most. The compassionate prince thought immediately of his followers. He asked that all the monkeys and bears, who had given their lives for his honour in battle, should be brought back from the dead; and that there should be flowers, fruit and clear water in abundance, even out of season, wherever those noble creatures went. His wishes were granted. The monkeys and bears all rose up rejoicing, their wounds healed, 'like sleepers who wake at the end of night'. Then the gods bowed low to Rama and returned to heaven in their chariots blazing like the sun.*

## ೞ ೲ

## Rama's Coronation

*Rama was anxious to return to his Kingdom of Ayodhya, so King Vibhisana put Pushpaka at his disposal. This was an aerial* chariot, swift as thought, made by Vishvamitra, the Architect of the Universe, for the God Kuvera, but Ravana had stolen it from him and it was now in Lanka. The gold of its framework gleamed bright as the sun, its rooms were of silver decorated with golden lotuses, its floors were of crystal and around its windows, set with pearls and the rarest gems, hung rows of bells, which pealed melodiously in flight. Rama, Sita and Lakshmana climbed on board, but just as they were about to take their leave, Sugriva and Vibhisana begged to accompany them, with all their followers, to see Rama crowned. There was room in Pushpaka for everyone, so the monkeys and demons took their seats on emerald thrones and the chariot soared into the sky, drawn by its team of swans.

Rama sat at a window beside Sita, pointing out all the landmarks – the places where the battle had raged, where Ravana and the other wicked demons had been killed, the wild shark-infested sea where Nala and the monkeys had built their bridge, and Rameshwaram with its purifying waters. When they flew over the Kingdom of Kishkindha, Sita asked Rama if they could land there for a while. Ever thoughtful for others, she said, 'I want to enter your royal capital, Ayodhya, with Tara, the beloved wife of Sugriva, and the wives of all the other monkey leaders.' The monkey wives were delighted at the invitation. They dressed themselves in their finest robes and leapt swiftly on to Pushpaka, happy to meet Sita at last. Then they all flew on together, over Lake Pampa, Mount Rishyamuka, the Godavari River, the Dandaka Forest and Chitrakuta, until they came to the hermitage of the Sage Bharadvaja at Prayag.

Rama had now completed the fourteen years of his exile and was eager for news of his family. He questioned Bharadvaja closely. 'Is Bharata fixed in his duty?' he asked. 'Are my mothers still alive?'

The sage reassured him. All was well at the palace and Bharata was ruling the country wisely, in the best interests of everyone. He was still living the life of an ascetic in Nandigrama and ruling in the presence of Rama's sandals, to which he always paid homage.

Rama and his followers spent the night at the hermitage. When they set out again in the morning, Bharadvaja caused the countryside to burst into bloom, though it was not the season, so that the monkeys could feast on honeyed fruits, dripping with nectar.

When Pushpaka drew near to Shringavera, Rama sent for Hanuman. He had given great thought to his situation and had a most delicate mission for that shrewd monkey. He instructed him to go on ahead to Nandigrama. When he introduced himself to Bharata and told him that Rama was on his way home and already within sight of Ayodhya, Hanuman must pay special attention to the expression on Bharata's face. 'You will know by his gestures, his colour, his glances and his words. Whose mind would not be moved by the thought of ascending a throne, to a kingdom abounding in prosperity, with hosts of elephants, horses and chariots? If the fortunate Bharata wishes to reign in his own right, let that descendant of Raghu govern the entire earth!' said Rama.

Hanuman took on human form for his mission and flew with the speed of Garuda to Nandigrama. There he hid behind a bush, so that he could observe Bharata from a distance. He saw him looking sad and emaciated, his hair matted, his limbs covered in dust, dressed only in a black antelope skin. He was outside his hermitage, where he lived on roots and practised penance. He had placed Rama's sandals in front of him and, as Hanuman watched, he was conducting the affairs of state in consultation with his ministers. He was so pure of soul that he shone like the God of Righteousness himself. Greatly moved, Hanuman came forward and bowed low, his palms joined.

'I bring you good news, O Prince,' he said. 'Your brother Rama, for whom you grieve, is enquiring about your welfare. Abandon your despair! The moment has come when you will be reunited with him, and with Lakshmana and Sita, Rama's devoted wife.'

Bharata was so overcome with joy that he fainted on the spot. When he came round, he embraced Hanuman, who gave him a full account of the fourteen years in the wilderness, Sita's abduction and Rama's victory over Ravana and the Rakshasas.

There was no doubting Bharata's devotion to Rama. He offered magnificent gifts to Hanuman, as the bearer of such good tidings. Then he sent for his brother Satrughna and together they prepared Ayodhya for Rama's triumphant return, levelling the highways, raising victory flags, scattering petals and draping all the temples and palaces with garlands of flowers. Then they set out to meet him. Preceded by his troops, who were mounted on thousands of elephants and riding in magnificent chariots, Bharata went on foot, still in his hermit's antelope skin. He placed Rama's sandals on his head and escorted the litters of the three Queens.

Rama received a rapturous welcome from Bharata, Satrughna, the Queens and all the people of Ayodhya. Then Bharata bowed low and personally fastened Rama's sandals on his feet. 'This kingdom, which I received in trust, I now hand back to you in its entirety,' he said. 'Today, when I see you as Lord of Ayodhya, the purpose of my existence has been fulfilled. Now inspect your treasury, your storehouses, your palace and your army. By your grace, I have increased them tenfold.'

When they reached Nandigrama, Rama dismissed the magic chariot Pushpaka, sending it back to its rightful owner, the God Kuvera. Satrughna brought in a team of barbers to attend to the exiles' long, tangled hair. Bathed and spruced, they mounted a magnificent chariot for their ceremonial entry into Ayodhya, accompanied by King Sugriva and Hanuman, 'whose beauty equalled Indra's, bathed and attired in robes of divine loveliness and sparkling earrings'.

The next morning, the monkey generals flew north, south, east and west, to the seas of the four quarters, to bring water in jewelled pitchers for the coronation ceremony. Then Rama was anointed by the gods themselves, crowned and dressed in his royal robes. He gave Sita a necklace of pearls and priceless gems. Sita unfastened the necklace she was wearing and looked for approval at Rama. He knew what was in her mind and said, 'Give the necklace to the one who pleases you.' So Sita leaned over and fastened it around the neck of Hanuman, 'in whom courage, strength, glory, skill, capability and reserve, prudence, audacity and prowess were ever to be found, and that lion among monkeys, adorned with the necklace, looked as radiant as a mountain covered with a white cloud, silvered by an aureole of moonbeams'.

For ten thousand glorious years, Rama reigned over the Kingdom of Ayodhya, with Sita at his side. During that time, there was no disease or anxiety and his people lived in happiness for a thousand years, each having a thousand sons. There were no criminals, but everyone attended to his duty, both civic and religious. Rain came down when it was needed, the winds were always fair and the trees bore flowers and fruit all the year round. It was paradise on earth.

'Hearing The Ramayana grants longevity and victory equal to Rama's, the hero of imperishable exploits. The one who, mastering his anger, listens with faith to this epic, formerly composed by Valmiki, overcomes all obstacles, and those who hear this story set forth by Valmiki will return from their journeys in foreign lands and rejoice the hearts of their kinsfolk. He who recites it with reverence will be freed from all evil and will live long. Rama is always pleased with the one who hears this epic or recites it in its entirety, and he who does so will obtain a felicity comparable to Rama's, who is Vishnu, the Eternal, the Primeval God, the Long-armed Hari, Narayana, the Lord.

This narrative, which promotes long life, health, renown, brotherly love, wisdom, happiness and power, should be heard in reverence by virtuous men desirous of felicity.'

# 15 The Malabar Coast

*Trivandrum – Quilon – Cochin – Ernakulum – Mahe –*
*Mangalore – Bombay*

IKE RAMA, I was on my way home. I had no intention of chasing his aerial chariot all the way back to Ayodhya, but I had three weeks left before my flight from Bombay to London, so there was ample time for me to cycle up the beautiful Kerala Coast. I had cycled that road before and loved it, but I hadn't realised at the time that there was a series of murals of *The Ramayana* in the Mattancherry Palace in Cochin. I particularly wanted to see those, to fill in my last remaining gap. Then I would continue cycling up the coast as far as time allowed, before jumping on the train to Bombay.

When I arrived back in Trivandrum from Sri Lanka, I went straight to the railway station, where I found Condor extremely dusty, but otherwise in good condition. The hotel gardener gave him a good hosing down, while I reclaimed all my cycling gear from the store room and struggled to repack my panniers. My luggage had swelled alarmingly, what with Christmas, gifts from Rani and her friends, and various books and guides which I had needed to buy. In the end, necessity overcame sentiment, and I had to leave an assortment of items behind, to the great delight of the cleaner.

After a month of cars and trains, it was good to be on the road again, on my own two wheels, in the cool of the morning. I stopped at a roundabout on the way out of Trivandrum, to check the route to Quilon with the traffic policeman on duty there. He pointed to the road, listed all the places along it, then said, 'My name is Benjamin.' 'My name

is Anne,' I said, and we shook hands solemnly in the middle
of the roundabout, while cars hooted and bullocks stamped.
Trivandrum's roads were crowded that Sunday morning with
families on their way to the beach at Kovalam and hordes of
Communists arriving for a rally, their coaches bristling with
red flags, hammers and sickles. Benjamin had stopped them
all. His conversation with me was far more fascinating than
a boring old task like keeping the traffic flowing. But no one
held it against me. The Communists interrupted their chant
of 'C-M-P Zindabad!' to shout 'Hello, Auntie!' and we all
waved. I was pleased to see that in this Communist State of
Kerala, with its 98 per cent literacy rate, there were as many
women as men going to the rally. Kerala is a state where
women really count – unlike the poor downtrodden creatures
in the north of India.

It was a beautiful ride that morning, through thickly
forested hills along a superb road. There were rice paddies,
bananas, coconuts and pineapples. As I cycled through the
villages, crowds were coming out of the churches. The
Catholic churches were like giant wedding cakes, with statues
of Christ on the steeple pinnacles and saints perched on the
lower tiers. St Antony of Padua with the Baby Jesus was very
popular, as was St Joseph leading a blond, curly-haired Child
Jesus by the hand, while St George slew his dragon in a
Ramayana-style crown and splendid mustachios. There was
the Protestant Church of South India, the Roman Catholic
Church, the Seventh Day Adventists, the Methodist Church,
the Salvation Army, the Syrian Orthodox Church and even
the Chaldean Syrian Church of the East. All these in addition
to the Hindu temples and the Muslim mosques, which were
painted in pastel shades, their white domes resting on open
pink lotus flowers – a very Indian touch. Not since my
cycle-ride across the American Bible Belt had I seen such a
choice of religions on offer!

What really impressed me about this array of temples,
mosques and churches was the large number and variety
of schools and charitable institutions which they were running. As well as the usual range of primary schools and
teacher-training colleges, many of the churches were running

computer colleges. I saw Schools for the Deaf, an Employment Institute for Deaf Girls and a School for Developmen-
tally Delayed Persons (political correctness has struck even
in south India). An old man sported a sky-blue T-shirt with
the logo, 'Jewish Home for the Aging'. There were
cooperative banks, gymnasia, charity hospitals, mother and
baby clinics and even family-planning clinics, with two
parents and two children happily smiling down from their
posters. It was a great area for charitable work and self-help.
The people of Kerala, who were already streets ahead of the
rest of India in literacy, were increasing their lead even
further. They were showing how a poor state, with no natural
resources beyond coconuts and fish, could prosper by developing its human potential.

There was just one disadvantage to all this religious
activity, as far as I was concerned. Hindu devotional music
was relayed throughout the villages on loudspeakers, often
continuing until one or two in the morning. I would just
manage to fit in an hour's sleep, and then the temples would
spring into action again. The chanting, drumming and
bell-ringing were absolutely ear-splitting, but the night-time
volume was as nothing compared with the dawn, when the
amplified muezzin joined in from all the mosques – not to
mention the church bells calling the faithful to early Mass.
The demon loudspeakers were attached to trees along the
main streets. If I was really unlucky, they were also attached
to the trees in my hotel garden. On my first night out of
Trivandrum, I had one directly under my window. After that,
I inspected the neighbouring trees before I accepted a room.
I wondered how the residents could stand it. Perhaps they
were impervious to noise? The loudspeakers blared out
sacred music in the daytime too, interspersed with popular
songs, and no one took the slightest notice.

The days were hot and humid, so I made an early start each
morning and reached my destination by about 11 a.m., before
the heat really built up. The temple brahmins must have
taken a long siesta, because the afternoons were relatively
quiet. They were also free of the mosquitos, which plagued
my nights. The afternoons were altogether a blissful time, the

best part of the day, when I could stretch out under the cool breeze of my ceiling fan and enjoy a long, deep sleep after the rigours of the night. Staying up late, rising early and doing my serious sleeping in the afternoon, I was probably adapting to the ways of the locals. They must have slept in the daytime, or they couldn't have carried on.

I could have reached Quilon in a day, but the countryside and the cycling were so pleasant that I cruised along slowly and broke my journey at the Attingal Tourist Home. 'Tourist Home' is the popular term for hotels in Kerala, where 'Hotel' normally indicates a local restaurant, as it does all over India. Only five-star tourists actually *stay* in hotels. In Attingal, I went to a 'hotel' for dinner and enjoyed a wonderful Kerala Chicken Fry, chicken coated in desiccated coconut and fried in coconut oil, with just a hint of cloves. Kerala Fish Fry, cooked in the same way, is equally delicious, provided you like a strong coconut flavour.

Quilon, or Kollam as it's called these days, marks the southern limit of Kerala's backwaters, the 40 rivers, 29 major lakes and over 1,000 canals and lagoons, where tiny fishing villages and coconut groves jostle for every inch of dry land. Phoenicians, Greeks, Romans, Arabs, Persians and Chinese have all traded in the port of Quilon and left their scattered wares for archaeologists to find. Today it trades chiefly in cashew nuts, unfortunately the one nut I don't much like. But between the cashew-nut stores, I found a supermarket, where I stocked up on snacks for my journey. It involved a lengthy drill: deposit shopping bag at door in exchange for token, select purchases, queue at desk for invoice (carbon copy kept), take invoice to cashier, queue to pay and get invoice stamped, present stamped invoice and pick up goods from delivery desk, take token to doorkeeper and reclaim shopping bag. How different from my local Sainsbury's!

After so much effort for a cake and a packet of biscuits, I revived myself with a 'coffee set' (a tray of coffee, with the milk and sugar separate) in the Indian Coffee House, where white-clad waiters in red turbans and sashes give an air of distinction to the service. A group of five young women were drinking coffee at the next table. One of them startled me by asking, 'Are you the new Engineering Professor? No? What a pity!' All five girls were engineering undergraduates. They said it was a popular profession among girls in India, though the job prospects were not brilliant in Kerala and they would probably have to move elsewhere to find work. They lamented the dullness of Quilon. 'There's so much more going on in Cochin and Trivandrum, more life than there is in this dump!' Kerala women are certainly not short of self-confidence.

I was taking the backwater passenger bus to Alleppey, which left in the early morning from a jetty on Lake Ashtamudi, so I transferred from my hotel in the town centre to the former British Residency. I cycled up across an enormous open space, which was probably a maidan or polo ground in the old days, but was nothing more than a dry, dusty, red-earthed emptiness that late afternoon. I entered the pleasant red-tiled building, noting that the royal coat of arms was still displayed on the fancy wooden eaves. At the rear, a covered path through gardens of cannas and bougainvillea led to a flight of stone steps down to the Residency's own boat jetty. It was a pleasant spot. Inside, the building was a repository for Victoriana. My bedroom had an enormously high ceiling, heavy mahogany furniture and a huge Royal Doulton bath with lion's claw feet. Unfortunately, the unconnected geyser leaked so badly that the bathroom floor was awash, and there were large holes in the mosquito netting round my monumental bed. Dinner was served in style at a vast round table with a white cloth and Victorian china.

For some reason, the obsequious waiter appeared at my bedroom door at 11.20 and asked me to hand over my padlock, so that he could secure my door from the outside. My windows had bars and I didn't fancy being locked in there, unless I held the key myself. In any case, I was dubious about his motives, so I sent him packing.

There were six of us in the Residency – three French girls, who were doing voluntary work in Pondicherry for the Order of St. Joseph of Cluny, a young Dutch chemistry graduate, an Englishman from IBM and myself. We all embarked on the Alleppey boat, with Condor lashed to the roof. It was an idyllic day, though a bit on the long side. The cantilevered Chinese fishing nets, which for some reason are billed as a tourist attraction, towered spidery over the shallow waters, where fishermen with hand nets stood waist-deep beside their boats and little boys tried to shoot fish with bows and arrows. Long dugouts glided by and a few traditional rice-boats, now converted into luxury houseboats for Westerners. Every spit of land had its village, with smart concrete houses, churches, schools and a post office, as well as more modest thatched huts. Kerala means 'Land of Coconuts' and it was coconuts which were providing most of the work. Men were shinning up the palms to collect them, or to tap the trunks to make toddy. There were small desiccation factories, open yards where men were separating the coir from the nut, weaving shops for coconut matting and vast waterside coir depositories. Even the empty shells were put to use. I was told that many were exported as biodegradable ice-cream cartons. They had shipped a vast consignment to Barcelona for the Olympics. Visually, it was all delightful. The water hyacinth looked beautiful, though its vast tangled expanses were clogging the navigation channels and robbing the fish of oxygen. Illegal land reclamation, excessive use of fertilisers and fishing with dynamite were destroying the natural balance and the water levels were falling alarmingly. But none of this was visible that lazy day on the boat, when the sun shone and we drifted idly in the shade of the coconut palms.

It was late evening by the time we pulled into the inevitable chaos of Alleppey's landing stage. A flock of hotel touts and rickshaw wallahs swooped down on us in the pitch blackness. With no street lamps, anxious passengers were striking matches, trying to read their guide books in the dark. Condor was unroped from the roof and a freight charge demanded. No one had mentioned charges before, so I was unprepared and had no suitable change. Jostled and flustered, I was trying to deal with the money problem, while keeping an eye on my baggage. Just as I was on the verge of panic, a quiet voice asked, 'Do you have a particular hotel in mind?' It was Mr. IBM, demonstrating the folly of early judgements. In the Residency, he had struck me as rather conceited, holding forth sententiously about the antique furniture, and I had ignored him on the boat. Now, on the Alleppey jetty, he turned out to be kindness itself. He guarded my panniers while I dealt with the freight charge, hired us a rickshaw, heaved Condor on board with all the other baggage and checked out a few hotels. We had a couple of most agreeable dinners together in Alleppey. I last saw him leaning out of a bus window, waving encouragement as I pedalled along the road to Cochin.

As I was going there to see the *Ramayana* frescoes in the palace, I decided to stay in Fort Cochin, the historical quarter on the southern promontory of the harbour, rather than in the modern mainland city of Ernakulum. That was a mistake. The road surface deteriorated after the Ernakulum fork and the streets grew scruffier, with goats, cats and garbage. The one presentable hotel was full and I was too hot and tired to face the Ernakulum ferry. I ended up in a concrete kennel with a hole in the mattress, a poster of the Sacred Heart of Jesus and shared facilities. I was going to turn it down, but two Australians with backpacks, who stood behind me in the entrance, advised me to snap it up. They had been tramping the town for over an hour and this was the first place they had found with any free rooms.

'Where've you come from on that bike?' asked one of them.

'Alleppey.'

'Crikey! We've just walked 4 kilometres and we're knackered. I'm 25 and Kev's 24.'

'I'm a bit older than that.'

'No! You're kidding!'

We dumped our gear and went off for a coffee together at The Chariot Fast Food Café, in the easy kind of companionship that riding a bicycle always produces.

Fort Cochin is as cosmopolitan as any place in India. An ancient spice port on the sea route to China, it housed the body of Vasco da Gama for fourteen years, until he was transferred to Lisbon. His tombstone remains in St Francis Church, where Cochin's more recent history is reflected. Founded as the Catholic church of Saõ Antonio by the

Portuguese around 1510, it was converted to a Protestant church by the Dutch, when they took control of the port. In 1804 it became an Anglican church and since 1949 it has belonged to the Church of South India.

While I waited in the morning for Mattancherry Palace to open, I cycled through the spice market, heavy in the heat with the mingled aromas of pepper, cinnamon, ginger and cumin. Some of the business names were Jewish, for this was Jewtown, where Jews have lived since the Diaspora. There are only a handful left now, but they still have their synagogue, the oldest one in the British Commonwealth. Jewtown is also the area for antique shops, where Indian artifacts are stacked in dusty profusion among Georgian tea caddies, portraits of King Edward VII, porcelain from China and Victorian dining chairs. The Kerala tribal figurines were particularly delightful and, as they were small, I had room for them in my panniers. I bought myself a lovely set of four little bronze musicians, all in strange tall headdresses, playing the drum, flute, tambourine and bagpipes; and I bought a tiny bronze elephant on wheels, a tribal toy, as a present for a friend in Oxford, who had just been burgled and lost her childhood companion, Elephant, also wheeled and Indian, though of brightly painted wood.

Mattancherry Palace was built by the Portuguese in traditional Kerala style around 1557, as a gift to the Raja of Cochin in return for trading rights. Most of the *Ramayana* murals date back to the end of that century, 45 of them, illustrating every incident in the epic. They are lively tempera paintings on wood panels, in rich colours, predominantly green and gold. Like most Indian devotional art, they are extremely complicated pictures, where every millimetre of space is covered in decoration, so that it is difficult at first sight to read the scene. Unlike Western painting, which uses light and perspective to focus attention on to the key elements, traditional Indian painting seems to melt into some kind of organic whole, where hundreds of faces loom, plants merge into draperies and fire flames into gods. There are no planes, no background, just more figures, more trees and more plants pressing down on the bewildered viewer. There is a sensuous, mesmeric, almost dreamlike quality about Indian art, both Hindu and Buddhist. Looking at a picture is a sensory experience, rather than an intellectual exercise.

The *Ramayana* murals were magnificently exuberant. Had I not gone round with the detailed guide produced by the Archaeological Survey of India, I doubt if I could have distinguished my demons from my monkeys. Fortunately, Rama was always larger than the other figures and his face a darker green, so that I could start with him and work outwards. But the detail was quite overwhelming and I found my concentration slipping after only three of the murals. There was far too much to take in on one visit. I should need at least a week to give the *Ramayana* series the attention it deserved. And that was only a part of it. There were magnificent murals of the major gods too, and a series on Krishna. What a good excuse for a return visit to Cochin!

I took a cursory look at the remainder of *The Ramayana*, then moved on to see the most famous of the Krishna murals. It was a Krishna Lila, Krishna at play. It showed this most popular of Vishnu's avatars reclining in the lap of one milkmaid, caressing seven others with seven of his hands, and playing the flute with the eighth. Again the detail, down to the smallest petal of the smallest golden flower, was just too much to take in and I escaped to the simplicity of the Coronation Hall, to rest over the portraits and regalia of the Rajas of Cochin.

Cochin, like Travancore to the south, was extremely fortunate in its Rajas. While the others shot tigers and collected Rolls-Royces, Cochin's rulers seem to have been Sanskrit scholars and philosophers to a man, interested far more in the scriptures and public works than in private display. They founded schools and hospitals and encouraged economic development. Their progressive administration gave the people of Kerala a flying start, which explains why Kerala's educational standard is higher today than that of any other Indian state.

The Rajas of neighbouring Travancore had even less incentive to be extravagant. As rulers in a matrilineal society, they administered the state as the eldest son of the Rani who held the property. She passed it down to her eldest daughter, whose son succeeded as Raja. This neat arrangement provided the perfect balance of power, separating wealth from political authority. Although this system is less prevalent today than it used to be, there are still families in Kerala where property passes down through the female line, on the principle that it is the women who need secure homes where they can bring up their children. Husbands move into their wife's family property on marriage, and can presumably be ejected from it if they prove unsatisfactory. Kerala women are noticeably more self-confident than those in other states. Hardly surprising, when they have both property and education behind them.

I was pleased to see that most of those excellent Cochin Rajas were called Rama and the Ranis Lakshmi. Obviously, Rama's high-mindedness had spilled over into his namesakes. The Travancores too were Vaishnavites and their elegant palace at Padmanabhapuram, south of Trivandrum, has fine murals of Vishnu, Rama and Krishna. Even the name of the palace (padma – lotus; nabha – navel; puram – town) alludes to the creation of the universe from Vishnu's navel.

Once I had visited Mattancherry Palace, I was in a hurry to leave Fort Cochin. Cycling to the Ernakulum ferry, I couldn't help contrasting the place with Malacca in Malaysia. Both were spice towns with a similar Portuguese–Dutch–British history, both are still major ports, yet Malacca is clean and well maintained, its history lovingly preserved, while Fort Cochin is dilapidated and dirty. Its situation is splendid. There are some fine old buildings and a sea-front promenade. But the concrete has crumbled into treacherous, wobbly chunks and the palatial houses, with names like The Anchorage, which stand in prime positions on the beach, are peeling and gently decaying. There is one block of smart new flats, but the rest of the town is a monument to neglect and unrealised potential. The only good feature of life there is the lack of motorised transport. Spices are light enough to be carried on human heads, so that coolies, cyclists and pushers of handcarts take precedence over trucks.

Over in Ernakulum, a much smarter place, I checked with
great relief into a clean, airy hotel, where I had hot water, an
armchair, a writing desk and a sloping bedhead, which was
perfect for reading in bed.

Ernakulum was in disarray. To begin with, there was a
statewide Hindu general strike in support of Swami
Prakasananda, who was on the thirtieth day of a fast unto
death in protest against the government takeover of a
religious school. It was Ramadan, which always causes some
disruption to services. Preparations were being made for a
huge Congress Party rally to be addressed by Sonia Gandhi.
And on top of all that, the city was flooded out with black-clad
Ayappans on their way home from Sabarimalai, where the
great annual pilgrimage had just reached its climax.

There were only two other Westerners in the hotel, an
English couple who were travelling the exciting way, on an
Enfield Bullet motorbike. They had hired it in Goa to tour the
whole of India, but having biked as far as Ernakulum, they
were having second thoughts.

'It's the most terrifying experience,' they said. 'It's not just
the traffic and the potholes, though they're bad enough. It's
not knowing which bit of the bike is going to fall off next!'

I liked Ernakulum. Apart from its rather dusty museum,
there was no sightseeing to be done, so I was free to enjoy
my leisure and a few good meals. 'Posh Refreshments' and
'Lovely Corner' didn't attract me so much as the Metropolitan
Hotel, where I could actually get a bottle of Kingfisher with
my dinner. So I had no need of the bell boy's conspiratorial
offer of 'Special beer? Whisky? Brandy?' whenever I crossed
the hotel lobby, at whatever time of day. Indian non-drinkers
have very strange ideas of foreign drinking habits.

In the evening I went to watch *The Ramayana* being
danced in a display of Kerala Kathakali. The hero of these
dances, who always has a green face (green for fertility and
goodness) and a flouncy skirt, is a familiar figure these days
on Indian tourist posters. The villain is black and red.
Applying the make-up before the show takes about two
hours, as the paints are all freshly mixed from natural
substances, blended together with coconut oil: sulphur for

yellow; add indigo for green; turmeric for red; burnt coconut oil for black. The dance dramas themselves are highly stylised, each gesture, facial expression and eye movement heavy with significance. They are traditionally performed in temples, where they go on all night, but you would need to be a Hindu devotee or a dance fanatic to watch for that length of time, so the Ernakulum performances are abbreviated for tourists to theatre length. I was lucky enough to see an enactment of the final battle between Rama and Ravana, which was carried on with much beating of drums and rolling of eyes. Rama's green face reminded me of the green Ramas in the Mattancherry murals.

The Tourist Office advised me to take National Highway 47 north through Trichur rather than the coast road, as accommodation would be easier to find. Trichur was only 75 kilometres from Ernakulum and I could have made it quite easily the first morning, but the sun was strong and when I passed a very pleasant hotel in Chalakudy at 11 a.m., I decided to call it a day. In India, it's best to play safe.

When I reached the temple city of Trichur the next morning, I didn't like it at all. It was a dusty, noisy place, with narrow streets and no decent hotels. As it was only 10.30, I decided to move on. Twenty hours in a dump like that would be far too long, even for a laid-back cyclist whose life had slowed down to a snail's pace – particularly as Kerala temples don't normally admit non-Hindus, so that I couldn't while away a couple of hours with the gods. But my problems began soon afterwards. There were two nice-looking hotels along the highway at Kunnamkulam, but they were both full. The same at Edappol. By this time, I was off the NH 47 and the countryside was growing poorer, with shabby, overpopulated little villages. Off the tourist track, I was an object of wonder, to be stared at and shouted after. Some of the people had never seen a Westerner before, except on television. I passed a group of children playing and one of them, aged about five, took to his heels and ran screaming into the woods when he saw my white face, to the great amusement of his older, more sophisticated siblings. The road seemed to get hillier as my tiredness grew. I watched the sun growing redder and sinking dangerously close to the horizon. Ponnani, a small town sandwiched between the sea and a lagoon, would be my last chance of a bed before darkness fell, and I was getting desperate. But as so often happens, just as I was starting to panic, I reached Ponnani and spotted the Masirah Lodge. I cycled up, followed like the Pied Piper by all the town's children, and found that they had a vacant room. What a relief!

There were women peeping at me round the edge of a curtain in reception. A young man took me up to inspect my room, which was sparsely furnished but surprisingly clean, and when I went down again to sign the register, the women appeared and invited me into a very formal lounge, with plush and gilt dining chairs all round the walls. There were seven of them: the mother, four daughters and two daughters-in-law. They offered me a glass of fresh lemonade, sent a little boy out for a Limca, then produced a tray of tea. With the youngest daughter as our interpreter, we went through the inevitable families, ages and professions. I was so hot, dusty and exhausted that I could think of nothing except the shower and bed which awaited me upstairs, but they were such a kind family that I had to make polite conversation and toy with my tea and biscuits. I was just beginning to think that I could make a tactful exit, when one of the girls came in beaming behind a mountain of mutton curry, rice, pickles and chapattis, all for me. I hadn't even had chance to wash my hands and I was far too weary just at that juncture to eat a heavy meal. Exercise is an appetite suppressant. But I had to do my best. They were a Muslim family, obliged by Islam to offer hospitality to a travelling stranger. The food was delicious. Only the timing was wrong. Had they brought in the curry at 7 o'clock, when I was showered and rested, I would have wolfed it down. As it was, I just picked at it, then had to scour the town later to find a passable meal.

The Masirah Lodge was an interesting hotel. It consisted of a row of six bedrooms over six shops, with the extensive family accommodation and hotel reception area off a large courtyard behind. The paterfamilias had earned the money to build this complex by working in one of the Gulf States, and he was able to provide employment for all the young men in his family, both sons and sons-in-law, each of whom ran one of the shops. The women supervised the hotel from the seclusion of their residence, sending one of the young men to deal with the customers.

The well-educated Kerala Muslims are favourite employees in Saudi Arabia and the Gulf. They go there in large numbers, make a pile of money and come back to Kerala to invest it in homes and businesses. Ponnani had three restaurants named 'Kuwait Hotel', 'Gulf Hotel' and 'Emirates Hotel', and like most villages, it had one or two quite spectacular houses, which stood out like fantasies from the Arabian Nights in the middle of the thatched huts.

My family of Kerala Muslims were extremely kind and solicitous. I'd just got back from my chicken dinner, when one of the sons came knocking on my door, with his own toddler in tow to give the visit respectability. He'd come to check that I had everything I needed and to remind me to lock my door.

'Did you have a drink with your dinner?' he asked.

'Yes. I had a Limca.'

'No hot drink?'

'Yes. I had a coffee afterwards.'

'I mean the other sort of hot drink,' he said coyly.

'Hot drink' was evidently the local term for alcohol and, being a foreigner, I was obviously one of those racy people who indulged in it constantly. It was a dry Muslim town and I thought the chance would be a fine thing! But perhaps if I'd asked the family, even Kingfishers would have been available.

The women insisted on plying me with tea before I set out the next morning, though I'd already had coffee and chapattis in a palm-roofed shack. They tried hard to persuade me to stay on as their guest. When I pleaded lack of time, they invited me to come back the next year for a long holiday and bring my family. They were amazingly hospitable and being Muslims, they were able to entertain me freely without the problems of caste, which make social life so difficult for Hindus. They were even able to fling their arms around me and kiss me without fear of pollution by an outcaste.

Ponnani, which had seemed so unpromising at first sight, turned out to be one of the most delightful experiences of that trip, thanks to my seven plump and generous hostesses.

I somehow managed to miss the turning to Tirur, which would have taken me across flat coastal land, and ended up on NH 17, where I had gruelling mountain climbs with no shade. To make matters worse, the cold which had been brewing for the last couple of days began to stream uncontrollably. I struggled on as far as Kottakkal, where attractive roadside billboards advertised a Tourist Lodge. It proved to be a disappointing tip, but the helpful village pharmacist directed me to the Reem Palace.

The Reem was a palace of faded dreams, built on Dubai money. A photograph of the Emir of Dubai graced reception and beside it the minister who had opened the hotel was photographed in his astrakhan hat, sitting on a settee with the owner and his small daughter. I was given a whole suite, lavishly furnished in Middle Eastern style. In my bedroom were two double beds with mirrors for headboards, a chandelier, a tapestry of two horses gambolling in Alpine scenery, plastic flowers and a great deal of complicated built-in furniture, gleaming with black veneer and gold paint. The giant television came with video, a canned muzak line and the most intricate wiring, but none of it worked. Neither did the chandelier, nor the two fluorescent lights, so I had to rely on one dim bedside lamp. This exotic room, with its en suite bathroom, led off from my very own vestibule, where a row of deck chairs and a coffee table faced another television set. Two other double bedrooms, one with a golden cot in the corner, a single room and another bathroom completed my night's accommodation. There was dust everywhere, the paintwork was stained and the windows were so filthy that I could scarcely see the road outside. I was the only guest. I couldn't help feeling sorry for the owner. He had come home from Dubai and invested all his savings in what he hoped would be a magnificent international hotel. But he had not done his market research. His home town of Kottakkal was a poor little place off the beaten track, which could never support such a grandiose enterprise. His dreams had faded, he had lost heart, and now he couldn't even be bothered to supervise the cleaning. The simple Masirah Lodge with its row of shops was a much shrewder investment.

Calicut (now called Kozhikode) was where I nursed my cold for a couple of nights. Over Kerala chicken fry in my hotel restaurant, I chatted to a most enterprising young local, who had seen me cycling around the town. His income came from the textile business, for which Calicut is still famous, but his heart was in his hobbies.

'I am a folk dancer,' he told me proudly. 'I am studying folk dances from many lands. And I am playing the violin also. Every day I am practising for two hours. And what about you? Are you having nice hobbies? Are you playing instruments?'

'I play the piano.'

'Wonderful. Have you brought your piano to India with you? We can play duets.'

'Bring my piano on a bicycle? How would I do that? I should have to hire a large trailer for it.'

'Or an elephant to walk behind you,' he grinned.

That was not such an outlandish suggestion. Kerala's roads were busy that month with gaily decorated elephants marching to various temple festivals. When I stopped for a Limca at a roadside stall and parked my bicycle in the shade, it would often be joined by an elephant. The keeper would produce some sugar cane to keep her quiet, while he took a coffee himself. Parked elephants were as common as parked cars and a much more cheerful sight.

Their only rivals in gaiety were the lorries, which in south India almost matched the fairground vividness of Pakistan. Most had a yellow background, with friezes of small birds and garlands on the sides and the tailgate. The back of the cab was where imagination really blossomed – tigers, lions, Krishna with his flute, colts in a meadow, blond babies in a shower of petals, prancing horses, Jesus pointing to His Sacred Heart and the ever-popular Saint George, mustachios and all, spearing his dragon. Carriage painters lined the approaches to every town, along with the motor mechanics.

Bicycles were less elaborate, being mostly gearless and black. I got quite excited in Ernakulum when I saw a display of mountain bikes. I rode up for a closer look and found that they were certainly chunky in design and bright in colour, with knobbly tyres, but they still didn't have any gears. All that extra weight and drag on the road, with no compensating technology! They must have been as hard to ride as the treadle sewing machines on wheels pedalled round the villages by itinerant tailors.

The roads in this part of Kerala were comparatively quiet outside the towns, which perhaps made some parents over-confident. I was overtaken at speed one morning by a child, who could not have been more than ten years old, riding a Yamaha motorbike. It was too big for him to control effectively and I was not at all surprised, a few miles further up the road, to see a smashed Yamaha lying beside a dented car and an overturned cycle-rickshaw. There was no sign of the boy, just a crowd of people standing round staring.

Almost at the northern end of the long thin State of Kerala was another former French enclave, Mahe. It was handed over to the Indian Government in 1954 along with Pondicherry and is in fact administered as part of the Union Territory of Pondicherry – a very awkward arrangement, given that the two towns lie on opposite sides of India. Mahe and neighbouring Tellicherry are interesting little towns historically, because it was along this strip of shore that the East India Company set up its first depot on the Malabar Coast in 1683, for the export of pepper and cardamom.

Both towns have seen more prosperous days. I spent the night in Mahe, where I saw only two signs of its former French occupancy – 'Le Café' and an off-licence called 'Bon Maarchey'. From my third-floor window in the Rivera [sic] Tourist Home, I had a spectacular view of the river, where lines of men with rods and nets were fishing along the banks, and fleets of fishing boats sheltered in the lee of a sandy spit across the river mouth. Beyond was a wild sea, with daunting breakers, where sea gulls wheeled and cried. They looked as big as hawks and were ginger-brown in colour, with black tips to their wings. The shallows directly under my window were home to a colony of dark-grey cranes. It was fresh and breezy up there and I enjoyed being able to sit by my open window in the evening, watching the swallows over a bottle of really cheap, tax-free Pondicherry beer, without fear of being eaten alive by mosquitos. It was a nice, almost idyllic place to spend the night. Except that, in India, there's invariably something to spoil the romance. In Mahe, it was the sight of the entrails of slaughtered cattle from the upstream abbatoir, which drifted slowly past my window to the sea and quite put me off my breakfast. No wonder the sea birds were so huge!

North of Mahe, the road ran along the coast through a parrot-green landscape of coconut groves, giving glimpses of blue sea and thatched fishing villages. It was a predominantly Muslim area, colonised by the Moplahs, of Arab descent. There were beautiful beaches, but the landscape was unchanging and there was rural poverty all the way to Mangalore, which made for rather a dull ride. As always in the tropics, I started out in the cool of the early mornings and was amazed to find the Indian fields empty. The farmers seem to have inherited British civil service hours. They don't start work in the fields until the sun is already high, and then they carry on through the heat of the day. Southern Europe manages things so much better, with an early start and a siesta.

My time was up when I wheeled into Mangalore, the city of palmists. 'If you have any qustion consult: Bussiness, Abrod, Job, Love, Marrage, Fucher' said a notice in my hotel. I took the bus over the Western Ghats to Bangalore. There was a full moon, which showed the contours of the land quite clearly, the misty ghats, then the arid desolation of the Mysore Plateau. As soon as I arrived in Bangalore, the computer capital of India where our telephone bills are processed for BT, I went straight to the railway station to book my ticket to Bombay.

The tourist quota was already fully booked and I was placed at No. 46 on the waiting list for a berth. But I knew that stations held a VIP/emergency quota, so I pushed my bicycle along the platform to see the assistant station manager, who turned out to be a very pretty girl playing the part of a tycoon, talking on two telephones, handing work to her secretary, answering the queries of male subordinates and signing letters, all the while dealing with my request. She

gave me a form on which I had to fill in 'special reasons'. I
was obviously a foreigner and a woman, both points in my
favour, but to clinch the matter in a society where age is
respected, I thought it prudent to play the old age card. 'As I
am a pensioner,' I wrote, 'I am too old to stand for forty hours
and need a sleeping berth.' She read the form, glanced out of
the door at my bicycle and grinned.

'So you aren't strong enough to stand for forty hours?'

'No. I'm too old.'

'I see you've been cycling around India.'

'Yes. But I have to go very slowly. I'm an old lady.'

Still smiling, she gave me a chitty for the conductor and I
was soon ensconced in sleeping car 6, berth 17, on my way
to Bombay. Indians have a nice sense of humour.

I shared my compartment with three others and we had
ample time to get to know one another on the long journey.
There was a young Indian nurse on her way from Kerala to
Bombay for a job interview. She had applied to a new hospital
in Kuwait, which was recruiting 500 Indian nurses. They had
received over 2,000 applications and she was one of the
1,000-strong short list. Then there was a middle-aged man in
the steel business, who said little, because his English was
shaky. And there was a most frightening young Muslim. He
was a handsome boy, probably just a little over twenty, who
was studying for his MBA while working in his uncle's spice
exporting firm. He was learning the Koran by heart, in order
to become a 'hafiz', and spent most of the journey hunched
up over his copy (Arabic on one page and the English
translation opposite), rocking backwards and forwards and
intoning quietly to himself. Between his learning sessions, he
did his very best to needle me, always with the greatest
courtesy and the most charming smile. He was deadly as a
viper. He needled me about Christianity, about Islam in
England and about the role of the British in India. Topics
would always be introduced in an innocent way:

'Have you been to Pakistan? What's it like there?' would
turn into an anti-British argument about 'divide and rule' and
the damage that policy had done to India. 'Jinnah helped,' I
said. 'We didn't want to split the country.'

'Have you seen the Koh-i-Noor diamond?' became a tirade against British plunder of Indian wealth. 'I expect you were sorry about Princess Di' led to accusations of an anti-Muslim plot because, he claimed, 'she was engaged to be married to a Muslim and the Palace wouldn't have it.'

But worst of all was the religious fanaticism. He was a clever boy, almost Jesuitical in argument. We discussed a number of issues, like consumption of alcohol and the veiling of women. He wore his convictions like a suit of armour and refused even to consider other points of view. 'Sharia Law will come to England eventually,' he crowed, 'because Muslims don't practise family planning. In a few centuries, England and the whole world will be under God's law.' He had all his arguments off pat, because he had obviously rehearsed them many times before. I did my best with impromptu responses and, as usual, it was only later that I thought up the perfect answers. For an hour or so, I endured his dogmatic ranting and managed somehow not to rise to his insolent baits. Then I returned to my book.

'It's been very interesting talking to you,' I said politely. 'You obviously have your point of view on these matters and I have mine.'

'No. You have your point of view. I have God.'

Despite his religious arrogance and his conviction that I lived in a godless country, he still asked me to help him find a job here!

We were turned out of the train at 4.30 in the morning at Dadar Station, fourteen kilometres out of Central Bombay. 'Work on track'. I collected Condor unscathed from the guards van and despite the protests of touts, who were determined to fix me up with a taxi and a hotel, I hooked my panniers on to the rack and cycled off into the dark, with 'It's too far! It's fourteen kilometres!' ringing in my ears.

It was a magical run into town. There was scarcely any traffic on the dual carriageway. I stopped at an early-morning workmen's café and had a coffee, then gave my tyres a bit of a pump. The rag-pickers were out, sifting through the garbage before the dustmen came to collect it. A queue of patient bullocks stood in pairs, yoked to their empty carts, waiting for loads of timber. Once commissioned and loaded up, they set off smartly into the city, to cross it before the traffic built up. There's no time or space for ambling bullocks in this city of Mercedes, once the business day begins. My nose told me I was passing the fish market, where chaos was somehow getting organised. Then I cycled through the streets near Victoria Terminus Station, where the open-air markets were just beginning to come to life. Finally, I reached the Gateway of India and Apollo Bunder, in time to see the great red globe of the sun rising over Bombay Harbour.

My Ramayana pilgrimage ended, as it had begun, with a prayer. I leaned my bicycle against the harbour wall and sat down to watch the sunrise. A bundle of rags stirred on the pavement beside me and a man emerged. Utterly indifferent to my presence, he closed his eyes, raised his hands to the sun and began the Gayatri Mantra, the prayer from the Rig Veda which is so sacred that many people will not write it down: 'Earth, sky, heaven. We meditate on the excellent light of the divine sun. May he illuminate our minds.' He prayed, then he gathered up his rags and set off along Strand Road with a light step.

The ragged, barefoot man who was praying to Hanuman in a crowded Ujjain street started me off on my search for Rama, while a ragged pavement dweller, praying to the rising sun in Bombay, greeted me at the end of my journey. Their prayers were my prologue and epilogue. In the years between the two encounters, the years spent travelling in India, studying *The Ramayana* and writing this book, I have come to have a deep respect for the ancient religion of the Hindus, its traditions, its tolerance and its metaphysical elegance. It is a religion for everyone, just as accessible to a poor bundle of rags on a Bombay pavement as it is to the most learned, high-caste gurus of Varanasi. Hanuman and Rama have given me the key to the temple's outer courtyard and led me to a dim understanding of this complicated faith. But I doubt if I have time in one lifespan to reach the temple's inner sanctum, or the subtlety of mind to embrace its numen if I do.

## ☙ ❧

## The Alternative Ending

*In what is considered to be Valmiki's original story,* The Ramayana *ends with the coronation of Rama. Sita has under-gone the ordeal by fire, her virtue has been proved and she and Rama live happily ever after. But there remains the problem of the Uttara Kanda, the last book of the epic. Although it is undoubtedly a later version, and although it makes very uncom-fortable reading, it is still a part of the epic which has come down to us, so I had better summarise it.*

*(In this version, it is Rama, not Sita, who gives Hanuman the wonderful necklace, which is often seen glittering around his neck.)*

After the coronation, Rama and Sita resumed their lives together in Ayodhya, delighting in each other's company. They entertained their allies in beautiful palaces for a whole month, feeding them on the choicest fruits and showering them with diamonds. Then King Sugriva led his monkeys and bears back home to Kishkindha, and King Vibhisana left with his Rakshasas for Lanka.

Rama ruled wisely, with the beautiful Sita by his side, and his kingdom prospered. One day, Sita expressed a wish to visit the Rishis who lived in hermitages on the banks of the Ganges. Always eager to please her, particularly as she was soon to give birth to their first child, Rama asked Lakshmana to accompany her to the Ganges, so that she could spend a day with the holy men.

While Lakshmana was making preparations for the trip, Rama entered his throne room and enquired of one of his friends, 'What do they say of me in the town and the countryside?'

With great hesitation, his friend replied, 'The people are saying that Rama has achieved the impossible. He has thrown a bridge over the sea and defeated the invincible demon Ravana. But they wonder how he can bear to take Sita back into his house again, when she has been sitting in Ravana's lap? They worry that they will now have to tolerate the same sort of behaviour from their own wives, for where a king leads, his subjects must follow.'

*Rama was devastated, but his reputation and his duty as king were paramount. He changed his instructions to Lakshmana. He ordered him to take Sita across the Ganges and leave her there. So it fell to the unfortunate, grief-stricken Lakshmana to tell Sita that she had been banished. Weeping bitterly, Sita at first complained of her treatment. 'What sin can I have committed in days gone by that I, who am virtuous and chaste, should be cast off by the king?' But then she recollected her duty and, full of wifely devotion, accepted her fate. She sent a message to Rama: 'The husband is as a god to the woman. He is her family and her spiritual guide. Therefore, even at the price of her life, she must seek to please her lord. It is for you, Rama, to keep your fair name untarnished.'*

*Sita was taken into his hermitage by the Sage Valmiki, and there she gave birth to twin sons, Kusha and Lava. The two boys grew up as Valmiki's disciples. They had sweet voices, and Valmiki composed an epic poem about the wanderings and exploits of Rama, which he taught them to sing. Then he sent them to Rama's court, with instructions to perform* The Ramayana *before him, accompanying themselves on their stringed instruments. Everyone was amazed at the beauty of their song and commented on their likeness to Rama. Rama was so enchanted that he offered the boys eighteen thousand gold pieces each, but they rejected them airily. 'Grain, fruit and roots are enough for ascetics like us. What should we do with gold and silver in the forest?'*

*Rama listened for many days and nights to the sublime epic, so melodiously sung, and little by little it dawned on him that these were his own twin sons. He learned from the boys that Sita was living in the hermitage of the Sage Valmiki and he immediately sent messengers to her. 'If Sita is without sin, let her prove her good faith. Tomorrow at dawn, let the daughter of Janaka attest her purity on oath in my presence, before the assembly.'*

*When Valmiki led Sita into Rama's crowded throne room, he had some sharp words to say to him. Rama tried to justify himself. He said to the Sage, 'Though wholly convinced of her innocence, it was from fear of the people that I cast off Sita. Please pardon me. I acknowledge these twins, Kusha and Lava, as my* sons, and I wish to make my peace with the chaste Sita before the assembly.'

The monkeys, bears and Rakshasas had all flown to Ayodhya to hear Sita's defence. Now they were joined by the gods themselves, led by Brahma. A hush fell over the great hall. Sita came forward, dressed in a yellow robe, and approached Rama with joined palms and bowed head. 'If I am pure,' she said, 'if my mind has never dwelt on any man but Rama, may the Great Goddess receive me!'

No sooner had she spoken, than the earth opened and the goddess herself appeared. She took Sita in her arms and placed her on a celestial throne. The gods shouted with joy and a rain of blossoms fell down from the skies as Sita descended into the earth from which she had sprung. At that moment, a great tremor passed through the whole world.

Rama was overcome with grief. He begged the earth to restore Sita to him, and when Sita did not reappear, he became wild with anger. He threatened to plough up the whole earth, with its mountains and forests, until nothing but water remained. But Brahma calmed him down. 'Remember that you are Vishnu, Invincible Hero!' he said. 'You will be reunited with the chaste and virtuous Sita in the Celestial Kingdom.'

Without Sita, the world was a desert to Rama. He never took another consort, but every time he performed a sacrifice, he set up a golden image of Sita. The three Queens eventually died and joined their husband, King Dasaratha, in heaven.

When Rama had ruled for eleven thousand years, Yama, the God of Death, came to him one morning, disguised as an ascetic. He told Rama that his message was so confidential, that no one else must hear it. Rama must promise to kill anyone who came into the room and interrupted them. Rama promised and sent Lakshmana to guard the door. Yama had come at the request of Brahma, to inform the Protector of the Worlds that his time on earth was nearing its end. He should prepare to join the immortals again as Vishnu. As the two gods were conversing, the Sage Durvasa arrived on a visit and flew into a rage when Lakshmana would not admit him to Rama's presence, threatening to put a curse on the kingdom. Badly shaken, and fearing for the safety of Rama and Ayodhya, Lakshmana burst in upon his brother's conversation with Yama and so sealed his own fate.

As Rama wept, the ever faithful Lakshmana tried to comfort him. 'Do not grieve on my account,' he said. 'This event was ordained and has its roots in a past cause. Be faithful to your vow. If you find any merit in me, then kill me without hesitation and fulfil the law.' Rama could not bring himself to kill his brother. Instead, he commuted the sentence from death to banishment, on the ground that both were equal punishments for a man of honour.

Lakshmana left the city in great sorrow. He walked to the River Sarayu, where he performed his ritual ablutions, then sat down on the bank to meditate. As he subdued his senses, he was buried in a shower of blossoms and became invisible. Then Indra himself came down to the river bank and carried him skywards. So a part of Vishnu returned to heaven, to the great delight of the gods.

Rama made preparations for his own departure. He divided his extensive Kingdom of Ayodhya into two and enthroned his sons, Kusha and Lava. All the citizens begged to accompany him on his journey, as did Sugriva and Vibhisana, who had arrived with their monkeys, bears and demons. Rama welcomed them all. Anyone who followed him on his journey could enter heaven with him. Only three must remain behind: Vibhisana to rule his Rakshasas; Jambavan, the wise old King of the Bears; and his faithful friend Hanuman.

'Foremost of Monkeys,' he said, 'Resign yourself to continuing to live. As long as my story is told in the world , so long will your fame endure.'

Hanuman replied, 'As long as your purifying history is circulated in the world, so long shall I remain on earth submissive to your will. I shall always hold you in the greatest affection. I shall never give my allegiance to anyone else. Listening to your divine exploits will dispel my anxieties, as the wind chases away a flock of clouds.'

Greatly moved, Rama embraced his friend tenderly. Then he took off his string of pearls with an emerald bright as the moon and fastened it round Hanuman's neck. 'Let it be so. Be happy and remember my words.'

The next morning, Rama set out for the River Sarayu with his remaining brothers, Bharata and Satrughna. The city emptied as the whole population, with their birds and beasts, followed rejoicing. Rama, clothed in silk, radiant as the sun, walked barefoot between the Goddess Lakshmi and the Goddess of the Earth; and assuming human form, his weapons followed devoutly in his train, together with the Vedas and the sacred word, aum.

When the multitude reached the river, the gods appeared in their aerial chariots 'and the whole firmament glowed with a transcendent splendour, a marvellous radiance emanating from the lustre of those heavenly beings'. To the accompaniment of celestial choirs and orchestras, Rama stepped into the water, to be welcomed by Brahma: 'Hail, O Vishnu! With your godlike brothers, enter the shining ether! You are the Inconceivable One, the Great Being, the Indestructible, the Ageless One.'

Everyone who entered the river with Rama gave up their lives in a wave of ecstasy. They took their places in golden chariots and ascended to heaven, their bodies resplendent. The monkeys and bears resumed their original forms as the children of the gods, Sugriva merging with the disk of his father, Surya, the God of the Sun. And so the Lord Vishnu, He who Pervades the Three Worlds and all they contain, returned to his celestial kingdom, his mission on earth accomplished.

This conclusion to the epic is unambiguous. Rama and his brothers are clearly shown to be earthly forms of the God Vishnu and Sita to be Lakshmi. The Demon King has been slain. Good has once again triumphed over Evil, and the heroes and heroine are free to resume their seats among the Immortals.

For the modern reader, this ending presents even more problems than the earlier one. It is difficult to reconcile Rama's divine wisdom and virtue with his shabby treatment of Sita. If he really is God, how can he be such a slave to public opinion as to disown his wife for a second time? Sita and Lakshmana, in their unquestioning devotion to Rama, seem to us to be much more godlike in character than Rama himself.

I suppose this ending needs to be viewed in the context of Hindu tradition. A man's first duty is the sacred one of playing out his destiny. His second is his duty towards his caste. Rama is a king, a member of the kshatrya caste, and must therefore be the perfect ruler, above reproach in his relationship with his subjects. His third duty is towards his family of birth. Rama again is perfect in this regard. He obeys his father and continues to love and respect all three Queens, even though one of them has engineered his banishment for fourteen years. Rama is the ideal man within this divine and social framework, where personal affections are less important than status. Within this framework, his love for his wife comes lowest in his list of priorities. His reputation, and that of his office and his parents, are more important than his behaviour towards Sita.

There are many situations in real life where people have to make agonising choices between conflicting duties. What is so annoying about Rama is that, in his self-righteousness, he seems almost unaware of the conflict. He weeps a little, but never really hesitates. His own good name is paramount. Perhaps a god, being omniscient, can resolve these problems more easily than mere mortals!

Sita's behaviour in this ending is interesting. She states throughout The Ramayana that a husband is as a god to his wife and no matter how badly he treats her, it is her duty to go on loving him. She has already proved her virtue by submitting to an ordeal by fire. Now, after ruthlessly banishing her to save his reputation, Rama expects her to give another public proof of her innocence. This is too much, even for the long-suffering Sita. She finally rebels and chooses to descend into the earth, rather than suffer the humiliation of a second test.

Legend does not relate what happened to King Vibhisana and Jambavan, the King of the Bears, when they were made to stay behind on earth. Presumably, they ruled wisely and well for the rest of their natural span.

Hanuman retired from the Kishkindha army and, according to the Indonesians, went to live on the Hindu island of Bali. He is a popular figure there and also on Java, where he features prominently in the shadow puppet plays and traditional dances based on The Ramayana. In Yogyakarta, the cultural capital of Java, there is a Ramayana Ballet, and when I visited the city, I dined in a restaurant called Hanuman's Forest, where Hanuman and his monkey army gyrated throughout dinner to the accompaniment of a gamelan orchestra.

Hanuman flies from Bali to be present, whenever and wherever in the world the story of his hero Rama is told. If you turn your head quickly, you may just catch a fleeting glimpse of him now, listening quietly in the corner.

# Appendix A: Bicycle Specification

I rode my sea-green Condor on all my journeys in India. I had a new chainset with extra gears and converted from randonneur to straight handlebars, to make room for convenient handlebar flick-switches.

| | |
|---|---|
| Frame | Reynolds 531 twin-tube (mixte) |
| Wheels | Dedra 6060 alloy rims, Shimano hubs, Sapim Alpina spokes |
| Tyres | Vredestein Perfect |
| Tubes | Vredestein |
| Mudguards | Esge |
| Gears | Shimano |
| Brakes | Shimano |
| Bars and Stem | Raised stem, straight handlebar, curved bar ends |
| Headset | Stronglight |
| Cassette | 12–28 |
| Seatpin | Shimano |
| Saddle | Brooks |
| Chain | Sachs |
| Chainset | Sugino triple with gear ratios 28–38–48 |
| Pedals | Shimano ATB |
| Rack | Topeak |
| Panniers | Karrimore Iberian |
| Barbag | Topeak |
| Pump | Zefal hp X 3 |
| Odometer | Tri-Pro Cyclocomputer |

Spares carried: 2 inner tubes, 6 spokes, 1 gear cable, 1 brake cable, selection of nuts, bolts, screws and washers.

Tools: spanner, screwdriver, set of Allen keys, puncture repair kit, 2 valve adaptors.

# Appendix B: Luggage List

**Cycling Clothes** (layers worn as required)

Lightweight wool jersey
Long-sleeved cotton/polyester shirt
Loose cotton trousers
Trainers, socks, baseball cap, cycling gloves
Anorak, waterproof trousers, woolly hat
Silk longjohns, silk long-sleeved polo-necked vest, silk balaclava.

**Additional Clothing**

2 changes of underwear and socks
1 long-sleeved shirt
1 short-sleeved blouse
1 nightdress
1 pair of flat sandals, doubling up as slippers
1 pair of smart cotton trousers
1 smart top
Liberty silk suit, black silk T-shirt, black petticoat, black tights,
high-heeled black sandals, small black handbag (for special
occasions)
1 large all-purpose cotton square (as scarf, laundry bag, emergency
pillow-case, sarong, etc.)
1 swimming costume and small towel.

**Medicines and Toiletries**

1 course of Amoxycillin (wide spectrum antibiotic)
Prescription medicines for polymyalgia
Imodium capsules
Aspirins, Senokot, Rennies
Paludrine and Avoclor tablets (malaria prophylaxis)

Antihistamine cream
Savlon antiseptic cream
Canesten cream (for fungal infections)
Cicatrin antibiotic powder
Anti-inflammatory gel
Selection of plasters
Clarins Sun Block (factor 25) for face
Ambre Solaire (factor 20) for arms and legs
Basic cosmetic kit
1 tablet Roger et Gallet soap (my small luxury).

## Miscellaneous

Light down sleeping bag
Thermarest sleeping mat
Universal plug
Swiss Army knife
Knife, fork and spoon set
Electric water boiler, mug, Nescafé, herbal teas
Torch
Sewing kit
Nail file, clippers, tweezers
Airmail writing pad, envelopes and three notebooks
Compass
Nelles maps
Pentax Espio 115 camera and four slide films
Nepal Handbook, India Handbook, Lonely Planet India, Lonely
Planet Sri Lanka (as required)
*The Ramayana*, Horace's *Odes*.
Stack of *Times* crosswords. Copies of *Tough Puzzles*.

# Bibliography

All publishers based in London unless otherwise stated.

**General Reading and Reference**
Ali, Tariq, *The Nehrus and the Gandhis: an Indian Dynasty*. Picador, 1985
Baker, Sophie, *Caste*, Jonathan Cape, 1990
*Bhagavad Gita*, Penguin Books, 1962
Bumiler, Elizabeth, *May You be the Mother of a Hundred Sons*, Penguin India, 1991
Coleman, S and Elsner, J, *Pilgrimage*, British Museum Press, 1995
Collins, L and Lapierre, D, *Freedom at Midnight*, Tarang Paperbacks, India, 1975
Craven, Roy C, *Indian Art*, Thames and Hudson, 1976
Dalrymple, William, *The Age of Kali*, Flamingo, 1999
Dowson, J, *A Classical Dictionary of Hindu Mythology and Religion*, Rupa & Co., India, 1982
Edwardes, Michael, *The Sahibs and the Lotus*, Constable, 1988
Gandhi, MK, *The Story of My Experiments with Truth*, Navajivan Karyalaya, India, 1933
Hartsuiker, Dolf, *Sadhus*, Thames and Hudson, 1993
Housden, Roger, *Travels through Sacred India*, Thorsons, 1996
Klostermaier, Klaus K, *Concise Encyclopaedia of Hinduism*, Oneworld Publications, 1998
Koestler, Arthur, *The Lotus and the Robot*, Hutchinson, 1960
Lannoy, Richard, *The Speaking Tree*, Oxford University Press, 1971
Mehta, Gita, *Snakes and Ladders*, Secker and Warburg, 1997
Mitchell, AG, *Hindu Gods and Goddesses*, Victoria and Albert Museum, 1982
Mitter, Sara S, *Dharma's Daughters*, Penguin Books, 1992

Moorhouse, Geoffrey, *India Britannica*, Harvill Press, 1983

Moorhouse, Geoffrey, *OM: an Indian Pilgrimage*, Hodder and Stoughton, 1993

Nabar, Vrinda, *Caste as Woman*, Penguin Books India (P) Ltd, 1995

Naipaul, VS, *An Area of Darkness*, Andre Deutsch, 1964

Naipaul, VS, *India*, Heinemann, 1990

Naipaul, VS, *India: a Wounded Civilization*, Andre Deutsch, 1977

O'Flaherty, Wendy (ed.), *Hindu Myths*, Penguin Books, 1975

Paz, Octavio, *In Light of India*, Harvill Press, 1997

Singh, Daram V, *Hinduism: an Introduction*, Travel Wheels, Jaipur, 1991

Spear, Percival, *A History of India*, Penguin Books, 1965

Strabo, *Geographica, Book XV*, William Heinemann Ltd, 1930

Stutley, Margaret, *Hinduism: the Eternal Law*, Crucible, 1985

Sullivan, Bruce M, *Historical Dictionary of Hinduism*, Scarecrow Press Inc., 1997

Thapar, Romila, *A History of India*, Penguin Books, 1966

Wood, Michael, *The Smile of Murugan*, Viking, 1995

Zaehner, RC (ed.), *Hindu Scriptures*, JM Dent & Sons Ltd, 1966

### The Ramayana

Aiyar, VVS, *Kamba Ramayana: a Study*, Bharatiya Vidya Bhavan, Bombay, 1965

Aryan, KC, *Hanuman: Art, Mythology and Folklore*, Rekha Prakashan, New Delhi, 1994

Gowen, HH, *A History of Indian Literature*, D Appleton & Co., 1931

Narayan, RK, *The Ramayana*, Penguin Books, 1972

Pargiter, FE, *The Geography of Rama's Exile*, Journal of the Royal Asiatic Society, 1894

Pillai, MSP, *Ravana, King of Lanka*, Asian Educational Services, New Delhi, 1993

Shastri, Hari Prasad (trans.), *The Ramayana of Valmiki*, Shanti Sadan, India, 1953

Winternitz, M, *A History of Indian Literature*, University of Calcutta Press, 1927

# Index